AF446430

Trading *Values* For Greater *Virtues*

(Determining the magnitude of *virtues* by the level of *values*)

OLA JONES DUYILE

Tulip Publications
"bring concepts to life"
Ceintuurbaan 23B
Rotterdam The Netherlands
Reach out to us - info@tulippublication.com
Visit our websites - www.tulippublications.com

Dedication

This book is dedicated to everyone who lives and demonstrates practical love, reverence and Godly fear.

To that individual who exhibits a lifestyle of value toward God and His Agents on earth. It is God's worth that announces your worth in life. Thank God for your life and your knowledge of His worth. I pray that your value for God shall keep promoting you until you are lifted above your peers in life.

Contents

Acknowledgement

"Behold, what manner of love the Father hath bestowed upon us, that we should be called the sons of God: therefore the world knoweth us not, because it knew him not." I want to appreciate the Giver and Preserver of life, Father God, for His grace, love and mercy over my life. I want to also thank the Lord Jesus for the price He paid to bring me out of the miry clay to the throne of honour *"And hast made us unto our God kings and priests: and we shall reign on the earth"* I so much value His price on my life and His worth as the Lord of all. Thank you, Lord, for this great privilege to be called the son of God.

I acknowledge the Helper who consistently teaches, leads, guides and instructs me in every step and decision I make in life. Precious Holy Spirit, I appreciate your ever presence and help. Indeed, you are the Author of this book and your worth is immeasurable. You are the gift of God in the Saints through our Saviour.

I acknowledge all my teachers, particularly my mentor Bishop David Abioye, who keeps nurturing me in the word of faith, discipleship and practical discipline, teaching me how to take personal responsibility by walking in the fear of God and esteeming His worth in my privileged position. Your stewardship training is incomparable and your level of humility and focus which I learn on a daily basis cannot be overemphasized. You are indeed a great teacher and a true leader. You keep showing us that it is possible to live what you teach and teach what you live! Thank you for availing and making yourself a ladder for the younger ones to climb to their higher height in life.

I appreciate all those who have been part of my strength. Those who criticized to strengthen my weakness and those who praised to enhance my strength. Thank you all for the part you played in my life and ministry.

I appreciate every member of Victory House, Denmark who are the main trainees for my daily growth. I learn and grow feeding you as the flocks of God in His vineyard where I have been privileged to serve. Thank you for giving me the opportunity to serve you.

To my wife, my best friend and channel of inspiration; thank you for your care, support and love. Thanks for creating quite an atmosphere around me when needed and thank you for taking good care of the heritages of God in the house. Indeed, your unswerving support helps strengthen my daily walk with God and in God which enhances my working for the promotion of His kingdom here on earth. Your commitment as a *'help meet'* enables me to understand that calling is profitable, achievable and fulfillable when you choose to walk with God rather than focusing on working for Him.

Finally, I want to appreciate those who made themselves available for the editing, proof-reading, reviewing and updating of this book. Thank you for your time, support and love.

Thank you all and God bless.

One Thing is Needful

"But one thing is needful: and Mary hath chosen that good part, which shall not be taken away from her" [Luke 10: 42]. Salvation is needful; it must be chosen today and not allowed to be taken away from us. Now is the accepted time; behold, today is the day of salvation for you. Hallelujah!

Hello friends, I am excited to introduce to you the Source of value, the Colour behind our worth and the Strength that produces virtues in us. His name is Jesus Christ the Saviour of the world. This is a lifetime opportunity for you in case you are yet to receive Him into your life as your personal Saviour and Lord. Jesus Christ is the path designed for our rescue from destruction, for all have sinned and come short of the glory of God; but thanks be to God who in His mercy made His Son to become the sacrificial lamb needed for our rescue *"And he is the propitiation for our sins: and not for ours only, but also for the sins of the whole world"* [1 John 2:2].

The word of God revealed the depth of His love to all mankind thus:

"For when we were yet without strength, in due time Christ died for the ungodly. For scarcely for a righteous man will one die: yet peradventure for a good man some would even dare to die. But God commendeth his love toward us, in that, while we were yet sinners, Christ died for us. Much more then, being now justified by his blood, we shall be saved from wrath through him. For if, when we were enemies, we were reconciled to God by the death of his Son, much more, being reconciled, we shall be saved by his life. And not only so, but we also joy in God through our Lord Jesus Christ, by whom we have now received the atonement. Wherefore, as by one man sin entered into the world, and death by sin; and so death passed upon all men, for that all

have sinned: (For until the law sin was in the world: but sin is not imputed when there is no law. Nevertheless death reigned from Adam to Moses, even over them that had not sinned after the similitude of Adam's transgression, who is the figure of him that was to come. But not as the offence, so also is the free gift. For if through the offence of one many be dead, much more the grace of God, and the gift by grace, which is by one man, Jesus Christ, hath abounded unto many. And not as it was by one that sinned, so is the gift: for the judgment was by one to condemnation, but the free gift is of many offences unto justification. For if by one man's offence death reigned by one; much more they which receive abundance of grace and of the gift of righteousness shall reign in life by one, Jesus Christ.) Therefore as by the offence of one judgment came upon all men to condemnation; even so by the righteousness of one the free gift came upon all men unto justification of life. For as by one man's disobedience many were made sinners, so by the obedience of one shall many be made righteous." [Romans 5: 6 - 19]

We are only restored into righteousness through the obedience of Christ Jesus. He is all in all for us. There is no point wasting your time seeking for value elsewhere. Christ Jesus said *"I am the door: by me if any man enter in, he shall be saved, and shall go in and out, and find pasture"* [John 10:9]. He is the Possessor of the values for mankind! He is the worth of our life and through Him we generate virtues to impart our world. But until He makes us free, we are not free indeed. How do we get our freedom in Him and through Him?

By coming to the knowledge of the truth *"And ye shall know the truth, and the truth shall make you free"* and the truth is that, grace is made available for everyone who desires to be saved. *"For the grace of God that bringeth salvation hath appeared to all men, Teaching us that, denying ungodliness and worldly lusts, we should live soberly, righteously, and godly, in this present world; Looking for that blessed hope, and the glorious appearing of the great God and our Saviour Jesus Christ;* [Titus 2: 11-13]. God already made the provision for your redemption by the power of His love for you personally and the entire world. *"For God so loved the world, that he gave his only begotten Son, that whosoever believeth in him should not perish, but have everlasting life. For God sent not his Son into the world to condemn the world; but that the world through him might be saved. He*

*that believeth on him is not condemned: but he that believeth not is condemned
already, because he hath not believed in the name of the only begotten Son of God.
[John 3: 16 - 18].*

Therefore, to be freed indeed is to accept Jesus Christ as your personal
Saviour and Lord, having believed that God sent Him as the Lamb that takes
away the sins of the world. You need to consciously accept Him into your life
before continuing your journey to the secret treasures in this book.

HOW DO I RECEIVE JESUS CHRIST INTO MY LIFE?

*"But what saith it? The word is nigh thee, even in thy mouth, and in thy heart: that
is, the word of faith, which we preach; That if thou shalt confess with thy mouth
the Lord Jesus, and shalt believe in thine heart that God hath raised him from the
dead, thou shalt be saved. For with the heart man believeth unto righteousness;
and with the mouth confession is made unto salvation. For the scripture saith,
Whosoever believeth on him shall not be ashamed"* [Romans 10: 8 - 11]. Believe
in your heart with the understanding of the grace that has been released to you
for the salvation of your soul. Having understood the price He paid for your sins
and the opportunity given to you to return back to your Father and become His
righteousness, all you need is to confess your faith with your mouth and you
shall be saved.

You may ask me, 'what about my sins? I do not think I deserve His forgiveness,
or I was not born a Christian how will He receive me?' Well, congratulations
for your present position, I want to announce to you that you are in your best
position to be cleansed, forgiven, accepted as the beloved of the Father and be
made new as a child of God. Never bother about your status, Jesus already paid it
all. All that is required from you is to believe that Jesus Christ is the Son of God
and be willing to allow Him to come into your life. If you are convinced with
this simple truth kindly pray this prayer of faith:

*Father God, I come to you in the name of your Son Jesus Christ, to submit
my life to you. I acknowledge my sins and disobedience and I am here to ask
for your forgiveness. I ask you to cleanse me from all unrighteousness by the
precious blood of your Holy Child Jesus Christ. I consciously accept the price*

Congratulations for your new life and new beginning. I rejoice with you today as a new creature and heaven rejoices too for your sake. "*Therefore, if any man be in Christ, he is a new creature: old things are passed away; behold, all things are become new*" [*2 Corinthians 5:17*]. I pray that the same grace that led you out of your old life into the new life shall preserve, protect and defend you to the end in Jesus name. God richly bless you in Jesus name.

Prologue

For I am the Lord thy God, the Holy One of Israel, thy Saviour: I gave Egypt for thy ransom, Ethiopia and Seba for thee. Since thou wast precious in my sight, thou hast been honourable, and I have loved thee: therefore will I give men for thee, and people for thy life. Fear not: for I am with thee: I will bring thy seed from the east, and gather thee from the west; I will say to the north, Give up; and to the south, Keep not back: bring my sons from far, and my daughters from the ends of the earth; [Isaiah 43:3-6]

With this notable scripture, the worth of man can easily be appraised, as it is obvious that no one in his right sense pays a huge price to acquire valueless items, but every wise man takes delight in investing on items that are valuable to him. *"Since thou wast precious in my sight, thou hast been honourable, and I have loved thee: therefore, will I give men for thee, and people for thy life."* The value of man in the sight of God stands as the eternal cord that draws mercy, provokes grace and releases salvation. The worth of man was comparatively defined and proportionally measured by the efforts God invested on man when He formed him. It was recorded that man was wonderfully, delicately and fearfully made. *I will praise thee; for I am fearfully and wonderfully made: marvellous are thy works; and that my soul knoweth right well. [Psalm 139:14]*

This indicates that God invested so much on man that He could not afford watching him being molested, buffeted and or destroyed by circumstances. God made several provisions to restore man and retain his quality and potency in creation with the expectation that man will generate virtues to Him as the end products of the values placed on him. *"For ye are bought with a price: therefore, **glorify** God in your body, and in your spirit, which are God's"* [1 Corinthians 6:20].

Man is worth more than anything to God. God values man more than any other creatures. He made man to be His sole representative on earth. Man became the apple of His eye *"For thus saith the Lord of hosts; After the glory hath he sent me unto the nations which spoiled you: for he that toucheth you toucheth the apple of his eye"* [Zechariah 2:8] and He leads man with delicacy, *"He found him in a desert land, and in the waste howling wilderness; he led him about, he instructed him, he kept him as the apple of his eye"* [Deuteronomy 32:10] simply because He values man!

You see, treasures are delicately preserved based on the level of their worth to us. However, such items are disposed-off when they are worthless since they are now inconsequentially valueless and can no longer produce virtues to their owners. *"…but if the salt have lost his savour, wherewith shall it be salted? it is thenceforth good for nothing, but to be cast out, and to be trodden under foot of men"* [Matthew 5:13]. Treasures are preserved to generate virtues with the philosophy that the higher the expectation, the more the value we display towards such treasure which ultimately determines how great the virtues we derive.

Man is mandated to dedicate his life to appreciate, glorify, praise, worship and serve God with honour and reverence. *I will praise thee, for… marvellous are thy works; and that my soul knoweth right well[1]*. My soul knows that you are worthy to be honoured because of your marvellous works in my life! God values man with the expectation that man will generate the virtues of service and praise in return. That was why God placed emphasis on these two virtues: service and praise! *"let my people go that they may **serve** me"* for *"This people have I formed for myself; they shall shew forth my **praise**.[2]"*

The value exhibited toward God and the honour conferred on Him by us stand as the driving forces that compel His sovereignty and commit His integrity to act beyond our expectation. Our value for God is interpreted as honour to Him and *"for them that honour me I will honour, and they that despise me shall be lightly esteemed."* [1 Samuel 2:30]. Ultimately, when we attribute value to God, He empties His virtues on us and manifests His power as the all-sufficient, ever reliable and dependable God. He displays the supremacy of His glorious light

---

¹ *Read Psalm 139:14;*

² *Read Exodus 4:23 and Isaiah 43:21*

amidst our dark world, thereby releasing His worth as virtues to demonstrate His manifold Godhead bodily.

The value attributed to God by the three Hebrew boys in Babylon paved way to the release of God's virtue, which resulted in victory and generated eternal honour and glory to the boys in the kingdom of Nebuchadnezzar

> *Nebuchadnezzar spake and said unto them, Is it true, O Shadrach, Meshach, and Abednego, do not ye serve my gods, nor worship the golden image which I have set up? Now if ye be ready that at what time ye hear the sound of the cornet, flute, harp, sackbut, psaltery, and dulcimer, and all kinds of musick, ye fall down and worship the image which I have made; well: but if ye worship not, ye shall be cast the same hour into the midst of a burning fiery furnace; and who is that God that shall deliver you out of my hands? Shadrach, Meshach, and Abednego, answered and said to the king, O Nebuchadnezzar, we are not careful to answer thee in this matter. If it be so, our God whom we serve is able to deliver us from the burning fiery furnace, and he will deliver us out of thine hand, O king. But if not, be it known unto thee, O king, that we will not serve thy gods, nor worship the golden image which thou hast set up. [Daniel 3: 14 - 18]*

Summoning up their courage and confidence in God, they declared 'Oh *Nebuchadnezzar*, we are not careful of your mere golden image and your frenzy threat! Our God is worthy to be praised and only Him shall we bow to worship. In case you do not understand our stand with Him, even if He does decide not to save us from your hands, we vow not to let down the value we place on Him' (*paraphrased*). These young chaps despised what they did not value and esteemed their God. They risked their life because of their value for God. Their value for the God of Israel provoked their faith and caused their faith to be unstoppable, making their eyelids look straight before them to confront the threat of the king on their temperament. Their faith became hyperactivity zealous, desperate to please God and God only! You see, value strengthens faith, making faith piously enraged when anything contrary to what you have confidence in rises to challenge its value. Value determines action, as it is no respecter of a person. When there is no value, kings are treated as common citizens, but when value is in place servants will be honoured.

Trust is the product of believe, while believe is the evidence of value. You naturally believe what you value and simply trust what you believe. We believe God because we value His supremacy and we trust Him because we value the worth of His sovereignty.

<blockquote>

And when he was come into the house, the blind men came to him: and Jesus saith unto them, Believe ye that I am able to do this? They said unto him, Yea, Lord. Then touched he their eyes, saying, According to your faith be it unto you. And their eyes were opened; and Jesus straitly charged them, saying, See that no man know it. [Matthew 9: 28 - 30]

</blockquote>

In the school of the supernatural, we trade our faith on the platform of our value for the vessel and when values are traded, virtues would be released for manifestation. Reading the account of the leper in Mark 1:40-42, it was obvious that his value for Christ was the secret strength behind his healing. He said, 'I know you carry what can make me whole, I value your capability and omnipotence. However, all I require from you is your willingness to exercise that sovereignty over my situation and I will be made whole instantly' (*paraphrased*). That is, "*If thou wilt, thou canst make me clean*" And the Lord said to him 'by the reason of your value for me, my willingness is at your service, let my virtue be released according to the level of your value for my capability to heal you' and it was so that "*immediately the leprosy departed from him, and he was cleansed*".

<blockquote>

"And there came a leper to him, beseeching him, and kneeling down to him, and saying unto him, If thou wilt, thou canst make me clean. And Jesus, moved with compassion, put forth his hand, and touched him, and saith unto him, I will; be thou clean. And as soon as he had spoken, immediately the leprosy departed from him, and he was cleansed" [Mark 1: 40 - 42]

</blockquote>

His faith was measured by the level of the value he placed on Christ for his instant release from the siege of leprosy.

God's totality that we enjoy is directly proportional to the level of value we exhibit towards Him! Take for instance, the issue of Lazarus and the reaction of his sisters when the Saviour arrived at the scene on the fourth day of his burial.

Mary and Martha reciprocally said to the Lord, Master if you were around our brother would not have died. We value you so much to the intent that your presence would have been enough to keep our brother alive. Nevertheless, your worth is still the same though you came at this seemingly late hour. We have the assurance that even though he is dead and buried, whatever you desire for him from your Father (even now) will be the final answer to our situation.

> *"Then said Martha unto Jesus, Lord, if thou hadst been here, my brother had not died. But I know, that even now, whatsoever thou wilt ask of God, God will give it thee…*
>
> *Then when Mary was come where Jesus was, and saw him, she fell down at his feet, saying unto him, Lord, if thou hadst been here, my brother had not died." [John 11: 21-22, 32]*

They were of one mind and in unity declared their values for Christ and their confidence in His worth. And the Lord replied, because of this magnitude of value you exhibited towards me ***"Thy brother shall rise again"*** Listen, I am the resurrection and life, and anyone who dares to value me this way, though he were dead will live again

> *"Jesus saith unto her, Thy brother shall rise again. Martha saith unto him, I know that he shall rise again in the resurrection at the last day. Jesus said unto her, I am the resurrection, and the life: he that believeth in me, though he were dead, yet shall he live: And whosoever liveth and believeth in me shall never die. Believest thou this? She saith unto him, Yea, Lord: I believe that thou art the Christ, the Son of God, which should come into the world"* [John 11: 23-27]

Friends, that was the secret behind the miracle of a four-day old dead, stinking man who rose up with no trace of sickness or the smell of grave in his life. Understand therefore, that the declaration of God's worth is the master provoker of His sovereignty in turning your world around! Those who value God don't die! You cannot value God and not be attended to in your desperate situation. You cannot value God and not be dignified in life, *'for my people shall not be ashamed'*.

The question is, what is God's worth to you and how much value do you exhibit towards Him? How much of service do you render for the promotion of His kingdom? How much praise do you offer to the Lord for His marvelous works both in your life and around you? How much do you align yourself to walk in the fear of God and maintain ceaseless release of the honour due to Him amidst turbulent situations and the valley of decision, when trials and temptations rage against your faith and integrity?

These questions among others are the major subjects in this book. Listen, you are not an ingrate so don't live like one. You are the apple of God's eyes and everything around you is earnestly waiting to see you speaking and declaring God's worth in your life. Ingratitude is the breeding ground for frustration and failure in life. People tend to backslide because they fail to see the faithfulness of their Maker and tend to rob God of the honour due to Him. What defines your living on earth is the ability to recognize God and who He is in your life. Your value for God is the only answer to your fulfilment in life. Colossian 1:27 talks about one of the mysteries that has been kept secret for long but now made manifest to us through grace, and that mystery is the indwelling of Christ in us, the hope of glory.

> *"Even the mystery which hath been hid from ages and from generations, but now is made manifest to his saints: To whom God would make known what is the riches of the glory of this mystery among the Gentiles; which is Christ in you, the hope of glory:"* [Colossian 1:26-27]

God is what people see in us to recognize and appreciate our worth. So, an attempt to despise or refuse to cultivate the habit of value for God and His kingdom is to devalue and reduce yourself to nonentity in life. For the word says, *"To whom God would make known what is the riches of the glory of this mystery among the Gentiles; which is **Christ in you, the hope of glory.**"* His presence in us is the only hope that generates glory and virtue, turning us to the envy of the world.

David, a man full of passion for God, enjoyed the fullness of heaven on earth throughout his life because he gave God everything at his disposal, both in praise, in service, in fear, reverence and honour. He placed the highest value on God, with fear and trembling; reverencing, honouring, serving and praising

God always despite the wars and trials that surrounded him. He dedicated his life to valuing God and the works of His hand. Hear what he (David) said concerning God:

> *"O Lord our Lord, how excellent is thy name in all the earth! who hast set thy glory above the heavens."* [Psalm 8:1] and while making analysis of the secret of men, he declared: *"How excellent is thy lovingkindness, O God! therefore the children of men put their trust under the shadow of thy wings.* [Psalm 36:7].* What pronounces your worth in the society is the level of God's recognition in your life, *"For in him we live, and move, and have our being; as certain also of your own poets have said, For we are also his offspring.* [Acts 17:28]

Apparently, as it appeals to the things of God, so is it to the natural paradigm of life. You need to start seeing God and His glory in people instead of evaluating them with their self-worth. David saw the element of God in Saul and resisted from hurting him. No wonder, he could not be destroyed by the king and the whole nation that turned against him. He valued the God whose anointing was poured on Saul – he dared not touch the anointed of God because he valued God's anointing, the evil acts of the man notwithstanding.

> *"And he came to the sheepcotes by the way, where was a cave; and Saul went in to cover his feet: and David and his men remained in the sides of the cave. And the men of David said unto him, Behold the day of which the Lord said unto thee, Behold, I will deliver thine enemy into thine hand, that thou mayest do to him as it shall seem good unto thee. Then David arose, and cut off the skirt of Saul's robe privily. And it came to pass afterward, that David's heart smote him, because he had cut off Saul's skirt. And he said unto his men, The Lord forbid that I should do this thing unto my master, the Lord's anointed, to stretch forth mine hand against him, seeing he is the anointed of the Lord. So David stayed his servants with these words, and suffered them not to rise against Saul. But Saul rose up out of the cave, and went on his way. David also arose afterward, and went out of the cave, and cried after Saul, saying, My lord the king. And when Saul looked behind him,*

David stooped with his face to the earth, and bowed himself. And David said to Saul, Wherefore hearest thou men's words, saying, Behold, David seeketh thy hurt? Behold, this day thine eyes have seen how that the Lord had delivered thee to day into mine hand in the cave: and some bade me kill thee: but mine eye spared thee; and I said, I will not put forth mine hand against my lord; for he is the Lord's anointed. Moreover, my father, see, yea, see the skirt of thy robe in my hand: for in that I cut off the skirt of thy robe, and killed thee not, know thou and see that there is neither evil nor transgression in mine hand, and I have not sinned against thee; yet thou huntest my soul to take it. The Lord judge between me and thee, and the Lord avenge me of thee: but mine hand shall not be upon thee. As saith the proverb of the ancients, Wickedness proceedeth from the wicked: but mine hand shall not be upon thee." [1 Samuel 24: 3 - 13]

The virtue an individual possesses will be released into your direction when you start seeing such an individual as God's vessel, heaven's agent on earth, strong, value-based and trusted personality with great integrity. But if your perception about people is nonchalant, you will deny yourself of the great virtues they possess. As it is commonly stated in the philosophy of life, that *handling life casually is what ends people in casualty!* Dealing with people without cultivating a heart or sense of value for them is what dries up the virtues due for our glorification. Consequently, God took the virtues of kingship, honour and protection from Saul and placed them on David because he honoured the value of God and preserved its worth in Saul. Favour is cunning and beauty is deceptive, but those who value God and the works of His hand shall be dignified.

The purpose of this book is to expose you to the secret treasure of accomplishment without stress in life. This material contains the life-gate for accomplishment and the secret trigger of God's manifold presence in every situation in life. By the time you are through with this book, my strong perception is that the strategies for a return to the initial agenda of God for your life would have been unveiled and the path made known to you. I pray for your spiritual eyes to be opened as the Holy Spirit quickens your understanding mind and helps you to embrace the new way of life to the fullness of God's purpose on earth. All that heaven requires from us is to cultivate a heart that values and treasures God and all that has to do with His kingdom. This is the key to all-round fulfilment in life. It delivers grace and makes God's mercy so real and obtainable at every point in life. As the scriptures say *"Let us therefore come boldly unto the throne of grace, that we may obtain mercy, and find grace to help in time of need"* [Hebrews 4: 16]

Hear this, any prayer you pray without first building confidence in God for an answer is a waste of time and effort. The confidence is the end result of the value you have for Him in securing His capability to answer your prayers and His integrity to deliver your desired requests according to His will. So, when this confidence is built, you approach him with boldness because you trust His sovereignty to act and value His integrity to perform and deliver.

> *"And this is the confidence that we have in him, that, if we ask any thing according to his will, he heareth us: And if we know that he hear us, whatsoever we ask, we know that we have the petitions that we desired of him"* [1 John 5: 14 – 15]

Whatever succeeded in making you lose value for the things of God has robbed you of the virtues due for your breakthrough and fulfilment in life. That is why I believe that your understanding of this material will help strengthen your spiritual perception to the minor things that matter in life which have been regrettably ignored and neglected in our day to day life and endeavours.

I see a change of story for you by the virtue of the light that will break forth in your life through this material and I pray that your mind be opened to receive and embrace the engrafted word of truth communicating to you this season in Jesus name.

I decree that every virtue you have lost as a result of pride, arrogance and or due to ignorance of this simple daily lifestyle shall be restored in manifold form in Jesus name. I command the light of the truth to penetrate every dark place of your life through this material, and all your inheritances in Christ be restored fully in the course of your studying this book in Jesus name.

Welcome to your season of visitation and divine enablement. Jesus is Lord.

Chapter 1

Faith, Value And Virtue

> *And a woman having an issue of blood twelve years, which had spent all her living upon physicians, neither could be healed of any, Came behind him, and touched the border of his garment: and immediately her issue of blood stanched. And Jesus said, Who touched me? When all denied, Peter and they that were with him said, Master, the multitude throng thee and press thee, and sayest thou, Who touched me? And Jesus said, Somebody hath touched me: for I perceive that **virtue** is gone out of me. And when the woman saw that she was not hid, she came trembling, and falling down before him, she declared unto him before all the people for what cause she had touched him, and how she was healed immediately. And he said unto her, Daughter, be of good comfort: thy faith hath made thee whole; go in peace. [Luke 8: 43 - 48]*

"Someone touched me" the Lord Jesus said, and His disciples exclaimed 'Master, what do you mean? How can you say someone touched you when multitudes are thronging you?' And the Lord replied, 'I know that people are thronging me, and I can feel the heat of their thronging, I can hear their screaming and see their overwhelming excitement. However, somebody 'values' my presence, my position, and conceivably my capability, not as a celebrity but as a Carrier of solutions to the devastating state of humanity. Someone in the congregation esteems the anointing on me and such an individual just touched me now because **virtue** has gone out of me to confirm the **value** this fellow has for me'

Majority gather in churches, conferences or crusades on a daily basis, jerking, screaming, jumping and exercising all sorts of physical exertion to demonstrate their faith and believe in God, yet find it difficult to experience change. There is the need to understand that those who approach the throne with valueless heart end up virtue-less in return; physical and religious exercises notwithstanding. God is not mocked, man can be deceived by all these religious acrobatic activities in the name of kingdom commitment and services, but only God knows those who really place values on what they are doing in the house; "*for* the LORD seeth *not as man seeth; for man looketh on the outward appearance, but the LORD looketh on the heart.*" [1 Samuel 16:7]

Thronging does not draw virtues, it only promotes excitement and enhances religious bigotry or narrow-mindedness, but 'someone drew something peculiar from me and I can feel it.' Said the Saviour! And He turned Him about and saw the enfeebled now being strengthened by the reason of the **value** she placed on the Vessel that compelled the **virtue** to be released into her direction for the quickening of her destiny. She was released from the siege upon her life simply by trading values. Friends, it is not the rigor of your religious commitment nor the energy of your shouting and screaming that command virtues, it is simply, the value you cultivate in the heart toward the vessel that determines and commands the release of virtues to your direction "*… for by strength shall no man prevail*" *[1 Samuel 2:9]*

Therefore, value is the master determinant of virtue. The secret of the release of virtue was the value she (the woman of the issue of blood) placed on the vessel… "*For she said within herself, If I may but touch his garment, I shall be whole.*" [Matthew 9:21]. The greater the value you place on a thing the stronger the virtues you command. So, in the school of manifestation, value is the master key to the secret treasure house of virtues.

Faith is the substance of things hoped for, the evidence of things not seen[3] – we have not seen it, yet we believe that we have received it. Why, because something is actively working between our faith and the expectation of the release of our desired virtues. This is where values come into play. We have faith to receive because we value the source of supply and by the level of our value for the source, virtues are determined.

Now, between the time you pray and the time you receive, three things

---

[3] *Read Hebrews 11*

should be in place to sustain your faith: **hope, assurance** and **expectation**. However, these three essential qualities of faith are sustained by confidence and confidence is the product of the value you place on the source of the expected answers to your requests. For *…this is the confidence that we have in him, that, if we ask any thing according to his will, he heareth us: [1 John 5:14].* We ask with all confidence building our trust, hope, expectation and assurance according to the **worth** of God's ability, faithfulness and principally, the value we attribute to *His will (according to his will)* regarding that issue.

The inevitability of value is that when it is cultivated, it produces greater virtues but when it is neglected it strains the flow of virtues. In Luke 6:19, the whole city came to Christ with great value desiring the release of healing virtues and it was recorded that *all* were healed of whatever type of sickness or disease *"And the whole multitude sought to touch him: for there went **virtue** out of him, and healed them all."* This same all-powerful, virtue-carrier Saviour, Healer and Deliverer (Christ Jesus) arrived in Nazareth and virtues could not be released, why? Simply put, the place of value is what determines the release of virtues. They could not receive because they did not value the source and by the reason of their valueless act, they lost their confidence and ultimately, faith became impotent.

We celebrate faith so much that we forget that the strength of faith is the value we ascribe to God in return for our desired expectation. Faith has no root to bear if value does not precede it. The Lord Jesus could not do so much because the people never value His worth. A vessel is a container and carrier of virtues, only your value for the vessel can guarantee your access to its content. Listen, no matter how endowed and powerful a vessel is, when you don't recognize its worth, you render such a vessel impotent to function and deliver effectively. Value when cultivated sets expectation on and worth when recognized makes strength available to generate virtues in return. *"And he could there do no mighty work, save that he laid his hands upon a few sick folk, and healed them. And he marvelled because of their unbelief. And he went round about the villages, teaching." [Mark 6:5-6]*

So *"…he did not many mighty works there because of their unbelief."* *[Matthew 13:58].* Because they placed no value on His personality, rather they saw Him as the son of Joseph whom they all knew. I decree that every habit of religious familiarity that is set to rob you of God's virtues shall be destroyed in your life right now in Jesus name. Listen attentively, God has no uncle, neither does He have special respect for any man *(For there is no respect of persons with God [Romans 2:11]).* He is no respecter of persons *"...But in every nation he that feareth him, and worketh righteousness, is accepted with him"* [Acts 10: 35]. His principle is simply "whosoever will" whosoever recognize His worth, whosoever appreciate and value Him for who He is and what He is able to do, such an individual or group will experience His supernatural acts. So, in God's ethics, it is whosoever *'values'* that commands whatsoever *'virtues'* on the platform of faith which must be principally driven by worth and value.

You need to understand therefore, that, as a child of God and by redemptive delivery, you have your root of value in God. One of the vital reasons why God places so much value on man is primarily because man was made in His image and fashioned after His likeness. So, you carry God's worth as your personality and wisdom demands that you start seeing God, who is the main Source of values and virtue with a great sense of worth in order for you to enjoy His great virtues. The people of Nazareth had no confidence in Christ because they had a heart of insignificance and familiarity toward the vessel that God sent to liberate them. Faith functions effectively on the platform of value for the vessel. Faith is strengthened through the confidence we build towards our expectation and this confidence is sorely dependent on the worth and value ascribed to the vessel in view! Therefore, operating faith without cultivating a heart of worth and value is likening to living without breathing. I pray therefore that your confidence in exhibiting a heart of value towards God shall not be lost in Jesus name.

WHAT THEN IS FAITH?

Faith is recognizing God's value, appreciating God's worth, acting on His worth/ value to attract and compel the release of His virtues. Faith can also be defined as the ability to believe that all things are possible and taking responsibility to act based on the belief, thereby committing God's integrity to perform His part. In other words, receiving instructions from God, jumping to obeying them and confidently acting on the instructions with excitement and a sense of expectation for the release of virtues as the end-result of the obedience.

 OLA JONES DUYILE ◆

How do you believe and act? You act based on the perception that the source cannot fail, lie or deny Himself or His integrity to fulfil His part in your life. That is why it is written that even when our belief system fails, God abides faithful because of the value we have placed on Him and hence cannot deny Himself to command the release of His virtues on us. This is simply by the reason of the values we have for Him even in the midst of our faithlessness because *"It is a faithful saying: For if we be dead with* him, *we shall also live with* him: *If we suffer, we shall also reign with* him: *if we deny* him, *he also will deny us: If we believe not, yet he abideth faithful: he cannot deny himself."* [2 Timothy 2: 11 - 13].

Therefore, faith can be summed up as the ability to earnestly approach God with great sense of **value** in order to command the release of His virtues. This value is not determined or influenced by the position, situation and or circumstance of a man, rather it is an inbuilt nature cultivated right in the heart and not deterred by the waves of circumstances. Value is inherent in a man's personality; the condition of things around him notwithstanding. *"Though he slay me, yet will I trust in him: but I will maintain mine own ways before him"* [Job 13:15]. Job said my situation does not affect my value for God, I am not moved by the condition; I stand upon my integrity, I will maintain the level of value I have for Him and I am confident that His virtues will be released to my direction sooner than I can ever imagine!

Where is the Strength of Faith?

As it is written *"And this is the confidence that we have in him… "*, the strength of faith is the **confidence** you exhibit in the midst of turbulence. It is your stand in the time of seemingly impossible circumstances. A man that has his confidence in God does not look back. He is never influenced by the situation. His eyelids are looking straight before him; he keeps celebrating the faithfulness of God because he is already settled with God's sovereignty and maintains consistency in appreciating God's worth. He is never moved by the complexity of the unfinished assignment, but his focus is on God, trusting Him to perfect His will regarding the burning issues. *"Being confident of this very thing, that he which hath begun a good work in you will perform it until the day of Jesus Christ"* [Philippians 1:6].

He maintains his boldness and strengthens his faith through the confidence he has in the God of all possibilities. He turns his song to the assurance in God, exclaiming, proclaiming and declaring his faith in the Lord with full assurance saying *"For the Lord shall be my confidence, and shall keep my foot from being taken"*

In Romans chapter four, the bible reveals to us the secret strength of Abraham's faith that kept him on an excited journey for twenty-five years without looking back. The scriptures recorded that: *"He staggered not at the promise of God through unbelief; but was strong in faith, giving glory to God; And being fully persuaded that, what he had promised, he was able also to perform"* *[Romans 4:20-21]*. Despite his age and the deadness of Sarah's womb, Abraham was not moved, nor was he weak in faith, but was fully persuaded and confident. He was at peace, resting on God's faithfulness to deliver his expectation at His (God's) own appointed time. The Amplified version helps us to simplify the effectiveness of Abraham's confidence while demonstrating his trust and celebrating God's worth in preparation for the delivery of His promise, though it seems late by human nature.

> *Without becoming weak in faith he considered his own body, now as good as dead [for producing children] since he was about a hundred years old, and [he considered] the deadness of Sarah's womb. But he did not doubt or waver in unbelief concerning the promise of God, but he grew strong and empowered by faith, giving glory to God, being fully convinced that God had the power to do what He had promised. Therefore his faith was credited to him as righteousness (right standing with God). [Romans 4:19-22: AMP]*

He knew God's worth, so his confidence in God was without doubt; no wonder it was accounted to him for righteousness and he became the father of faith. His secret strength was the confidence he built in God. Faith feeds on confidence to establish our conviction in the invincibility power of God that turns impossibilities to testimonies. Confidence becomes the portal where faith acquires the strength needed to function effectively in the field of manifestation.

Look at the case of Job in his state of pain and agony, while his closest friend in life, his help-meet said to him, Job why are you still holding God with this great value, despite what He had allowed to happen to us as a family? See all our children are dead, the houses and all the treasures are burnt, all your acquired wealth is gone. Our life no longer worth anything and I equally believe that God should worth nothing in this family. So, curse God and let Him know we have lost respect for Him! Curse Him and confirm He has no value in your hand and in this family anymore. And Job said to his wife "Thou *speakest as one of the foolish women speaketh*" I don't rate God by my wealth, achievement or circumstance, I rate God by His worth and value for my soul, the breath of life He gave me, and as long as I breath, His worth and value can never depreciate.

> *"So went Satan forth from the presence of the Lord, and smote Job with sore boils from the sole of his foot unto his crown. And he took him a potsherd to scrape himself withal; and he sat down among the ashes. Then said his wife unto him, Dost thou still retain thine integrity? curse God, and die. But he said unto her, Thou speakest as one of the foolish women speaketh. What? shall we receive good at the hand of God, and shall we not receive evil? In all this did not Job sin with his lips."* [Job 2:7 - 10]

This man (Job) was facing coordinated attack from the pit of hell, Satan taken hold of all his substances with strong direct oppression, affliction and molestation yet he remained calm, for *"Thou wilt keep him in perfect peace, whose mind is stayed on thee: because he trusteth in thee."* He kept esteeming God's worth and with his unmovable confidence in God despised the deeds of Satan. He lost focus on his predicament and set his eyes on God's sovereignty for total restoration. Friends, there is an end to those burning issues if only you can maintain your integrity and not curse God in your heart. If you can hold on to God's worth, the scent of waters will be released to your direction for your transformation.

Always remember that faith is the substance of things hoped for… *"For there is hope of a tree, if it be cut down, that it will sprout again, and that the tender branch thereof will not cease. Though the root thereof wax old in the earth, and the stock thereof die in the ground; Yet through the scent of water it will bud, and bring forth boughs like a plant"* [Job 14:7-9]. Learn therefore to patiently build your faith and confidently hope in God's ability by recognizing and appreciating His worth and value. Be strong in the Lord, be bold, be confident and be courageous to declare God's worth at every point in your life. This is the secret strength of faith that produces the wisdom and energy to draw virtues from the Vessel.

Faith makes its boast in God

Psalms 34:2 declares *"My soul shall make her boast in the Lord: the humble shall hear thereof, and be glad."* This is the secret lubricant of faith. It boasts of the sovereignty and the capabilities of God at all times and in all situations. Hezekiah boastfully said concerning God when Sennacherib was threatening Israel *"O Lord of hosts, God of Israel, that dwellest between the cherubims, thou art the God, even thou alone, of all the kingdoms of the earth: thou hast made heaven and earth."* He continued to distinguish the God of Israel among gods by declaring *"Of a truth, Lord, the kings of Assyria have laid waste all the nations, and their countries, And have cast their gods into the fire: for they were no gods, but the work of men's hands, wood and stone: therefore they have destroyed them."* Yes, he can destroy other so-called gods because they are no gods, BUT *"thou art the God, even thou alone, of all the kingdoms of the earth:"* and no one can molest you[4]. Faith strongly declares that 'no man can handle my God and as long as *"all my springs are in thee"* I cannot be moved by the threat of mere men'. I am confident that very soon your virtues will be released to my direction for the quickening of my feeble life.

God in His capacity declared His level of supremacy over the heaven and the earth so that everyone who associates with Him might make his/her boast in the God of all power and authority. He declared *"See now that I, even I, am he, and there is no god with me: I kill, and I make alive; I wound, and I heal: neither is there any that can deliver out of my hand. For I lift up my hand to heaven, and say, I live for ever"* [Deuteronomy 32: 39 - 40]. This is where believers should draw strength and enhance their faith in the worth of their God. Faith builds on values while understanding exposes the worth of God to establish the root for our faith and strengthen the cord of our hope. Building your faith in God and making boast of His capabilities helps your faith to rise to the reality of the victory and

---

[4] " [Read Isaiah 37]

 OLA JONES DUYILE ♦

triumph you aspire to get in any situation. Make boast of your faith in your God today, that is how to trade value for the release of virtues.

Faith Awakes to the Reality of Life

Faith can likewise be defined as the immeasurable value we place on God with the confidence built on the platform of our trust, hope and expectation, making us cultivate an immovable heart of belief without any aorta of doubt for the release of the expected virtues from the Vessel. Joseph enjoyed the presence of God both as a slave and prisoner because of the value he had for the God of his fathers. Hear what he said concerning God. *"There is none greater in this house than I; neither hath he kept back any thing from me but thee, because thou art his wife: how then can I do this great wickedness, and sin against God?"* [Genesis 39:9]

It was recorded that God was with him in all his situations (*Genesis 39 verses 2 and 23*), God was with him when he was a slave; God was with him in the dungeon of prison. Honourably, God showed up when Joseph stood before Pharaoh in the palace and gave him insight, wisdom, revelation and solution to the plight of the king (*Genesis 41 verses 38 and 39*). His secret was that he woke up to the reality of who God is and said: I value God! I tremble at His presence! His word shakes me to the bone! I love Him, and I want to reverence Him both in private and in the public no matter the situation. *"How then can I do this great wickedness, and sin against God?"* And this man Joseph became the carrier of God's Spirit and took over the rulership of a strange nation, determining what happens in his generation.

The secret was not because he was from the loins of Jacob, but the secret was the value he placed on the God of his fathers; Abraham, Isaac and Jacob. While other sons of Jacob were celebrating the covenant and thronging God in the name of being covenant children, Joseph was busy trading values and maintaining a right sense of worth for God in fear and trembling. No wonder he became the father of Pharaoh and the lord of the entire land of Egypt.

> *"And Joseph said unto his brethren, Come near to me, I pray you. And they came near. And he said, I am Joseph your brother, whom ye sold into Egypt. Now therefore be not grieved, nor angry with yourselves, that ye sold me*

Faith creates no room for gimmick rather, faith awakes to the reality of life most importantly when it is consciously built on the platform of God's worth and value. Friends, it's high time for you to understand the difference between thronging and touching in your Christian journey. Yes, you are a covenant child, but that should give you a sense of responsibility to acquaint yourself with God's principles and ethics of His kingdom more willingly than merely celebrating your position in the covenant and turning reality to religion.

Christianity is not a religion, rather it is all about relationship, fellowship, covenant walk and kingdom perspective. Though there seems to be some religious vacuum that earnestly desires to be filled, but Christianity fills this vacuum with spirituality and not with religious activities. Christianity is about becoming part of God's kingdom, walking in the knowledge of God to truly manifest the kingdom on earth with great peace and adequate wisdom to match. As it is *written "Grace and peace be multiplied unto you through the knowledge of God, and of Jesus our Lord"* [2 Peter 1:2] Also, as an *"Elect according to the foreknowledge of God the Father, through sanctification of the Spirit, unto obedience and sprinkling of the blood of Jesus Christ: Grace unto you, and peace, be multiplied."* [1 Peter 1:2]. Christianity implies 'Christ in you' which by divine election qualifies you as an heir of the kingdom, representing Him here on earth as the ambassador of the kingdom, bringing the kingdom to functional reality here on earth.

However, there is no ambassador that can effectively and positively represent a country without first cultivating the habit of value for such country and equally understanding her worth. What an ambassador of a nation trades in another country is the worth and value of his country, but when he does not recognize and or has value for his country, he is ultimately not qualified to represent such country. The same applies to us as believers, we are not expected to be called

Christian if we don't see the worth of the kingdom of God and or have value for God, our religious activities notwithstanding. Remember that it was the worth and value of Christ that the people of Antioch saw in the lives of the Apostles that brought about the name Christians [Acts 11:26], which literally means "Christ - in – them". Let Christ be seen in you therefore, both in capacity and in character so people can appreciate His values in you while you continue to generate great virtues.

Empty yourself to be filled by God

People throng because they want to feel the celebrity and show that they belong, but those who touch came because they do not see themselves as qualified to belong, rather they esteem the vessel and value His capacity to impart their lives. Those who touch believe and value the anointing upon the anointed and therefore obtain mercy and gain access to the treasure house of the virtues that the anointed one possesses. Majority are thronging not for the faith at work but for a mere showcase. Your time and effort shall not be wasted in the school of faith in Jesus name.

> *"And he went out from thence, and came into his own country; and his disciples follow him. And when the sabbath day was come, he began to teach in the synagogue: and many hearing him were astonished, saying, From whence hath this man these things? and what wisdom is this which is given unto him, that even such mighty works are wrought by his hands? Is not this the carpenter, the son of Mary, the brother of James, and Joses, and of Juda, and Simon? and are not his sisters here with us? And they were offended at him. But Jesus said unto them, A prophet is not without honour, but in his own country, and among his own kin, and in his own house. And he could there do no mighty work, save that he laid his hands upon a few sick folk, and healed them. And he marvelled because of their unbelief. And he went round about the villages, teaching."* [Mark 6: 1 - 6]

Empty yourself! bury your pride, re-organize your mentality! Open your heart and welcome the Spirit of God to help you build a heart that craves for

God's worth and appreciate God's value. This is the only way to get yourself out of the thronging mentality to the reality of faith driven touch that releases the virtues from the vessel. You need to have value for God and the things of God, so you can benefit from the virtues He carries.

WHAT IS VALUE?

"And Pharaoh said unto his servants, Can we find such a one as this is, a man in whom the Spirit of God is?" [Genesis 41:38]. Value is the determinant of the worth of an item, while virtue is the inveterate evidence of the worth and the impact it generates in return. Value makes virtues out of a vessel and derives benefit or gain advantage through submissive disposition to the quality, capacity and capability of the vessel. As soon as Pharaoh saw Joseph, he affirmed the quality and the worth of Joseph and that in return released to his kingdom all the virtues that Joseph carried.

I have spent some time studying the subject of value and it amazes me to discover that people cherish what they esteem and despise what seems insignificant to them. In the normal world's norms, familiarity is the degrading tool for values. He is my brother and what can he add to me! We have been friends for years and so what can he offer? We came from the same loins, we are from the same place, the same house, the same city, we even went to the same school, we were in the same class and I know his capacity; therefore, knowing him in and out, I have concluded that nothing good can come out of him. *"And Nathanael said unto him, Can there any good thing come out of Nazareth? Philip saith unto him, Come and see"* [John 1:46].

These are the common norms in our society today and most pathetically, among the saints of God. We doubt people's calling into ministry, we despise prophecy, we demean utterances and we reduce the strength of our faith to mere religious practices; hence we lose all the virtues of the glory of heaven.

Christ sent His disciples to a certain city (specifically, to the lost sheep of Israel) to preach the gospel and to rescue them from their misplaced position. They were principally sent to *"Heal the sick, cleanse the lepers, raise the dead, cast out devils..."* among them. He instructed them to freely distribute the grace and mercies of God that have brought salvation to the lost: but hear the rule: *"And into whatsoever city or town ye shall enter, enquire who in it is worthy; and there abide till ye go thence. And when ye come into an house, salute it. And if the house be worthy, let your peace come upon it: but if it be not worthy, let your peace return to you. And whosoever shall not receive you, nor hear your words, when ye depart out of that house or city, shake off the dust of your feet"* [Matthew 10: 11 - 14]

If the house recognizes your worth, values your presence and appreciates the anointing you carry, then release your virtues upon the house. But *"if it be not worthy, let your peace return to you!"*

Value is of the heart and when it is cultivated, it becomes a force that helps us to stretch for the virtues contained in the vessel. Always be reminded that we human beings are only permitted to experience the release of virtues on the platform of worth and the measure to which we value things. Whatever you are demeaning will result in depreciation, only what you value appreciates. So, the virtue at your disposal is proportional to the value you exhibit toward the vessels around you.

Value is the high regard you have for someone, his/her worth, importance and or usefulness to you. English dictionary defines values as *"Principles or standards of behaviour; one's judgement of what is important in life[5]."* In other words, your action towards the quality and capability of someone brings about the worth and importance you place on such an individual to determine what you can benefit from him/her based on the worth and in disparity to the general view. Pharaoh saw God in Joseph and realized that all he needed to sustain his kingdom at that crucial time was God, so he exclaimed *"…Can we find such a one as this is, a man in whom the Spirit of God is?"* Now, see what Pharaoh did after he recognized the value of Joseph:

> *"And Pharaoh said unto Joseph, Forasmuch as God hath shewed thee all this, there is none so discreet and wise as thou art: Thou shalt be over my house, and according unto thy word shall all my people be ruled: only in the throne will I be greater than thou. And Pharaoh said unto Joseph, See, I have set thee over all the land of Egypt. And Pharaoh took off his ring from his hand, and put it upon Joseph's hand, and arrayed him in vestures of fine linen, and put a gold chain about his neck; And he made him to ride in the second chariot*

---

[5] https://en.oxforddictionaries.com/definition/value

which he had; and they cried before him, Bow the knee: and he made him ruler over all the land of Egypt. And Pharaoh said unto Joseph, I am Pharaoh, and without thee shall no man lift up his hand or foot in all the land of Egypt. And Pharaoh called Joseph's name Zaphenath-paneah; and he gave him to wife Asenath the daughter of Poti-phera priest of On. And Joseph went out over all the land of Egypt" [Genesis 41: 39 - 45]

No wonder, he enjoyed full heaven on earth all through his reign in Egypt. By this recognition, he gave Joseph free hand to operate and coordinate the affairs of Egypt by the Spirit of God which was visible in his life. Even till today, Pharaoh still possesses the major portion of Egypt. God's wisdom and discretion worked through Joseph and virtues were released to the extent that he virtually bought the entire Egypt to Pharaoh.

Peter was astonished that He could have an encounter with Christ. He saw himself as someone who is not worthy to come near to Christ, seeing Christ as the Holy Lord and Master. He valued Christ even in the state of his distressful toiling and disappointment. He recognized the worth of Christ and when he saw the act, he submitted to the Lordship of the Saviour " *When Simon Peter saw it, he fell down at Jesus' knees, saying, Depart from me; for I am a sinful man, O Lord. … . And Jesus said unto Simon, Fear not; from henceforth thou shalt catch men"* [Luke 5:8, 10]. That was the beginning of his fulfilment. This man later became the carrier of the same order of virtues to the end that his shadow was healing the sick and raising the dead. He valued Christ and then received a full deposit of the virtues of Christ to function in his career as the preacher of the gospel.

Value discharges virtues on those who cultivate it. You are created a chosen generation, a royal priesthood, an holy nation, a peculiar people; a priest and a king on earth, purposely to show *forth the praises (in order word to practically manifest the worth and value) of* him who hath called you out of darkness into his marvellous light. You are by creation a producer of great virtues by the reason of your inherent values in God. It is also expedient that you value things around you, so you can benefit immensely from the virtues they carry. Most importantly, God, who is the source of all virtues. You need to place value on the things of His kingdom. You need to understand and dwell in the worth of God both in your life and for the entire world, so you can be ushered into the great virtues that flow from His throne.

WHAT IS A VIRTUE?

In traditional Christian angelology, virtue is referred to as the seventh highest order of the nine-fold celestial hierarchy. Some bible dictionary describes virtues in two distinct meaning; firstly as "manly power," "valor," "efficacy" as derived from the Latin word (Latin: *virtus,* "manly strength" or "excellence," *from* vir: "man"): and secondly used in its ordinary modern meaning of "moral goodness"[6]. Scripturally, Christ referred to virtues as the unusual power released to terminate ailing issues and restore dignity to destiny. He described this release as the benefit derived based on the recognition and honour attributed to Him as the Vessel of the virtues. *"And Jesus said, somebody hath touched me: for I perceive that **virtue** is gone out of me"* [Luke 8: 46] This can also be interpreted as 'healing power' (*see AMP*).

Virtues can therefore be defined as the highest order of the power of God generated in Christ (the Vessel) and released to attend to any situation at the instance of faith and value. The value for the vessel determines the level of virtues (i.e. power) released to attend to the circumstance. The worth of the vessel pronounces the excellence of the manifold grace which is released as virtues to cater for the need of those who recognize the worth of the vessel.

RELATIONSHIP BETWEEN FAITH, VALUE AND VIRTUE

Faith draws virtues from the vessel, value builds faith and determines the measure of virtues released from the vessel. While the vessel generates the virtues, the recipient is sorely responsible for triggering the virtues. This is where your faith and your sense of value needs to be built, developed, nurtured and enhanced so they can meet the required demand for qualitative release of virtues.

Rather than spending your time and energy debating religious ideology, it is more profitable to crave for spiritual enlightenment, building your most holy faith, treasuring God's grace and ability to turn things around for your favour. I give more of my time building and enhancing my understanding of God's worth

---

[6] *Read more about definition of virtue here: https://www.biblestudytools.com/dictionary/ virtue/*

and taking advantage of the privilege I have through redemption to be called the son of God, rather than celebrating religious dogma.

If we truly believe that His love is being shed abroad, making us sons and daughters, then wisdom demands that we appreciate His worth and proclaim His value at all times. Your faith and the position you place God in your life is the brotherhood of the virtues of God which are released to your direction. Faith and value when they marry together, produce virtues which are from the loins of the vessel that we entrust faith and ascribe value to. This is simply the sum of their relationship!

When you know the worth of God, you will realize that there is no case too small or big for Him to address. The miniature or magnitude of the situation notwithstanding, when you know your God and reverence His worth, you are bound to command greatness. That is why the bible states that "those who **do** know their God will be strong and do great exploits" Sometimes ago, I had an urgent need from the foreign office and looking at the time of the day, it was absolutely impossible to receive any attention. The usual time to be in the foreign office was 06.00am even though the door would be opened at 10.00am. You need to be there on time otherwise it would be eternally impossible to secure an appointment.

Here was I, a faith driven man in the office, planning to go to a foreign office that was already congested with people. By my schedule, I was to leave my office at 9.30am and arrive at the foreign office at about 10.15am. So, my concerned colleagues said to me 'Ola, are you beside yourself? Why do you want to waste your time and energy going to the foreign office at this time?' I replied 'I am not going to the foreign office; God is going with me to the foreign office and He decides when to go. Once He arrives there, everything will stand at attention' They laughed at me to scorn for this sort of statement that to them was the most ridiculous statement, but to me was the perfect way to express the worth of the God in me.

Friends, I summoned courage and said; 'Oh God of heaven and earth, I recognize your worth, therefore go before me and settle the issue in the foreign office; thank you Jesus, Amen!' It will surprise you that I left my office at 9.45am and as soon as I arrived at the foreign office, a strange hand was stretched towards me from the reception desk, beckoning that I should come forward and under fifteen (15) minutes, the issue that brought me there was settled. I was out of the place fully accomplished. I didn't need to take numbers and be on queue, just by simply recognizing the worth of Christ and confidently positioned my faith, everything was settled for me, virtues needed were released and I worked out majestically.

Surprisingly, I met some pastors and friends there and most of them have been waiting for hours. When they saw me leaving, they said Brother Ola, what? You just came in now and you are already attended to and on your way out again, what is the magic? I said to them humorously, 'life is not magical! Life is a mystery and it's been given to us to know the mysteries of life so we can lay hold on the packages that are contained in it through redemption' for *"The wind bloweth where it listeth, and thou hearest the sound thereof, but canst not tell whence it cometh, and whither it goeth: so is every one that is born of the Spirit."* *[John 3:8]* I am not regenerated into carnality; therefore, I don't operate with a carnal mind. I recognize my God, I understand His worth and all I just did now was to employ His capability to settle me in an impossible situation and He has manifested Himself as the All-Faithful God" I am grateful to God for being such a valuable, reliable and worthy Father to trust.' Please walk in faith, show your worth (value) for God and allow Him to manifest His virtues.

What I am conveying to you right now is that, when value is in place, faith flows in the supernatural and when faith is active, God's sovereignty is triggered for delivery. Just recognizing the worth of God in your situation makes Him step forward ahead of you to ensure all crooked ways are made straight. Apostle Paul once said that he is not ashamed to be called a preacher of the gospel of Jesus Christ, an apostle, and a teacher of the Gentiles. *"For the which cause I also suffer these things: nevertheless I am not ashamed: for I know whom I have believed, and am persuaded that he is able to keep that which I have committed unto him against that day"* *[2 Timothy 1:12]*. Because only those who **do** know their God, those who **do** value their God, those who **do** understand the worth of their God will be strong and will receive the virtues to do exploits in life. Not those who confess and celebrate when things are going well but infuriate when there are trials of their faith. You need to maintain your trust in God no matter what! You need to ascribe glory to your Father in every situation. Don't let your circumstance dictate your stand with God, never allow sentiment to dictate the tune of God's worth in your life. Stay committed to celebrating God's worth and values, you will never lack the release of His virtues. I decree a new beginning for you from this hour in Jesus name.

I strongly believe that our Saviour and Lord, Jesus Christ did not only come to this earth to save us from our sins, but, He came both to save our souls and to show us the pathway to the plan and purpose of our Father, so we can experience His manifold glory and virtues. He knew the worth of His Father and He practically demonstrated this worth which enabled Him to release such tremendous virtues to mankind in all ramifications. He said to the father *"Father, glorify thy name. Then came there a voice from heaven, saying, I have both glorified it, and will glorify it again."* [John 12: 28]. He understood the glory and knew that all the glory belongs to the Father, but for Him to experience the glory, He ascribed all to the Father with great sense of value. No wonder He enjoyed the virtues of the Father always and in every phase of His ministry while on earth and later possessed eternal glory forever. He traded God's worth and value to eternally possess the right hand of the Father.

Christ knew the capacity of His Father and He rode on the wings of His worth and value to get things done so cheaply. *"Then answered Jesus and said unto them, Verily, verily, I say unto you, The Son can do nothing of himself, but what he seeth the Father do: for what things soever he doeth, these also doeth the Son likewise…. I can of mine own self do nothing: as I hear, I judge: and my judgment is just; because I seek not mine own will, but the will of the Father which hath sent me. [John 5:19, 30]*

Also, in John 8:29, Jesus recognized God in His activities while He said, *"And he that sent me is with me: the Father hath not left me alone; for I do always those things that please him."* This is the pattern that He (Christ) came to establish for us who believe in Him, that we might be one with the Father even as He was and eternally is. Until we arrive at this same operational level with the right perspective, life will continue to be a thing of struggle. Nothing works in life without God in it and the earlier you recognize and embrace this truth the better for you to cultivate the heart of gratitude and value for God, so you can fulfil God's purpose for your life here on earth.

Now let us quickly look at the origin and the master inventor of these three attributes; *faith, value* and *virtue.*

THE ORIGIN OF FAITH, VALUE AND VIRTUE

God is the source and originator of faith, value and virtue. Talking about faith, God is full of faith and that is why He is a faith-full God. His faith determines the state of affairs around Him. His faith creates an atmosphere of all possibilities from the depth of impossibilities. By faith He called all things to be which were not in existence. *"And God said let there be…And God saw that it was good."*[7] Through His faithfulness, He daily preserves all creations. God is too faith-full that He cannot fail, disappoint and or deny Himself even in the state of faithlessness of man according to 2 Timothy 2:13 *"If we believe not, yet he abideth faithful: he cannot deny himself."* By the virtue of His faith-fulness, His values are conspicuously pronounced. He is all reliable, all dependable, undeniable, all possible, omnipotent, omnipresence, ever sure, unfailing, unchanging changer, always on time… name it! He will do what He says and always says what He will do.

Faith defines values and values provoke virtues; all these are traceable to the Creator. His expectation therefore is to see us walking in the same realm with the same perspective, practically manifesting His values and supernaturally commanding virtues on earth. God made us purposely to operate in the same frequency He operates and be as Christ is to perfect His love in us for *"Herein is our love made perfect, that we may have boldness in the day of judgment: because as he is, so are we in this world"* [1 John 4:17]. Therefore, beginning from this moment, I decree that your life shall start manifesting His true image and likeness all through the earth in Jesus name.

Now, after creation, the first pronouncement on all creatures was value. God defined the values of every creature, both living and nonliving. The sun takes care of the day and gives light to it while the moon takes care of the night and gives light to the night. The trees and herbs provide food for all living creatures, while man was to *dress* and keep the garden, and coordinate the affairs of all things created by God.

Man was made in the image and the likeness of God with the same values, purposely to produce the same order of virtues both in thought and action. *"And God said, Let us make man in our image, after our likeness: and let them have dominion over the fish of the sea, and over the fowl of the air, and over the cattle,*

---

[7] *Read Genesis 1:1 – 31 for the mystery of God's faith at creation*

and over all the earth, and over every creeping thing that creepeth upon the earth. So God created man in his own image, in the image of God created he him; male and female created he them." [Genesis 1: 26 - 27]

The values placed on man was that he should coordinate the affairs of all the earth, dominate it, replenish and take responsibility as the legal owner of the entire earth. He finalized the definition of value for all His creation thus: *"And God saw every thing that he had made, and, behold, it was very good…" [Genesis 1:31].*

Now when it comes to virtues, hear what God said: *"And God blessed them, and God said unto them, Be fruitful, and multiply, and replenish the earth, and subdue it: and have dominion over the fish of the sea, and over the fowl of the air, and over every living thing that moveth upon the earth" [Genesis 1:28].* After these declarations, God never expects anything less than what He pronounced. We can therefore conclude that faith, value and virtue have their origin in God, and they are the ultimate of life and godliness. God does not expect you and me to manifest or operate less than what He portrays.

Likewise, talking about His glory, He said *"And* the glory *which thou gavest me I have given them;* that *they may be one, even as we are one:" [John 17:22].* You mean the same level of glory? Yes! That was the original intention as well as His eternally established mandate for us and God cannot change *"For I am the Lord I changeth not"*

Hear this again, the worth of God cuts across salvation, blessing, curses, restoration and so on. Now the same virtue was released upon man to demonstrate the same order of virtues on earth. The spirit of these faith, worth and value of God that command His great virtues were practically deposited into man at creation *"And the Lord God formed man of the dust of the ground, and breathed into his nostrils the breath of life; and man became a living soul" [Genesis 2:7].* This was repeated by the Saviour after resurrection just to re-affirm the reality of its origin and re-establish our dominion in redemption. *"Then said Jesus to them again, Peace be unto you: as my Father hath sent me, even so send I you. And when he had said this, he breathed on them, and saith unto them, Receive ye the Holy Ghost: Whose soever sins ye remit, they are remitted unto them; and whose soever sins ye retain, they are retained. [John 20: 21 -23]*

May your faith produce the right result! May your value enhance your faith and provoke the virtues of God to your life in Jesus name.

Chapter 2

Why Are Things Not Working?

"Thus saith the Lord, Stand ye in the ways, and see, and ask for the old paths, where is the good way, and walk therein, and ye shall find rest for your souls. But they said, We will not walk therein" [Jeremiah 6:16]

Things are not working because we have lost value for the things of God. There are too much personal ego and pride among believers in this generation than what can be described. The philosophy of 'I can do it myself, I don't need anyone's assistance or contribution to achieve my goal in life' 'I am better off than you' 'I am more educated, intelligent and in fact have a better upbringing than you' among other ego are dominating people and spreading across our communities in a pace that is quite difficult to control. This habit is consciously eroding the trust we once built in God and replacing it with self-reliance which has now become the breeding ground for self-pride and arrogance, leading to the denial of the release of great virtues for man's accomplishment in life.

Things are not working because we have lost track of the steps our fathers laid down for us, and instead defined our own path to walk in, thereby turning the treasures on the pathway of greatness in life to threat to our lives.

We have by our acclaimed new generation faith, turn the principles of God to mere religion because of technological advancement. Listen, technology, innovation and what have you cannot and will never replace the principles of God which He laid down as the foundation for humanity. Advanced technology cannot fast and pray for any believer in order to get results on spiritual issues. The ways of God cannot be trodden by technology, it must be walked through with raw spiritual tenacity and kingdom consciousness before we are able to enjoy the full delivery of the packages in God. Thank God for technology, but thank God more for the old path, the ancient tracks that lead to integrity, righteousness, purity, uprightness and generates the lifestyle of holiness and peace without which no man shall see the Lord. God is still the Ancient of days and an attempt to expect Him to change because of our technological advancement will lead us to eternal frustration in life, *"For I am the Lord, I change not;" [Malachi 3:6]*.

Things are not working, and men are not accessing the virtues because we have laid aside God's instructions, and holding in high esteem the tradition of church, the philosophy of men and following the rudiment of our religion. Value for God has been eroded and for our lack of consciousness, men have succeeded in spoiling us through philosophy and vain deceit, after their own tradition, and the rudiments of worldliness, and not after Christ. We have lost the knowledge of the truth which scripturally enlightens us that in God dwells all the fullness of the Godhead bodily. We have equally lost His worth not seeing the reality of our total completeness and or recognizing the source of our accomplishment. We give ourselves to administrative activities and neglect spiritual needs, yet we claim to be running ministry in the name of Christ. Friends, we can only be seen through Christ as we are complete in him, which is the head of all principality and power. Anything less than these ancient principles will persistently settle man in a miserable lifestyle, which regrettably is the case for this generation at this present time. *[Read Mark 7:8 & Colossians 2:8-10]*

Now, one of the vital paths of this ancient spiritual technology is your diligence in hearing, hearkening and doing what the Ancient of Days tells you to do without rationalizing and or analyzing it with your new advanced technology. Hearing Him raw and executing the tasks assigned to you raw without compromise; this is the only way to show that you value God!

> *"And it shall come to pass, if thou shalt hearken diligently unto the voice of the LORD thy God, to observe and to do all his commandments which I command thee this day, that the LORD thy God will set thee on high above all nations of the earth: And all these blessings shall come on thee, and overtake thee, if thou shalt hearken unto the voice of the LORD thy God. Blessed shalt thou be in the city, and blessed shalt thou be in the field. Blessed shall be the fruit of*

thy body, and the fruit of thy ground, and the fruit of thy cattle, the increase of thy kine, and the flocks of thy sheep. Blessed shall be thy basket and thy store. Blessed shalt thou be when thou comest in, and blessed shalt thou be when thou goest out. The LORD shall cause thine enemies that rise up against thee to be smitten before thy face: they shall come out against thee one way, and flee before thee seven ways. The LORD shall command the blessing upon thee in thy storehouses, and in all that thou settest thine hand unto; and he shall bless thee in the land which the LORD thy God giveth thee. The LORD shall establish thee an holy people unto himself, as he hath sworn unto thee, if thou shalt keep the commandments of the LORD thy God, and walk in his ways. And all people of the earth shall see that thou art called by the name of the LORD; and they shall be afraid of thee. And the LORD shall make thee plenteous in goods, in the fruit of thy body, and in the fruit of thy cattle, and in the fruit of thy ground, in the land which the LORD sware unto thy fathers to give thee. The LORD shall open unto thee his good treasure, the heaven to give the rain unto thy land in his season, and to bless all the work of thine hand: and thou shalt lend unto many nations, and thou shalt not borrow. And the LORD shall make thee the head, and not the tail; and thou shalt be above only, and thou shalt not be beneath; if that thou hearken unto the commandments of the LORD thy God, which I command thee this day, to observe and to do them: And thou shalt not go aside from any of the words which I command thee this day, to the right hand, or to the left, to go after other gods to serve them" [Deuteronomy 28:1 -14]

These scriptural principles are the fundamental principles that everyone who claims to know God must strictly and fearfully adhere to and follow with all sense of commitment.

What you do not value will become a threat to your existence. Your approach to things is what defines the motive and your motive will always produce your expected result.

Our Lord Jesus Christ came in the New Testament dispensation and said clearly to everyone who desires to fulfil God's purpose in life 'if you want to be made, then follow me. If you dare to follow after me, I will be committed to making you become what God has ordained for your life in creation' *"And Jesus said unto them, Come ye after me, and I will make you to become fishers of men."* [Mark 1:17]

But how many are truly following the Lord these days. Even most of the so-called workers in the vineyard are now working to satisfy themselves, taking advantage of the innocent in the name of spirituality. They claim to have received from God and deceived people to believe their evil practices. Where do you belong in God? Are you *'following after'* Christ or you are following your 'man-designed' church ordinances, which in most cases are contrary to God's laid down principles and ethics of the kingdom? You see, people derive more pleasure working for God rather than walking with God. Working for God will only attract wages and in most cases the wages are not *'sufficient'* enough to meet the greed and covetously agitated needs of man. However, walking with God secures eternal inheritance, making you the heir of God and joint heir with His Christ.

As long as you keep walking away from God's ordinances because you see them as old versions and too slow for your jet age pace, things will keep degenerating. So, the earlier you wake up to the reality of the ancient principles that guided the patriarchs of old (and still new till tomorrow), the better for you to fulfil destiny. It is your choice sir/ma because the scriptures emphasis clearly that you need to *"Abide in me, and I in you. As the branch cannot bear fruit of itself, except it abide in the vine; no more can ye, except ye abide in me. I am the vine, ye are the branches: He that abideth in me, and I in him, the same bringeth forth much fruit: for without me ye can do nothing. If a man abide not in me, he is cast forth as a branch, and is withered; and men gather them, and cast them into the fire, and they are burned. If ye abide in me, and my words abide in you, ye shall ask what ye will, and it shall be done unto you."* [John 15:4-7]

Things are not working because we are no longer on the right track and until we come to terms with God's designed track things will keep deteriorating.

HAS GOD CHANGE?

Has God changed? Today, this question is commonly asked by so-called true believers who cannot figure out what they have lost along the path that they have chosen for themselves. Why are we not enjoying the same privileges just like our fathers of old? Why is God no longer showing up like the Mount of Gibeon and

Mount Perazim making His acts known, even His terrible act? Well, the answer is that God has not changed, He cannot change, and He will never change. *"For I am the LORD, I change not; therefore ye sons of Jacob are not consumed."* [Malachi 3:6].

You are *'absolutely'* responsible for any change around your life. God cannot change, we are the people that are susceptible unstable in our walk with Him. So, you need to come to term with the philosophy of discipline that if there is anything wrong around you, first check yourself to find out the root cause. You need to carry out personal root cause analysis on yourself, your faith, your character, conduct and your value for spiritual things and consider where or how you position yourself. *"Examine yourselves, whether ye be in the faith; prove your own selves. Know ye not your own selves, how that Jesus Christ is in you, except ye be reprobates?"* [2 Corinthians 13:5]

HAS GOD NEGLECTED HIS PEOPLE?

God has not neglected His people, rather it is His people that have neglected Him for another strange god. Sometimes ago, a woman walked into our church during the mid-week Victory Hour prayer meeting. Her appearance looked so frustrating, and her troubled face demanded an urgent attention. So, I hurriedly attended to her and asked what the matter was. She said to me 'Pastor, how many times must we pray to God on a particular issue before we receive an answer?' It didn't take me much time to understand her plight. And the Holy Spirit helped me with wisdom to give accurate answers and helped her out of her frustration. I said to her, 'sister, it all depends on the side you turn to God! Your stand with God determines how quick and or, how long you have to stay in prayer before an answer comes from God'.

The word of God makes it clear to us that *"The preparations of the heart in man, and the answer of the tongue, is from the Lord"* [Proverbs 16:1]. It absolutely depends on where your heart is; If your heart is in tune with God and well prepared to receive from Him, any prayer you make according to His will and in line with His principles is bound to receive a speedy response. The scripture says in Isaiah 65:24 that *"And it shall come to pass, that before they call, I will answer; and while they are yet speaking, I will hear."* Therefore, the question is: where is your heart and what have you been engaging to prove that you still belong to God? Your church activities cannot be used to measure your position, neither is your daily prayer a measuring tool for your part with God. It has to do with your heart! Many hearts have gone away from the ordinances of God yet still claim to belong to God and hold God accountable for the prayers that are not answered!

You see, many are calling God in prayers and even spending time to fast and subject their body to religious discipline, but their mind is far from God. You can't claim to be in God's camp and still have a relationship with witchcraft practitioners and expect God to answer you speedily. People are left on their own because they chose to go after a strange god. You can't be consulting priests of Baal such as diabolical priests, herbalists, sorcerers, soothsayers and evil spiritism *et cetera.*, and expect God to be part of your game. You cannot sell yourself to an idol and expect God to still have you in His list as His own people *"…For thou shalt worship no other god: for the Lord, whose name is Jealous, is a jealous God:"* [Exodus 34:14]. Also, *"God is jealous, and the Lord revengeth; the Lord revengeth, and is furious; the Lord will take vengeance on his adversaries, and he reserveth wrath for his enemies"* [Nahum 1:2]. He doesn't have neglect in His agenda for you, but your path is contrary to what He laid down for you and He is not happy that you have left the track of life.

This was the lifestyle of our dear sister! While she claimed to be a member of the body of Christ, she was still busy consulting the priests of Baal, who were helping her to build a special shrine for her safety and as long as she engages in this evil practice, her prayers remain noise and her petition an abomination before God. She sold herself to idolatry when God in His love and mercy had restored her from the mess of life. God has not neglected His own people, but He is jealous concerning every soul and wishes all could come to repentance and return *'back'* to Eden, His presence. *"For I am jealous over you with godly jealousy: for I have espoused you to one husband, that I may present you as a chaste virgin to Christ"* [2 Corinthians 11:2]

WHAT WENT WRONG HERE?

What went wrong? Ask yourself what value do you place on God's instructions? How do you respond to instructions from the word of God? How many of His

          OLA JONES DUYILE   ◆

servants have you torn apart with your thought, your action and your utterance? Remember your contribution to the promotion of Christian values in your community and the society at large and your answer will resolve the mystery of what went wrong. You see, God is not mocked, whatsoever a man sow, that he will equally reap. The society that honours God will be elevated and those who despise His capability will remain disabled for life.

Humanity is what went wrong! We have neglected the purpose of our existence and by this reason given ourselves to the contrary. We have embraced the 'fast by fast' way of life and neglected the 'precept upon precept' path of God because God now looks too slow for our speedy ambition! Nevertheless, God on His part still loves mankind and He has made all provisions to get man back to the right perspective of life, but remember He has no power over our will and choice. *"And even as they did not like to retain God in their knowledge, God gave them over to a reprobate mind, to do those things which are not convenient;"* [Romans 1:28]

You trust in your own ability so much that you 've virtually lost view of God in your endeavours. But the scripture says we should *"Trust in the Lord with all thine heart; and lean not unto thine own understanding"* [Proverbs 3:5].

Listen, *a*bsolute dependency on the Almighty is the only solution to man's plight. Dignity is naturally eroded in the absence of God. If you don't want to be naked in life, if you don't want to continuously experience defeat in your daily endeavours, simply return to God and stop acting like the Laodiceans church who had no value for God and His principles.

"And unto the angel of the church of the Laodiceans write; These things saith the Amen, the faithful and true witness, the beginning of the creation of God; I know thy works, that thou art neither cold nor hot: I would thou wert cold or hot. So then because thou art lukewarm, and neither cold nor hot, I will spue thee out of my mouth. Because thou sayest, I am rich, and increased with goods, and have need of nothing; and knowest not that thou art wretched, and miserable, and poor, and blind, and naked: I counsel thee to buy of me gold tried in the fire, that thou mayest be rich; and white raiment, that thou mayest be clothed, and that the shame of thy nakedness do not appear; and anoint thine eyes with eyesalve, that thou mayest see" [Revelation 3: 14 - 18]

They claimed to have believed in themselves and don't need God, without knowing that they were *"wretched and miserable, and poor and blind and naked"*

You are defeated in life because you took God's presence for granted forgetting that it is His presence that guarantees victory and triumph in every battle of life, for *"If it had not been the Lord who was on our side, when men rose up against us: Then they had swallowed us up quick, when their wrath was kindled against us: Then the waters had overwhelmed us, the stream had gone over our soul: Then the proud waters had gone over our soul." [Psalm 124:2-5].* Awake therefore and let Christ be seen in you otherwise you will continue to live a miserable life on earth. You are not created for groaning; rather, you are created to grow in wisdom, knowledge, strength and might; going from strength to strength, but only God in you can command its reality.

It is the God in us that transforms us to gods and when He is seen in us, mountains recognize and bow to Him. His presence energizes us and enhances our might to triumph in the race we are running. *"And the Lord shall be seen over them, and his arrow shall go forth as the lightning: and the Lord God shall blow the trumpet, and shall go with whirlwinds of the south" [Zechariah 9: 14].* So, the earlier you return to God and recognize His worth in your life the better for you to accomplish His will for your life.

Now, think of it, why are we not experiencing instance miracles just in the same frequency as the early church? Simply put, lack of obedience to God's move and instructions. In the early days of the New Testament movement, the simple rule was *"Whatsoever he saith unto you, do it" [John 2: 1 - 11].* Do what He says without re-thinking what it may mean. When He instructed the blind man to go wash in the pool of Siloam, he went seeking the way and with his eye completely blind obeyed without complaining about his situation. When He instructed the lepers to go show themselves to the priest, they simply obeyed. But in this new age! Alas, this computer age where we arrogantly celebrate earthly wisdom, boast of our academic achievements and built-up physical, political and financial muscles as strength! We tend to give God instructions instead of receiving instructions from Him. We dictate to God what we must do instead of receiving instruction on what He wants us to do.

We call ourselves into ministries and kingdom services without considering the Chief Executive Director of the corporation and the King of the kingdom.

We ordain ourselves to the priesthood office with our desired priesthood titles without considering the One who owns the ministry. We claim to have been made priest through redemption without considering that not all sons of Levi are entitled to priesthood office. Though, sons of Levi were called to do the service of the tabernacle and to minister to the congregation, yet there are those that are ordained by God to very sensitive positions in the ministry. There are those that were specifically called into the priesthood office to serve and conduct the oracles of God.

> *"And Moses said unto Korah, Hear, I pray you, ye sons of Levi: Seemeth it but a small thing unto you, that the God of Israel hath separated you from the congregation of Israel, to bring you near to himself to do the service of the tabernacle of the Lord, and to stand before the congregation to minister unto them? And he hath brought thee near to him, and all thy brethren the sons of Levi with thee: and seek ye the priesthood also?"* [Numbers 16: 8 - 10]

Yes, we all agree that everyone has a mission to fulfil in the kingdom. However, the fact that we are all born again and are now made to our God kings and priests does not erase God's ethic of calling. He chooses some to ministry and ordains some to occupy various offices for specific kingdom services. We failed to take time to seek His will before we covetously and greedily ordain ourselves to the office we lust after. These among other acts of men are the killers of instant miracles in our generation. We have deliberately wearied God out of interest in the affairs of life on earth, but we forgot that no man can weary Him.

Many so-called individuals and ministries have devised means of staging miracles to help God out of His 'precept upon precept' concept and launch the acts of 'fast by fast' speedy frequency to get things accomplished. They train people on how to pretend lameness, blindness, death, cripple and many vices simply to demonstrate healings and restoration power by themselves.

I need you to understand that God is not interested in what man can do. If it can be done by man's ability, then God is not needed. Consequently, since all these miracles can be performed by men as claimed by them, God is no longer needed to manifest His sovereignty among men. Do not be overwhelmed by the happenings around you and don't be surprised that many who are performing miracles around the world in the name of Christ are no longer enlisted in the sheepfold of Christ. They also know themselves that they no longer belong, but they keep pretending and deceiving their followers. What a horrible state of man in this generation!

Therefore, as an individual reading this truth right now, I want you to please take up your spiritual barometer and *"Examine yourselves, whether ye be in the faith; prove your own selves. Know ye not your own selves, how that Jesus Christ is in you, except ye be reprobates?" [2 Corinthians 13:5]*. Are you still enlisted in the sheepfold or are you now carried away by the inordinate affections and the deceitfulness of this world in the name of fame? Sheep do not need fame; sheep live on the virtuous wings of the Shepherd. That is their covering, that is their shield, their defense and strength. And these wings (which portray virtues) are only made available through the value we placed on the Shepherd. Sheep do not run after popularity! We are talking about values and worth that generate virtues through obedience!

THE SHEEP AND THE VOICE OF THE SHEPHERD

The Sheep hears the voice of the Shepherd and follows to affirm its belonging. Every sheep that wants to enjoy the fullness of the virtues of the Shepherd must learn to hear, hearken and abide by the voice. Simply put, sheep robe themselves with the values and worth of their Shepherd in order to command the release of virtues for their daily living! *"But he that entereth in by the door is the shepherd of the sheep. To him the porter openeth; and the sheep hear his voice: and he calleth his own sheep by name, and leadeth them out. And when he putteth forth his own sheep, he goeth before them, and the sheep follow him: for they know his voice." [John 10: 2-4]*

Your fellowship with God is measured by your obedience to His instructions. As was earlier stated, you cannot value God and not listen to Him and you cannot listen to Him and not experience His virtues. It all has to do with your level of obedience. Abraham walked with God based on these principles and he enjoyed the fullness of God's grace and blessings just by simply following God in every step of his life. No wonder, he became the friend of God. He stood to plead for Sodom and Gomorrah and God accepted his entreaties as many times as he requested, because he valued and revered God's worth.

MAN IS NOTHING WITHOUT GOD

People claim to believe in themselves without considering and recognizing their content. Man is typically empty without God. It is the spirit of God that quickens man and makes man a living being. God's wisdom in man is the ultimate promoter of man's destiny. We all function by the breath of the Almighty, so an attempt to praise your own personal effort without recognizing and ascribing the honour to God will make you a nonentity in the society. They say, just believe in yourself and the more you try to believe in yourself the less you see good things coming out of your own self.

Friend, until you recognize the presence of God in your life, you are not existing. Remember it is Christ in us who is able to do all things according to the power that works in us, that is according to the Spirit of God in us who doeth all things according to the power made available in us through Him. The Lord echoed that we should *"Abide in me, and I in you. As the branch cannot bear fruit of itself, except it abide in the vine; no more can ye, except ye abide in me. I am the vine, ye are the branches: He that abideth in me, and I in him, the same bringeth forth much fruit: for without me ye can do nothing. If a man abide not in me, he is cast forth as a branch, and is withered; and men gather them, and cast them into the fire, and they are burned"* [John 15:4-6]. Your worth in life is as contained in Christ Jesus.

HOW DO WE GET BACK ON TRACK?

Among others, the word of God advocates for our return to the original intent of God, walking in the path that was designed for our elevation. Some of these scriptures encourage us to get back on track so we can enjoy the fullness of God's presence and glory. According to *Malachi 3:7* we are not expected to see God's manifestation until we return to Him with all our hearts and souls *"Even from the days of your fathers ye are gone away from mine ordinances, and have not kept them. Return unto me, and I will return unto you, saith the Lord of hosts. But ye said, Wherein shall we return?"*

The book of Job expatiates on the benefits of returning to God and admonishes everyone saying *"If thou return to the Almighty, thou shalt be built up, thou shalt put away iniquity far from thy tabernacles. Then shalt thou lay up gold as dust, and the gold of Ophir as the stones of the brooks. Yea, the Almighty shall be thy defence, and thou shalt have plenty of silver. For then shalt thou have thy delight in the Almighty, and shalt lift up thy face unto God. Thou shalt make thy prayer unto him, and he shall hear thee, and thou shalt pay thy vows"* [Job 22: 23 - 27]. Likewise, in Jeremiah 4:1, God insists that we should desist from our abominable ways of life and cleave to His righteousness, recognizing and appreciating His worth and value for our true colour to emerge. *"If thou wilt return, O Israel, saith the Lord, return unto me: and if thou wilt put away thine abominations out of my sight, then shalt thou not remove.*

The following steps should be taken to fully return to the right track that God designed for man to walk in:

Think and Turn

There is a song that says *"Turn, turn, turn, turn everybody turn: turn, turn, turn and think: turn and think (see) the end of the way you are going: turn, turn, turn"* One of the ways to get back on track is to think and turn! Turn at God's rebuke so you can enjoy the outpouring of His virtues through grace! *"Turn you at my reproof: behold, I will pour out my spirit unto you, I will make known my words unto you"* [Proverbs 1:23]

Turn before God leaves you to your reprobate mind. Stop a lifestyle of pride! Give no room for ignorance to function – stretch forth to know the worth and the value of God. Give yourself wholly to following God's instructions with an obedient heart. Be ready to abide by the kingdom rules, principles and norms. Build a heart of appreciation and reverence.

Turn away from your own understanding and seek knowledge from on high. Open your heart and ask the Lord to forgive you both sinful acts and perhaps ignorance that may have caused a break in your fellowship and or relationship with Him. Then embrace the old path and reconcile with the Spirit of direction. This is the best way to get back on track. I will reiterate here that God on His part is ever merciful to accept us whenever we are ready to return to Him. See what He said despite our misbehaviours: *"I have blotted out, as a thick cloud, thy transgressions, and, as a cloud, thy sins: return unto me; for I have redeemed thee"* [Isaiah 44:22]

Give God your heart and fix your eye on His ways

My son, give me thine heart, and let thine eyes observe my ways. [Proverbs 23:26]

Sheep enjoy good and well-nourished grazing simply by submitting to the leading of the Shepherd. They are led by fixing their eyes on their leader. We are also expected to give our heart to God and fix our eye on Him if we want to experience His acts in our lives. Abraham became the blessing of God on earth by trading the wisdom of total dependency, fixing his heart and eyes on the Almighty God as the Source of supply of all his needs. He vowed not to take a thread even to a shoe latchet from any mortal man lest they claim to have made Abraham rich.

"And Abram said to the king of Sodom, I have lift up mine hand unto the Lord, the most high God, the possessor of heaven and earth, That I will not take from a thread even to a shoelatchet, and that I will not take any thing that is thine, lest thou shouldest say, I have made Abram rich." [Genesis 14: 22 -23]

What releases virtues from God to us is the enablement on our part to surrender all to Him and the ability to maintain consistent focus on Him alone for the actualization of all things. Abraham operated with this key and was able to provoke God's capability that compelled His virtues to supply his needs beyond expectation.

Remember the case of the Israelite when they were confronted by three nations, Ammonites, the Moabites and mount Seir: what gave them victory was their total dependency on God's sovereignty to fight the battle for them. They directed their cry to their source of hope: *"O our God, wilt thou not judge them? for we have no might against this great company that cometh against us; neither know we what to do: but our eyes are upon thee" [2 Chronicles 20: 12].* God won't release His virtues on you until He can see that you have no alternative to Him. Get rid of your alternative solutions if you don't want to alternate your destiny. Give your heart to God and let your eyes be single, totally fixed on God. Receive a heart of flesh right now in Jesus name.

Cultivate a new heart of Value for God

God cannot change and as earlier stated, He is still the Ancient of days, thus an attempt to expect Him to change will lead to failure and frustration on the part of man. Wisdom demands therefore that you renew your mind by educating it in the things and the ways of God. *"I beseech you therefore, brethren, by the mercies of God, that ye present your bodies a living sacrifice, holy, acceptable unto God, which is your reasonable service. And be not conformed to this world: but be ye transformed by the renewing of your mind, that ye may prove what is that good, and acceptable, and perfect, will of God."* [Romans 12:1-2]

Things will never work until you begin to see the values and the worth of God in your life and situation around you. Someone once asked me if God is pleased with this new generation and my answer was quick 'God cannot educate Himself to please man, it is man that needs to educate himself to please God'. God does not change, and He cannot change! The new generation lifestyle does not affect God's policies and or principles, God is only interested in people who care to hearken and to obey His instructions'. In order word, God cannot be bothered about your careless or carefree way of life. The choice is yours to either educate yourself to recognize and appreciate God's worth or deny yourself of the knowledge of God.

Decide the change you want

Life is a function of choice and not a matter of chance as people thought it to be. Nothing happens by accident; people make choices to get things to happen. God will never change His policy because of man's negligence to spiritual discipline. To get back on track therefore, you must decide the change you want. You need to make your choice just like the prodigal son, either to continue looking for an opportunity to eat with pigs in your prodigal journey or to return to your father where your dignity and colour will be fully restored. The woman of the issue of blood made the right choice to go after Christ for His worth and value in order to secure a final solution to her plight.

Must you wait until all your resources are wasted on riotous living or on physicians before returning to the Source of life? *Is there no balm in Gilead; is there no physician there? why then is not the health of the daughter of my people recovered? Return unto me, and I will return unto you, saith the Lord of hosts.* God is ready to accept and help you out of your distress.

> *"Wash you, make you clean; put away the evil of your doings from before mine eyes; cease to do evil; Learn to do well; seek judgment, relieve the oppressed, judge the fatherless, plead for the widow. Come now, and let us reason together, saith the Lord: though your sins be as scarlet, they shall be as white as snow; though they be red like crimson, they shall be as wool. If ye be willing and obedient, ye shall eat the good of the land: But if ye refuse and rebel, ye shall be devoured with the sword: for the mouth of the Lord hath spoken it."* [Isaiah 1:16 - 20]

There are always the paths to choose in life and this gives everyone the opportunity to make a choice:

Firstly, there is the choice to remain adamant and thicken your skin to adapt to this new age antipathy with God. In this perspective you deliberately and stiff-nakedly appoint a leader and or a captain for yourself who will lead you back to Egypt and ensure you are kept under bondage as a slave. *"And they said one to another, Let us make a captain, and let us return into Egypt"* [Numbers 14:4]

Another choice is to summon courage and start taking steps back to Eden, the presence of God where you will appreciate God's value and worth to produce His virtues in your life. *"Come, and let us return unto the Lord: for he hath torn, and he will heal us; he hath smitten, and he will bind us up"* [Hosea 6:1]

Therefore, *"See, I have set before thee this day life and good, and death and evil;"* Thus, *"I call heaven and earth to record this day against you, that I have set before you life and death, blessing and cursing: therefore choose life, that both thou and thy seed may live:"* [Deuteronomy 30: 15, 19]

In conclusion therefore, the only answer to this devastating state of mankind is to consciously subscribe to the old path and to do it right now not waiting for tomorrow. *"For he saith, I have heard thee in a time accepted, and in the day of salvation have I succoured thee: behold, now is the accepted time; behold, now is the day of salvation"* [2 Corinthians 6:2]. This is the only antidote to the endless struggles of humanity! *Come now, and let us reason together, saith the Lord*! Friend, you have this second chance to get back home where honour and dignity will become your garments. Make this hour your own hour of return. Get yourself together and reason with God right now!

May you make the right choice to value God and return to the center of His master plan for your life this season in Jesus name. You are not created to suffer; you are made to be the envy of heaven here on the earth. You are a delightsome son and daughter, specially made unto God a king and a priest not a destitute, poor and wretched being. From this moment I see God's worth delivering the right virtues on your life in Jesus name.

# Chapter 3

The Place of Value

One of the greatest treasures that has been lost in our society today is value. It is apparent that once a man has something to show off, he loses respect for other things including the things of God and the positive influence of other people in his life.

We have an account of a man who claimed to love God dearly, but when he was empowered with wisdom, riches and wealth, he lost value for God and turned his love to strange women. You see, love is not value, but love is one of the products of value as it demonstrates affection in its form. However, products are vulnerable when the producer is not appreciated, love is deadly susceptible when it is not rooted in fear and reverence; likewise, love wax cold when value is not appreciated. Love can be transferred; love shifts depending on circumstance. You can show love to someone today probably to get something from such an individual, but once your mission is accomplished such an individual may turn to become your worst enemy for life.

"And Solomon loved the Lord, walking in the statutes of David his father: only he sacrificed and burnt incense in high places. And the king went to Gibeon to sacrifice there; for that was the great high place: a thousand burnt offerings did Solomon offer upon that altar" [1 Kings 3: 3 - 4]

Solomon loved the Lord and offered a thousand burnt offerings to the Lord. But the question is, where is the value and the worth of God in his lifestyle? Absolutely zero! And Solomon loved strange women… and they turned his heart away from the Lord. His love for God had no root! He failed to build a good foundation, but he loved God for the fame of it and not for the fear of God, so he lost all the values he had for God and ended up in vanity.[8] Don't claim to love when there is no value in place. It is the measure of your value that dictates the level of your love.

> *But king Solomon loved many strange women, together with the daughter of Pharaoh, women of the Moabites, Ammonites, Edomites, Zidonians, and Hittites; Of the nations concerning which the Lord said unto the children of Israel, Ye shall not go in to them, neither shall they come in unto you: for surely they will turn away your heart after their gods: Solomon clave unto these in love. And he had seven hundred wives, princesses, and three hundred concubines: and his wives turned away his heart. For it came to pass, when Solomon was old, that his wives turned away his heart after other gods: and his heart was not perfect with the Lord his God, as was the heart of David his father. [1 Kings 11: 1 - 4]*

The value you place on a thing determines the virtues that are produced and released into your direction. There is no magic that will produce virtue from the vessel you do not value. Many are grounded today because they have despised the vessel of honour that God raised to sustain them. They evaluate them based on their age, education, popularity and eloquence and once they cannot see them rated to their expectation, they devalue them.

Friends, I want you to understand that God does not deal with the perfect to make for perfection. He takes the imperfect and transforms them that He might perfect His will, purpose and great plan through them. God designed His master plan and purpose to allow reality to derive its strength from impossibilities. He deliberately made foolish things to confound the wise. *"But God hath chosen the foolish things of the world to confound the wise; and God hath chosen the weak things of the world to confound the things which are mighty"* [1 Corinthian 1: 27]. He takes the unqualified and places them to lead nations. He raises a stammered man, dull in speech, to lead troops as their deliverer. He raises servants to become kings and brings slaves/prisoners to take over the affairs of nations.

Many could not tap into the great treasures of virtues in Christ because they lack the place of value for Him. Some judged Him based on how He was born

---

[8] *Read 1 Kings 3 and 11 for full account of Solomon's love and shift*

     OLA JONES DUYILE   ◆

(remember He was not born in the palace, but in a manger *[Luke 2:1-16]*), while others rated Him based on the family He was born into *[Mark 6:3]*. Majority evaluated His worth per His city and concluded that 'nothing good can come out of that city, therefore He possesses no value for us to believe and follow'. Please wake up and let your eyelid look straight before you to know that God does not judge by sight nor uses the strong in the battle to accomplish victory. The unqualified and the frailest are His weapons of war.

The focus in this chapter is to walk you through some notable biblical examples of how some people lost virtues while some enjoyed the fullness of it simply by the choice, they made in either understanding the place of **value** or demeaning its relevance. Now it was clearly established by God that no soul shall escape death, yet some men walked with God in fear and trembling, persistently proclaiming His worth and celebrating His value all through their lives. The end of the story was that they did not taste death, even though *"…it is appointed unto men once to die, but after this the judgment:"* [Hebrews 9:27]. They embraced God's worth and value in terms of purity, holiness and righteousness, living their life in the fear of God to the end that God took them alive.

In Genesis 5: 24 we learnt that *"And Enoch walked with God: and he was not; for God took him."* How? Hebrews 11:5, states that *"By faith Enoch was translated that he should not see death; and was not found, because God had translated him: for before his translation he had this testimony, that he pleased God."* God took him that he should not see death, why? because he simply traded the worth of God and embraced God's value in the school of righteousness. Through faith, he held unto God's worth and value and enjoyed direct entry to eternity by defeating death and the power of death. This indicates that value can secure anything including life when it is traded.

You won't have a problem with the case of Noah; *"The earth also was corrupt before God, and the earth was filled with violence"*. While the whole nation was swimming in corruption and defilement, Noah separated himself to please God. He got himself totally engulfed in purity and righteousness, pleasing God because of His value and worth. He lived in fear and reverence, celebrating God's worth and when it was time for the whole earth to be wiped out, God singled Noah out and preserved him from destruction. *"But Noah found grace in the eyes of the Lord."* His secret was that he *"(Noah) was a just man and perfect in his generations, and Noah walked with God" [Genesis 6: 8 - 9]*. You see, the nature of Christ is as contained in the values He possesses, and until you can reflect His divine nature in your daily life, you are not prepared yet to acknowledge His value and proclaim His worth to your generation.

Abraham grew from a man (in his father's house with nothing to show for life) to the servant of God and from the servant of God to the Prophet of God and from the Prophet of God to the friend of God, just by the instrument of value and the sense of worth he had for God. *"But thou, Israel, art my servant, Jacob whom I have chosen, the seed of Abraham my friend. Thou whom I have taken from the ends of the earth, and called thee from the chief men thereof, and said unto thee, Thou art my servant; I have chosen thee, and not cast thee away"* [Isaiah 41: 8 – 9].

He cherished God's value to the extent that he became the closest friend of God in his day. God took him as His own confidant, discussing His plans and actions with Abraham. God could not hide His agenda from Abraham any longer because of the value Abraham had for Him. *"And the Lord said, Shall I hide from Abraham that thing which I do; Seeing that Abraham shall surely become a great and mighty nation, and all the nations of the earth shall be blessed in him? For I know him, that he will command his children and his household after him, and they shall keep the way of the Lord, to do justice and judgment; that the Lord may bring upon Abraham that which he hath spoken of him"* [Genesis 18:17-19]

His value for God gave him his enviable place. He became the blessing of God and the father of faith on earth. It was once said by someone that 'the secret of a man can only be fully discovered inside his story'. People want the blessings of Abraham, but no one wants to take after Abraham's self-discipline and qualitative way of life as contained in his story. It is impossible to experience what Abraham experienced without finding out the path he took to get to where God positioned him. Instead of claiming Abraham's blessings are mine, please spend time to understand the place of value and how Abraham traded the worth of God and how he exhibited God's value in holiness, righteousness, purity, fear, and obedience to instructions without compromise. This will help you to climb the ladder to Abraham's height. *"Look unto Abraham your father, and unto Sarah that bare you: for I called him alone, and blessed him, and increased him."* [Isaiah 51:2]

Now, let us look at some biblical examples that would help us appreciate value as we explore the place of value and its outcome in people's life. Remember that value plays a major role in the position you attain in life. Barak the son of Abinoam enjoyed victory over Jabin king of Canaan by simply riding on the wing of prophetess Deborah. As a mighty army General, he was called to war against king Jabin whose hands God sold the children of Israel when they did evil in the sight of the Lord. Barak buried his military capabilities and embraced the worth of the prophetess of God in his days. *"And Barak said unto her, If thou wilt go with me, then I will go: but if thou wilt not go with me, then I will not go. And she said, I will surely go with thee: notwithstanding the journey that thou takest shall not be for thine honour; for the Lord shall sell Sisera into the hand of a woman. And Deborah arose, and went with Barak to Kedesh... So God subdued on that day Jabin the king of Canaan before the children of Israel. And the hand of the children of Israel prospered, and prevailed against Jabin the king of Canaan, until they had destroyed Jabin king of Canaan."* [Read Judges 4: 1 – 24]. Receive the wisdom needed to identify and value your God's ordained agent for your stress-free victory this time in Jesus name.

Abraham and Lot

When values are lost, virtues cease to flow! Lot did not value the privilege he had in Abraham and so, he lost everything. Even though Abraham who took him along was the blessing of God on earth, yet he could not partake of the ceaseless flow of God's grace on Abraham because of his inconsequential way of recognizing the virtues that Abraham possessed. Instead of recognizing the grace upon his uncle, he activated the spirit of competition, greed, and covetousness that ended him amidst evil society.

"And there was a strife between the herdmen of Abram's cattle and the herdmen of Lot's cattle: and the Canaanite and the Perizzite dwelled then in the land. And Abram said unto Lot, Let there be no strife, I pray thee, between me and thee, and between my herdmen and thy herdmen; for we be brethren. Is not the whole land before thee? separate thyself, I pray thee, from me: if thou wilt take the left hand, then I will go to the right; or if thou depart to the right hand, then I will go to the left. And Lot lifted up his eyes, and beheld all the plain of Jordan, that it was well watered every where, before the LORD

Lot lived like an accursed man because he had no value for the vessel of honour that God ordained to sustain him. You can be walking with a vessel without experiencing his virtues in your life. It all has to do with the value you placed on the vessel. Friend, it's about time you and I start picking things with our spiritual binocular and be sensitive enough to capture the true picture of and align with God's appointed vessels for our uplifting, so we can enjoy the full serenity and dignity that accompany greatness.

Laban and Jacob

Listen, your foundation and lack of philosophical relationship or fellowship with God notwithstanding, if you value His vessel you will reach His heart, and when you reach His heart, He responds to you as one of His own children. Valuing God's vessels or agents is the fundamental basis for honouring and reverencing God. This is basically because God's agents are positioned on earth to represent God and to manifest the power, honour, glory and more importantly, the capability of God in making all things possible.

Laban was an idol worshiper, yet he became rich simply by trading value. His coast was enlarged by the value he placed on the agent of God that was living with him. Hear what he said concerning Jacob when Jacob proposed his departure from his house:

"Give me my wives and my children, for whom I have served thee, and let me go: for thou knowest my service which I have done thee. And Laban said unto him, I pray thee, if I have found favour in thine eyes, tarry: for I have learned by experience that the LORD hath blessed me for thy sake. And he said, Appoint me thy wages, and I will give it. [Genesis 30: 26 - 28]

I pray thee, if I have found favour in thine eyes, tarry: for I have learned by experience that the LORD hath blessed me for thy sake. Please do not depart from me. I will keep the honour to you! Can you please tell me your wages and I am ready to pay you double because I value you and the God in you! Amen. This was the reason for his increase and enlargement irrespective of his idolatry.

We are not experiencing the glory, riches and honour from God because we despise His anointed, we esteemed Him not in our heart. We draw to Him through our mouth, our religious and church activities; we celebrate His presence while our heart is far from Him.

Elijah and Elisha

Elisha developed a deep passion for his spiritual father with the heart of fear and reverence. He esteemed Elijah as an oracle of God. He understood the worth of his master and he desperately positioned himself for the double portion of the power of God at work in his life.

Reading this long account (in 2 Kings 2) of what transpired between these two great prophets, it will amaze you that Elijah's position in Elisha's heart was extremely indescribable. He celebrated Elijah as a true father, he served him with all diligence, he humbled himself to sit at the feet of Elijah all through his days. Oh, he cherished his master and he knew his master's worth. He turned himself to a child, attached himself to his master even to the end. No wonder he was able to demand double of his master's capacity.

"And it came to pass, when the Lord would take up Elijah into heaven by a whirlwind, that Elijah went with Elisha from Gilgal. And Elijah said unto Elisha, Tarry here, I pray thee; for the Lord hath sent me to Beth-el. And Elisha said unto him, As the Lord liveth, and as thy soul liveth, I will not leave thee. So they went down to Beth-el. And the sons of the prophets that were at Beth-el came forth to Elisha, and said unto him, Knowest thou that the Lord will take away thy master from thy head to day? And he said, Yea, I know it; hold ye your peace. And Elijah said unto him, Elisha, tarry here, I pray thee; for the Lord hath sent me to Jericho. And he said, As the Lord liveth, and as thy soul liveth, I will not leave thee. So they came to

Jericho. And the sons of the prophets that were at Jericho came to Elisha, and said unto him, Knowest thou that the Lord will take away thy master from thy head to day? And he answered, Yea, I know it; hold ye your peace. And Elijah said unto him, Tarry, I pray thee, here; for the Lord hath sent me to Jordan. And he said, As the Lord liveth, and as thy soul liveth, I will not leave thee" [2 Kings 2: 1 - 6]

Now, by the reason of his consciousness for his master's worth and value, his master understood his need and was compelled to yield to his (Elisha's) earnest heartfelt expectation. Hear what the master said to him:

"And fifty men of the sons of the prophets went, and stood to view afar off: and they two stood by Jordan. And Elijah took his mantle, and wrapped it together, and smote the waters, and they were divided hither and thither, so that they two went over on dry ground. And it came to pass, when they were gone over, that Elijah said unto Elisha, Ask what I shall do for thee, before I be taken away from thee. And Elisha said, I pray thee, let a double portion of thy spirit be upon me. And he said, Thou hast asked a hard thing: nevertheless, if thou see me when I am taken from thee, it shall be so unto thee; but if not, it shall not be so" [2 Kings 2: 7 - 10]

Please, understand that the place of value for God and his ordained agents around you is what defines and settles you in your place in life. If I may ask you now, who is your God ordained teacher? Who can you point to as the one you are following to know how to go about your spiritual journey? What does this agent worth in your life and how do you follow *'after'* him/her to ensure you maintain ceaseless flow of the anointing he/she carries in your life? God will not come down to lead you, neither will Christ be here again to give direction. He has dispatched the Holy Spirit to do that and equally positioned His human agents to help lead, instruct, pastor, teach and give us direction in our spiritual journey in life as it is written *"And I will give you pastors according to mine heart, which shall feed you with knowledge and understanding"* [Jeremiah 3:15].

Elisha found his God ordained pastor and sold himself wholly to following him until the double anointing rubbed on him. The place of value and the worth of his master in his longing heart paved the way for supernatural delivery of the double anointing at work in Elijah to his life.

> *"And it came to pass, as they still went on, and talked, that, behold, there appeared a chariot of fire, and horses of fire, and parted them both asunder; and Elijah went up by a whirlwind into heaven. And Elisha saw it, and he cried, My father, my father, the chariot of Israel, and the horsemen thereof. And he saw him no more: and he took hold of his own clothes, and rent them in two pieces. He took up also the mantle of Elijah that fell from him, and went back, and stood by the bank of Jordan; And he took the mantle of Elijah that fell from him, and smote the waters, and said, Where is the Lord God of Elijah? and when he also had smitten the waters, they parted hither and thither: and Elisha went over. And when the sons of the prophets which were to view at Jericho saw him, they said, The spirit of Elijah doth rest on Elisha. And they came to meet him, and bowed themselves to the ground before him"*
> [2 Kings 2: 11 - 15]

Elisha valued his master to the intent that as soon as he no longer saw him physically, he tore his own mantle and took hold of his master's. What an honour and respect! This habit launched Elisha to the double anointing operational *modus operandi* of Elijah's capability. You need to position yourself for this unique impartation also if you really want to be known in life.

Elisha and Gehazi

While Elisha esteemed the worth of his master and received a double portion of the power and anointing at work into his life, Gehazi's case was the contrary. Though he had the opportunity to covet earnestly the best gift at work in his master's life and delicately position himself for the transference of the anointing, yet he failed to show any sign of interest in the worth of his master's ministry. Gehazi had no feeling nor did he care about how spiritually sensitive his master's office was. He failed to build his heart for spiritual things, rather he gave his heart to material possession. He lusted after gifts from mere men and lost track of the things of the kingdom of which he was trained to inherit. He despised the office of his master and received his reward *"The leprosy therefore of Naaman shall cleave unto thee, and unto thy seed for ever."* His soul burst asunder.

"But Gehazi, the servant of Elisha the man of God, said, Behold, my master hath spared Naaman this Syrian, in not receiving at his hands that which he brought: but, as the Lord liveth, I will run after him, and take somewhat of him. So Gehazi followed after Naaman. And when Naaman saw him running after him, he lighted down from the chariot to meet him, and said, Is all well? And he said, All is well. My master hath sent me, saying, Behold, even now there be come to me from mount Ephraim two young men of the sons of the prophets: give them, I pray thee, a talent of silver, and two changes of garments. And Naaman said, Be content, take two talents. And he urged him, and bound two talents of silver in two bags, with two changes of garments, and laid them upon two of his servants; and they bare them before him. And when he came to the tower, he took them from their hand, and bestowed them in the house: and he let the men go, and they departed. But he went in, and stood before his master. And Elisha said unto him, Whence comest thou, Gehazi? And he said, Thy servant went no whither. And he said unto him, Went not mine heart with thee, when the man turned again from his chariot to meet thee? Is it a time to receive money, and to receive garments, and oliveyards, and vineyards, and sheep, and oxen, and menservants, and maidservants? The leprosy therefore of Naaman shall cleave unto thee, and unto thy seed for ever. And he went out from his presence a leper as white as snow" [2 King 5: 20 - 27]

You see, what you run after reveals what you nurse in your heart. Elisha ran after the double anointing and returned fully empowered to manifest after the order of his master. But Gehazi ran after lust and greed, covetousness and worldly materials and ended up with leprosy. What you value determines the type of virtues that would be released into your direction. Whether to covet after the anointing of your master and receive a double portion or to run after material things and be baptized with irrecoverable plagues and eternal curses, make your choice!

Christ and the Disciples

There are ordained agents for our making on earth. We are expected to submit to their leadership and embrace them with our heart. We are to follow after and not follow beside or behind. They are ordained to take the lead while we follow. This is what illuminates our destiny with light.

Most of the Disciples of Christ were called out from their various professions into the ministry, yet they did not rebel but conducted themselves to be led. They passed through test and trial times which to most of us in this proud and arrogant generation would have seized the opportunity to rebel and dislodge from the ministry, but hear their response to their master: "*Then said Jesus unto the twelve, Will ye also go away? Then Simon Peter answered him, Lord, to whom shall we go? thou hast the words of eternal life. And we believe and are sure that thou art that Christ, the Son of the living God. Jesus answered them, Have not I chosen you twelve, and one of you is a devil? He spake of Judas Iscariot the son of Simon: for he it was that should betray him, being one of the twelve.*" [John 6: 67 - 71]

The Disciples clave to their Master at all cost! They turned themselves to servants under Him until His nature began to manifest in a practical form in their lives. It will amaze you that most of the disciples were older than the Master in age, yet, they were humbled despite the age difference and got all the virtues of Christ, the Master into their lives. They must have realized that "*The disciple is not above his master: but every one that is perfect shall be as his master*" [Luke 6:40]

Their humility, honour, obedience and respect for their master paved the way for them to function in the bishopric office above the frequency of their Master. Grace rubbed on them because of the value they placed on the Vessel. They committed themselves to the course of their Master and never thought of their own. No wonder they were promoted from servants to friends and above all from Disciples to the Apostles over their master's Ministry.

> *"Ye are my friends, if ye do whatsoever I command you. Henceforth I call you not servants; for the servant knoweth not what his lord doeth: but I have called you friends; for all things that I have heard of my Father I have made known*

> *unto you. Ye have not chosen me, but I have chosen you, and ordained you, that ye should go and bring forth fruit, and that your fruit should remain: that whatsoever ye shall ask of the Father in my name, he may give it you."* [John 15:14 - 16]

Power was delivered to them to do greater works for *"Verily, verily, I say unto you, He that believeth on me, the works that I do shall he do also; and greater works than these shall he do; because I go unto my Father"* [John 14:12]. Authority was vested on them to determine the state of affair in their generation as recorded in John 20: 21 – 23: *"Then said Jesus to them again, Peace be unto you: as my Father hath sent me, even so send I you. And when he had said this, he breathed on them, and saith unto them, Receive ye the Holy Ghost: Whose soever sins ye remit, they are remitted unto them; and whose soever sins ye retain, they are retained."*

What more can I say as time will not permit me to write about **Moses and Joshua!** Joshua was a servant to Moses, but his passion for service gave him his place in the ministry. He humbled himself as a servant, working tirelessly and fearfully, serving his master until he was approved by God. His master's baton was passed to him by the instrument of selfless service. He valued his master and equally celebrated his master's worth. He was nurtured and groomed by Moses without his knowledge of what God had for him. He kept himself under the ministry of his master and was never heard throughout his master's reign except on the account of his assignment to spy the land. No wonder, he gained full access to the anointing on his master which practically spoke in his life as a true follower.

Friends, what works in you is a function of who you value in life and who you consciously embrace as a true mentor of great worth. What rubs on you is a function of who you selflessly serve and wholeheartedly follow. Joshua valued Moses and served him diligently, therefore all the spirit of Moses was practically transferred to Joshua for manifestation *"And Joshua the son of Nun was full of the spirit of wisdom; for Moses had laid his hands upon him: and the children of Israel hearkened unto him, and did as the Lord commanded Moses"* [Deuteronomy 34:9]. His greatness in life was traceable to his value for his master.

Do you think you are serving that man with all these complaints and arguments and discord with his office? You challenge his authority on every issue and think you are now at the same level because you are now more educated and enlightened than him. I don't know how much education my master has, but all I know is He is my master and whatever is from above is above all. John insisted that Christ should increase while he decreased, though he was here before Christ to prepare the way for His ministry, yet he did not rob Him of His office, rather he honoured, reverenced and adored Him.

Where are you and who do you value in life?

Living without people to refer to as influences is living without a future. Life is all about influence, someone must be there as your mentor, guide, teacher and motivator otherwise, life will be void of light.

> *"And I will give you pastors according to mine heart, which shall feed you with knowledge and understanding. And it shall come to pass, when ye be multiplied and increased in the land, in those days, saith the Lord, they shall say no more, The ark of the covenant of the Lord: neither shall it come to mind: neither shall they remember it; neither shall they visit it; neither shall that be done any more. At that time they shall call Jerusalem the throne of the Lord; and all the nations shall be gathered unto it, to the name of the Lord, to Jerusalem: neither shall they walk any more after the imagination of their evil heart"* [Jeremiah 3: 15 - 17]

There are teachers, pastors and men with leadership potentials ordained by God and divinely positioned to mentor, teach, lead, guide and feed you with knowledge and wisdom that you may increase, multiply and turn from ordinary man to the city of God, the Ambassador of heaven on earth. Destiny is tanned without a teacher and life is eternally grounded without a guide.

We have learnt how the men of old aligned themselves with mentors for their great future. Men like Joshua, Elisha, Peter and Paul who discovered the place of value and subscribed to it for their greatness. Listen, there are two types of mentors ordained and approved by God to keep charge over you; first is the Holy Spirit, the Master Teacher, Guardian, Instructor and Director of life according to Psalm 32:8 *"I will instruct thee and teach thee in the way which thou shalt go:*

I will guide thee with mine eye." He is the sole Director of destiny (read John 14:25-26 and 16: 12 - 15).

Secondly, men chosen by God to mentor you in life and help train you to be sound and competent in your God given gifts until you become a valuable entity in the society. As it is written *"And though the Lord give you the bread of adversity, and the water of affliction, yet shall not thy teachers be removed into a corner any more, but thine eyes shall see thy teachers. And thine ears shall hear a word behind thee, saying, This is the way, walk ye in it, when ye turn to the right hand, and when ye turn to the left"* [Isaiah 30:20 - 21]. These are teachers in various fields of endeavours, be it mentors in your Christian journey, business, career, academic, family, *et cetera*. They are there waiting for you to be led and it is your responsibility to find them, value them and subscribe to their leading.

The question is, who do you value and who are your mentors? Life without a mentor will melt away without impact. Your worth is kept in your mentors and it will never be delivered to you until you are connected to them for mentorship. Joshua's future was hiding in Moses, Peter's destiny was wrapped in Christ while Timothy's hope for life was kept in the hand of Paul; and all these patriarchs found their mentors, aligned with them until they were lifted and fulfilled destiny in a grand style. It is impossible to jump the line! Get on-board right now and seek after your God ordained teachers and mentors before it is too late. You may claim to be hearing the Holy Spirit audibly every minute and every second, yet you still need His representatives here on earth whom He has appointed to lead and show you stuff that you cannot comprehend.

But, the problem with you is that you always think you can scale through without support, it is impossible! Take for instance, Lot who was divinely attached to Abraham for guidance; he thought he could outplay God's plan for his life, and he ended up in Sodom with nothing to show for his living. The earlier you deal with pride and start appreciating leaders around you the better for you to be elevated in life. God won't come down to mentor you neither will your Saviour Jesus leave His throne because you need a little direction here on earth. Listen, God, in His own wisdom, has appointed the Holy Spirit to take care of the tasks. In addition to this, He has rightly positioned His own ordained agents across the earth to mentor those who desire to be mentored, but if you fail to identify, recognize and value them you will lose all the virtues apportioned to you.

Christ the Saviour of the world, the Lord of Lords came to this earth for an assignment and kept having meetings with the elders, doctors and patriarchs of His time finding out how they operate, their *modus operandi*. I strongly perceive that He was learning the strategies of how they were able to handle issues among the complex multitude of people in the community. Remember, He had meetings with Moses and Elias at the mount of transfiguration probably to find out how they also were able to handle issues among the people during their time of ministry.

"And after six days Jesus taketh Peter, James, and John his brother, and bringeth them up into an high mountain apart, And was transfigured before them: and his face did shine as the sun, and his raiment was white as the light. And, behold, there appeared unto them Moses and Elias talking with him. Then answered Peter, and said unto Jesus, Lord, it is good for us to be here: if thou wilt, let us make here three tabernacles; one for thee, and one for Moses, and one for Elias. While he yet spake, behold, a bright cloud overshadowed them: and behold a voice out of the cloud, which said, This is my beloved Son, in whom I am well pleased; hear ye him. And when the disciples heard it, they fell on their face, and were sore afraid. And Jesus came and touched them, and said, Arise, and be not afraid" [Matthew 17: 1 - 7]

If I may ask you, who is your teacher at this present time? Who do you identify, recognize and value that you are now sitting and learning at his/her feet to enhance your gifts and calling? I challenge you to meditate on this and take the right step to give place to value so you can make impacts in life.

Chapter 4

Impact of Virtues

For I long to see you, that I may impart unto you some spiritual gift, to the end ye may be established; [Romans 1:11]

Every vessel is loaded with impacts and when the society cultivates the act of appreciating the values and the worth of the vessel, virtues are released, and the impacts are obviously manifested. Virtues are communicated to those who appreciate the values of the vessel and these flow through the vein called impartation. That was the intention of Apostle Paul to the Romans that his mission during this visitation would be to impart them with spiritual capacity that will help keep their faith strong, stable and unmovable on the day of trials. There is what is released upon your life that keeps you strong, fit and fulfilled. Among others, impact of virtues is notably salvation, healings, deliverances, divine [guidance, leading and direction], supplies (spiritual and or material), supernatural releases, spiritual empowerment as a seal of authority for the enhancement of kingdom manifestation, *et cetera*. All these can be seen through the scriptures and as displayed across pages of the book of life, the Bible. Virtues are released into our lives in the form of impartation and they culminate in the renewal of our strength and restoration of our purpose and dignity in life.

Zacchaeus embraced Christ's worth and sought to see Him that he may know who He is, then there was a release of virtue for salvation. Grace was imparted upon him for justification from all condemnation. And Jesus said *"Zacchaeus, make haste, and come down; for today I must abide at thy house. … This day is salvation come to this house, forsomuch as he also is a son of Abraham"*.

"And Jesus entered and passed through Jericho. And, behold, there was a man named Zacchaeus, which was the chief among the publicans, and he was rich. And he sought to see Jesus who he was; and could not for the press, because he was little of stature. And he ran before, and climbed up into a sycomore tree to see him: for he was to pass that way. And when Jesus came to the place, he looked up, and saw him, and said unto him, Zacchaeus, make haste, and come down; for today I must abide at thy house. And he made haste, and came down, and received him joyfully. And when they saw it, they all murmured, saying, That he was gone to be guest with a man that is a sinner. And Zacchaeus stood, and said unto the Lord; Behold, Lord, the half of my goods I give to the poor; and if I have taken any thing from any man by false accusation, I restore him fourfold. And Jesus said unto him, This day is salvation come to this house, forsomuch as he also is a son of Abraham. For the Son of man is come to seek and to save that which was lost" [Luke 19: 1 - 10]

Every time virtues are released from the vessel; the impact is conspicuously manifested. The effects of virtues cannot be kept secret because they are the products of faith. *"And a woman having an issue of blood twelve years, which had spent all her living upon physicians, neither could be healed of any, Came behind him, and touched the border of his garment: and immediately her issue of blood stanched. And Jesus said, Who touched me? When all denied, Peter and they that were with him said, Master, the multitude throng thee and press thee, and sayest thou, Who touched me? And Jesus said, Somebody hath touched me: for I perceive that virtue is gone out of me. And when the woman saw that she was not hid, she came trembling, and falling down before him, she declared unto him before all the people for what cause she had touched him, and how she was healed immediately. And he said unto her, Daughter, be of good comfort: thy faith hath made thee whole; go in peace"* [Luke 8: 43 - 48]. Virtue is gone out of me Jesus said and the impact must be visible, therefore who has been imparted among the people, let him/her show up now!

In another occasion, *"And Jesus answered and said unto him, What wilt thou that I should do unto thee? The blind man said unto him, Lord, that I might receive my sight. And Jesus said unto him, Go thy way; thy faith hath made thee whole. And immediately he received his sight, and followed Jesus in the way"* [Mark 10: 46 - 52]. More impact was recorded regarding a leper who came forward to express his desire to the Lord with great sense of value for Christ *"And there came a leper to him, beseeching him, and kneeling down to him, and saying unto him, If thou wilt, thou canst make me clean. And Jesus, moved with compassion, put forth his hand, and touched him, and saith unto him, I will; be thou clean. And as soon as he had spoken, immediately the leprosy departed from him, and he was cleansed"* [Mark 1: 40 - 42]. All these are the direct impact of virtues being released to individuals for the transformation of destiny. How did they get imparted? What was the cord that drew virtues and displayed the impact in the life of these individuals and visibly shown to the world?

DOOR TO VIRTUES

The costliest cost in life is change and the factory of change is the heart. An earnest, heartfelt desire for a change and the steps taken to back up the desire are the two combined forces that provokes virtues. With the heart man believes in righteousness and that results in the renewal of the mind to function in line with God's principles. With the heart, the steps to take to actualize our purpose and generate productive results are defined. The heart conceives and brings forth results as expected and if the change is not conceived in the heart it cannot attract virtues. The woman of the issue of blood *"said within herself, If I may but touch his garment, I shall be whole."* The prodigal son in Luke 15 came to himself and said within himself *"How many hired servants of my father's have bread enough and to spare, and I perish with hunger!* **I will arise and go to my father***, and will say unto him..."*

You will agree with me that, *"The preparations of the heart in man, and the answer of the tongue, is from the Lord"* [Proverbs 16:1], and *"as he thinketh in his heart, so is he"* The journey to supernatural release of virtues and the effects thereof begins with the heart. Therefore, your heart is the door to the release of desired virtues. The heart conceives the value and expresses the worth and when the pregnancy is due, it delivers the virtues through faith and the effects are known all around us.

     OLA JONES DUYILE   ◆

DIVINE VISITATION

Every transformation of destiny is preceded by divine visitation. Nothing can be compared with God's divine visitation in terms of worth, value and virtues. It is the cure for man's stagnancy and toiling in life. There is a distinct virtue released at the instance of divine visitation that culminates in instance termination of man's frustration, causing the bursting forth of joy and fulfilment. Peter was a professional fisherman but toiled all through the night without anything to show for his professional expertise. But an encounter with the Source of breakthrough brought abundance and overflow of fishes to the level of net breaking. *"Now when he had left speaking, he said unto Simon, Launch out into the deep, and let down your nets for a draught. And Simon answering said unto him, Master, we have toiled all the night, and have taken nothing: nevertheless at thy word I will let down the net."* [Luke 5:4-5] Nothing can be compared with divine visitation. It is God's ordained eternal solution to every impossible case.

Divine visitation culminates in the release of destiny from chain and bondage. In Exodus 3:7 - 8, The Lord announced to Moses the supernatural way of rescue for the children of Israel from their age long bondage *"And the Lord said, I have surely seen the affliction of my people which are in Egypt, and have heard their cry by reason of their taskmasters; for I know their sorrows; And I am come down to deliver them out of the hand of the Egyptians, and to bring them up out of that land unto a good land and a large, unto a land flowing with milk and honey; unto the place of the Canaanites, and the Hittites, and the Amorites, and the Perizzites, and the Hivites, and the Jebusites."*

The children of Israel experienced the impact of God's value (sovereignty) when He visited them. Divine visitation starred up their faith in preparing for their movement out of Egypt. *"And the people believed: and when they heard that the Lord had visited the children of Israel, and that he had looked upon their affliction, then they bowed their heads and worshipped. [Exodus 4:31]*

Every divine visitation ends up in the release of virtues as impartation on the privileged. Christ Jesus stepped into the pool of Bethesda and terminated the issue of thirty-eight years [John 5:1 – 15]. An encounter with Him brought an end to the plight of a man who was born blind without any traceable sin to either his parents or himself [John 9]. His visitation to the country of the Gadarenes frustrated the token of insanity and humiliated legions [Mark 5]. All these were the direct impacts of the release of virtues. And *"Blessed be the Lord God of Israel; for he hath visited and redeemed his people* [Luke 1:68]. You are next in line for divine visitation and the impact of His visitation shall be visible in your life this season in Jesus name.

In Genesis 21:1, we had this account that God promised to visit Sarah and make her a mother even in her old age *"And the Lord visited Sarah as he had said, and the Lord did unto Sarah as he had spoken"* However, faith is the predominant force that draws divine visitation and commands greater impact. So, the divine visitation was a function of faith that was earnestly and consciously cultivated in Sarah's heart, as it was recorded in Hebrews 11:11 that *"Through faith also Sara herself received strength to conceive seed, and was delivered of a child when she was past age, because she judged him faithful who had promised"*. Similar account was recorded about Hannah in 1 Samuel 2:21 *"And the Lord visited Hannah, so that she conceived, and bare three sons and two daughters. And the child Samuel grew before the Lord."*

This impact was preceded by the record that Hannah determined to trade on the spirit of faith by cultivating this act in her heart *"And she said, Let thine handmaid find grace in thy sight. So the woman went her way, and did eat, and her countenance was no more sad"* [1 Samuel 1:18]. When the heart is fully prepared, and the mind is set to receive, faith delivers the expectation. Faith demonstrates value and when value is secured, it attracts divine visitation which commands the flow of virtues.

Understand that, the impact of value is the release of virtues and the impact of virtues is the evident change in the position of the recipients. Virtues are released to transform the state of man to a new state. Virtues are released to change the position and circumstance of the recipients. Virtues set at liberty the prisoner, turns the sick to the healthy, transforms the weak to the strong and delivers hope to the hopeless. The virtues of heaven are the transforming power of God that changes the circumstances of man from mediocrity to the state of soundness of mind. Through divine grace and mercy, the man that was filled with Legion received an impartation for rescue from the spirit of lunacy and experienced a drastic change that all people in the community marveled at the strange transformation. *"And they come to Jesus, and see him that was possessed*

OLA JONES DUYILE

◆

with the devil, and had the legion, sitting, and clothed, and in his right mind: and they were afraid. And they that saw it told them how it befell to him that was possessed with the devil, and also concerning the swine. And they began to pray him to depart out of their coasts" [Mark 5:15-17]. You shall experience the impact of God's virtue this season in Jesus name.

HOW TO DRAW VIRTUES FROM THE VESSEL

Let me state again that virtue is impotent without a heart of value for the Vessel. You must first cultivate a heart of value for the Vessel, understand His worth and jealously guide your ways in line with His ethics and rules. Having done that, develop a desperate 'if I perish, I perish' kind of heart and go after the vessel for the release of your desired virtues. An earnest desire for a change is what compels change, you need to stretch forth toward your need to secure the change you crave for.

> *"O God, thou art my God; early will I seek thee: my soul thirsteth for thee, my flesh longeth for thee in a dry and thirsty land, where no water is; To see thy power and thy glory, so as I have seen thee in the sanctuary" [Psalm 63: 1 - 2]*

In this kingdom, nothing comes so cheap; spiritual gifts are not for sale, yet they are not delivered as a free lunch. Spiritual things must be sought for before they can be delivered. That is why Isaiah 55:1 cried earnestly to those who are ready to pay for the release of supernatural virtues *"Ho, every one that thirsteth, come ye to the waters, and he that hath no money; come ye, buy, and eat; yea, come, buy wine and milk without money and without price.* And in Psalms 42:2, David echoed *"My soul thirsteth for God, for the living God: when shall I come and appear before God?"* It takes desperation to get your portion in the kingdom. You must be ready to stretch beyond thronging and break through the multitude before you can access and draw virtues from the Vessel. Psalms 143:6 says *"I stretch forth my hands unto thee: my soul thirsteth after thee, as a thirsty land."* So, there is the need to stretch beyond the normal belief system.

TAKE IT BY FORCE

Luke 16:16 states that *"The law and the prophets were until John: since that time the kingdom of God is preached, and every man presseth into it."* In affirmation Christ continued to unravel the force that delivers the desire of man *"And from the days of John the Baptist until now the kingdom of heaven suffereth violence, and the violent take it by force"* [Matthew 11:12]. Virtues are not cheap commodities; they are as expensive as faith. Impartation of virtues is not about familiarity and friendship, but it is about desire and crave. People who desire a life encounter with virtues from above must violently press beyond religion and break through the multitude to reach the hem of the Vessel's garment for a release. Elisha engaged the tenacity of desperation to secure his glorious destiny in God. His crave for double portions of whatever was at work in Elijah's life and ministry was not taken lightly, but with all zeal he pursued with irresistible alacrity.

Remember that the sons of the prophets were about 50 in number, but only Elisha could receive impartation from the same father of these potential men of God. Please understand that life is neither fun nor competition, it is about desire, choice, personal crave and responsibility. Hence, the race is *"Ho, every one that thirsteth"* comes to the water of life! You don't wait to be imparted; you stretch for impartation at all cost. You earnestly and with desperation pursue after the vessel, holding tight and don't let go! You take it by force, not turning back until the desire is physically and practically delivered. *"And from the days of John the Baptist until now the kingdom of heaven suffereth violence, and the violent take it by force"* Only the violent in faith that desperately pursue the vessel shall have a delivery of their desired virtues released to them.

That was the philosophy of Elisha as recorded in 2 Kings 2.

> *And it came to pass, when the Lord would take up Elijah into heaven by a whirlwind, that Elijah went with Elisha from Gilgal. And Elijah said unto Elisha, Tarry here, I pray thee; for the Lord hath sent me to Beth-el. And Elisha said unto him, As the Lord liveth, and as thy soul liveth, I will not leave thee. So they went down to Beth-el. And the sons of the prophets that were at Beth-el came forth to Elisha, and said unto him, Knowest thou that the Lord will take away thy master from thy head to day? And he said, Yea,*

There are two distinct ways to describe everyone's position in life and either of these is what justifies every individual's profitability. No one is redundant in life! You are either creating an event for people to watch or you are watching people's events. That is simply the paradigm of life across every race, ethnicity, religion, colour and creed. While the sons of the prophets were busy asking and analyzing Elijah's flight, Elisha was busy chasing after the anointing with heartfelt desperation, consciously and bodily present; mentally and spiritually current with God's move regarding his master's flight. He followed with an opened eye and was scrutinizing every move of his master. Elisha was preparing for a new level of operation and an unusual dimension of greatness in the school of the prophetic. His heart was knit with his master's power, his eye was spiritually covetous towards the best gift in accordance with 1 Corinthians 12:31[9]. He longed to see himself manifesting and duplicating the grace at work in his master's life in a double dimension. He stayed focused and got imparted. You are not entitled to virtues if you are complacent. Only those who crave for change and take necessary steps toward the change they desire are permitted to experience change.

It takes a lion heart therefore, to possess your lion share of the glorious virtues of heaven on earth. You need to desperately secure the faith required for the flow of virtues in the areas of your needs. Take for instance the issue of healing; the desire to be healed and the desperation should be evidently seen in your action toward the supernatural acts of God. Nothing delivers outside the faith of man. It is therefore your faith that secures your healing. You cannot be desperate enough to receive healing and not experience the flow of virtues. God is not mocked; the level of your faith is what determines the amount of the virtues that flow to your direction.

> *"And when they were gone over, they came into the land of Gennesaret. And when the men of that place had knowledge of him, they sent out into all that country round about, and brought unto him all that were diseased; And besought him that they might only touch the hem of his garment: and as many as touched were made perfectly whole" [Matthew 14:34 - 36]*

Desperation is the answer! Take for instance the case of blind Bartimaeus. As soon as he knew that it was the Saviour passing by his street, he lost all sense of normalcy and went wild to reach the Vessel. His desperate move made room for him to the end that the Vessel stood still to attend to him as urgently as required.

> *"And they came to Jericho: and as he went out of Jericho with his disciples and a great number of people, blind Bartimaeus, the son of Timaeus, sat by the highway side begging. And when he heard that it was Jesus of Nazareth, he began to cry out, and say, Jesus, thou Son of David, have mercy on me.*

---

[9] *1 Corinthians 12:31 "But covet earnestly the best gifts: and yet shew I unto you a more excellent way"*

And many charged him that he should hold his peace: but he cried the more a great deal, Thou Son of David, have mercy on me. And Jesus stood still, and commanded him to be called. And they call the blind man, saying unto him, Be of good comfort, rise; he calleth thee. And he, casting away his garment, rose, and came to Jesus. And Jesus answered and said unto him, What wilt thou that I should do unto thee? The blind man said unto him, Lord, that I might receive my sight. And Jesus said unto him, Go thy way; thy faith hath made thee whole. And immediately he received his sight, and followed Jesus in the way" [Mark 10: 46 - 52]

And without faith it is impossible to draw virtues from the Vessel, for those who desire the release of virtues must first believe in the Vessel and secure the confidence needed for their reward. Friend, God has no uncle when it comes to the release of virtues. It has to do with your belief system, coupled with your consistent fellowship and desperation, once you have recognized His ability to resolve your ailing issues.

Nevertheless, at the root of desperation that attracts the Vessel is a heart of obedience. God is ready to avenge all disobedience around your life (sickness, career stagnation, oppression of the devil, release of your inheritances, *et cetera*) when your *obedience* is fulfilled. So, you need to consciously and committedly cast down all imaginations, and every high thing that exalts itself against the knowledge of God in your life and bring into captivity every thought to the *obedience* of Christ before God can be committed to your issues. Let God be confident in your daily walk in obedience to His principles, you will be attended to before you even call. I decree your release now in Jesus name.

COURAGE

Courage is the ability to operate bravery in a frightening situation, exercising strength in the face of pain and impossibility; acting with heartfelt hope, trust and expectation. It is an act of conscious belief with less consideration of the danger and high probability of failure or disapproval. Taking bold steps and making efforts to do something that is beyond human comprehension with full hope and confidence to generate positive results. Imagine a woman who had lost blood on a daily basis for twelve years; physical strength had reduced to zero, emotional capability had depreciated, and mental balance was out of range, yet she was courageous enough to break the security around the Vessel. She relentlessly broke through the thronging multitude and drew virtues out of the Vessel. It takes unshaking courage to draw such impact-generated virtues from the Vessel without formal notice or consultation.

It takes courage to access the deep things of God and to settle with it without compromise. It takes courage to stretch beyond your capacity to possess what you desire. God said to Joshua after Moses was taken to eternal rest *"Be strong and of **a good courage**: for unto this people shalt thou divide for an inheritance the land, which I sware unto their fathers to give them. **Only be thou strong and very courageous...,** Have not I commanded thee? **Be strong and of a good courage**; be not afraid, neither be thou dismayed: for the Lord thy God is with thee whithersoever thou goest"* [Joshua 1: 6,7 & 9]. God was strongly admonishing Joshua to build his faith upon the strength of courage, making the book of the law (which is the Word of God) his foundation. This shows the importance of the spirit of courage in our quest to fulfil God's master plan for our life and or receiving anything from God through our faith. We are instructed to approach the throne of grace with boldness before we can obtain mercy and find grace to help in time of need. The boldness here connotes courage and confidence (built on trust and believe) to approach the throne of God for the release of grace as the virtue that will make mercy available to help us through the issues of life at every point in time.

Courage is acting in an unrealistically but optimistic manner to compel the vessel to release the virtues we desire without delay. A woman came to Jesus crying for her daughter to be rescued from the torment of the devil and the Lord said to this desperate but courageous woman that children's meats are not meant for dogs. The woman admitted with desperation and courageously replied 'yes Lord you are right, I am a dog! But I am optimistic that dogs cannot be denied the crumbs that fell from the children's table. Just give me the one that fell from your children's table, that is sufficient enough for me Sir.'

It is courage that delivers the children's meat to the dog and supernaturally converts the status of a dog to a child. Her courage (without considering the insult on her personality) produced her desired expectation against the wish of the Vessel. Faith without courage is failure in disguise. It takes courage for faith to function on the delivery frequency. Faith functions effectively through process, but if you are easily offended, you will lose the process and deny yourself its end-product. You need to develop the spirit of courage as *a workman that needed not to be ashamed,* (but consciously, vigorously and with all tenacity, void of fear and offense), *rightly dividing the word of truth.* Standing by the truth, not terrified by the situation but bravely embracing and pressing forward with the strength of the truth until the vessel releases the virtues desired for your change of story. You are due for a greater impact.

Chapter 5

Responsibility

Life is a responsibility and only those who see through will make it through. Value is not a gift; it is a habit that every individual must cultivate. It is not an enforcement or an entity you are compelled to exhibit, but a choice to make. You chose to esteem what you value, and you chose to despise what you don't have value for, so it is your choice! *"Through desire a man, having separated himself, seeketh and intermeddleth with all wisdom"* [Proverbs 18:1]. You are responsible for everything around your life. What you permit will be retained and what you remit will be remitted to you, so it's all about your choice.

In the preceding chapter, we explored the forces of courage and desperation that secure the delivery of greater virtues and their impacts in our lives. However, no matter how desperate and courageous you may be, frustration will remain the product of your action until you are ready to accept responsibility and initiate a move to draw virtues from the vessels around you. The four lepers in 2 Kings 7 took it upon themselves to make a move and deliver themselves from the stagnant situation they were undergoing in the wilderness.

"And there were four leprous men at the entering in of the gate: and they said one to another, Why sit we here until we die? If we say, We will enter into the city, then the famine is in the city, and we shall die there: and if we sit still here, we die also. Now therefore come, and let us fall unto the host of the Syrians: if they save us alive, we shall live; and if they kill us, we shall but die. And they rose up in the twilight, to go unto the camp of the Syrians: and when they were come to the uttermost part of the camp of Syria, behold, there was no man there" [2 Kings 7: 3 - 5]

And as soon as they took responsibility to enforce their desired change, heaven responded with virtue that released them to their new beginning *"For the Lord had made the host of the Syrians to hear a noise of chariots, and a noise of horses, even the noise of a great host: and they said one to another, Lo, the king of Israel hath hired against us the kings of the Hittites, and the kings of the Egyptians, to come upon us. Wherefore they arose and fled in the twilight, and left their tents, and their horses, and their asses, even the camp as it was, and fled for their life."* That was the end of their reproach as lepers! *"And when these lepers came to the uttermost part of the camp, they went into one tent, and did eat and drink, and carried thence silver, and gold, and raiment, and went and hid it; and came again, and entered into another tent, and carried thence also, and went and hid it"* [2 Kings 7: 6 - 8].

You cannot claim desperation and courage when you are not ready to take responsibility. They took their lives into their hands and made a move to end their shame and reproach in life. There is a time that you need to say to yourself, 'I am going after this vessel and will not look back until I receive the desired virtues from the vessel' It is called 'if I perish, I perish' order of desperation which is born out of compulsion! *"Then Esther bade them return Mordecai this answer, Go, gather together all the Jews that are present in Shushan, and fast ye for me, and neither eat nor drink three days, night or day: I also and my maidens will fast likewise; and so will I go in unto the king, which is not according to the law: and if I perish, I perish"* [Esther 4: 15 - 16]. This is the responsibility we are talking about here. Responsibility to initiate a positive move backed up with desperation and courage; responsibility to separate yourself for an encounter that will bring about the change you desire in your area of endeavor.

Responsibility is about making the difference in your decision, taking steps contrary to human disposition and enforcing the right principles against all odds. Responsibility is driving yourself out of the convenient box of life to secure the will and purpose of God in your endeavours. Daniel and his friends were taken to the king's palace to be groomed for service. Naturally, those who are selected to serve in the king's palace are nourished and nurtured with the king's food to meet the physical standard set for workers in the palace. But these four young chaps took responsibility for their lives and purpose in their heart not to defile themselves with the king's food. They defined the line of connection to the Source of virtues. *"But Daniel purposed in his heart that he would not defile himself with the portion of the king's meat, nor with the wine which he drank: therefore he requested of the prince of the eunuchs that he might not defile himself. Now God had brought Daniel into favour and tender love with the prince of the eunuchs"* [Daniel 1: 8 - 9]. Friends, favour is far if you are running away from responsibility. It takes a lion-hearted discipline to draw the virtues called favour.

Every comfort zone of life is a trap in disguise to secure failure and frustration. Many are sitting down indolently blaming their brothers, sister and uncles or cousins who are not helping them, while others who are sold to slavery summoned courage, embraced responsibility and took advantage of the seemingly discomfort of their slavery to become the head of nations. Joseph was never heard blaming his brothers for selling him to slavery, rather he thanked them for their bravery in sending him to a place of his fulfilment. *"And Joseph said unto his brethren, Come near to me, I pray you. And they came near. And he said, I am Joseph your brother, whom ye sold into Egypt. Now therefore be not grieved, nor angry with yourselves, that ye sold me hither: for God did send me before you to preserve life. For these two years hath the famine been in the land: and yet there are five years, in the which there shall neither be earing nor harvest. And God sent me before you to preserve you a posterity in the earth, and to save your lives by a great deliverance. So now it was not you that sent me hither, but God: and he hath made me a father to Pharaoh, and lord of all his house, and a ruler throughout all the land of Egypt"* [Genesis 45: 4 - 7]. Joseph took responsibility to enforce the release of virtues from above in providing solutions to every ailing situation around his life. He said to his brethren, 'You sold me to slavery, but I took responsibility of my life to secure God's backing in fulfilling His purpose for my life. The God of our fathers, Abraham, Isaac and Jacob has attended to me and helped me out because I went after Him to secure a place of honour and glory as against your planned reproach for me.'

Joseph determined in his heart to make God his eternal focus. He accepted responsibility to walk in that principle, placing value on God for answers to all bugging issues of life. He took responsibility as a slave and became the Director of his master's company; he took responsibility as a prisoner and was made the Overseer of the prison affairs. This same Joseph appeared before Pharaoh and became the Solution Provider to the agonizing plight of the king and the entire Egypt as a nation. His secret was that he took upon himself the responsibility of recognizing the God of his fathers and he stayed connected to the Source of solution to all situations. He kept walking in the principles of God to maintain His presence at all times. *"And Joseph answered Pharaoh, saying, It is not in me: God shall give Pharaoh an answer of peace"* [Genesis 41: 16]. So, it's all about responsibility and not luck or myth. Your lifestyle reflects in all your steps in life. Remember that his lifestyle of responsibility was shown when the king handed his kingdom and nation (Egypt) into his hand. He did not jump into celebration, but he went straight to the field and took responsibility with positive steps of action (Genesis 41: 45 – 48); *"And Joseph went out over all the land of Egypt... And Joseph went out from the presence of Pharaoh, and went throughout all the land of Egypt... And he gathered up all the food of the seven years, which were in the land of Egypt, and laid up the food in the cities:"* Please wake up and take responsibility of your life if you don't want to be left behind in this new wave of the release of God's virtues upon the last day armies of the kingdom.

KEYS TO ACCEPTING RESPONSIBILITY

The kingdom of God consists of responsible resources and agents, and everyone operates on a specific key to access a specific door for the release of virtues. As much as all things are available, obtainable and attainable in the kingdom, nothing is enforced on anyone. The Vessel of the great virtues does not release virtues by automatic press of a button, rather He measures the release of virtues on the basis of values for Him. So, it's all about accepting the responsibility of cultivating a heart of values both for the vessel and His agents around you. Virtues are not enforced, however, if anyone determines in his/her heart to cultivate values for the things of God and humanity, that individual will enjoy the release of virtues from the vessels.

Among other ways to accept kingdom responsibility is to **Acquaint yourself with God.**

God is a God of principles who operates His kingdom on principles and ethics. Everyone who desires to draw virtues from Him must be willing to take the responsibility of aligning to the ethics and principles of His kingdom.

"Acquaint now thyself with him, and be at peace: thereby good shall come unto thee. Receive, I pray thee, the law from his mouth, and lay up his words in thine heart. If thou return to the Almighty, thou shalt be built up, thou shalt put away iniquity far from thy tabernacles. Then shalt thou lay up gold as dust, and the gold of Ophir as the stones of the brooks. Yea, the Almighty shall be thy defence, and thou shalt have plenty of silver. For then shalt thou have thy delight in the Almighty, and shalt lift up thy face unto God. Thou shalt make thy prayer unto him, and he shall hear thee, and thou shalt pay thy vows. Thou shalt also decree a thing, and it shall be established unto thee: and the light shall shine upon thy ways. When men are cast down, then thou shalt say, There is lifting up; and he shall save the humble person. He shall deliver the island of the innocent: and it is delivered by the pureness of thine hands" [Job 22: 21 - 30]

KEYS TO CULTIVATING VALUES

"And I will give unto thee the keys of the kingdom of heaven" The kingdom of God operates in keys and every door has its specific key used to secure access to the deep things within. But the master key to the main door (which is the heart of God) is knowledge. Before you seek any key to access the treasure house of virtues, there is the need to first build adequate knowledge of who God is and His capability to release virtues to your life.

"When Jesus came into the coasts of Caesarea Philippi, he asked his disciples, saying, Whom do men say that I the Son of man am? And they said, Some say that thou art John the Baptist: some, Elias; and others, Jeremiah, or one of the prophets. He saith unto them, But whom say ye that I am? And Simon Peter answered and said, Thou art the Christ, the Son of the living God. And Jesus answered and said unto him, Blessed art thou, Simon Bar–jona: for flesh and blood hath not revealed it unto thee, but my Father which is in heaven. And I say also unto thee, That thou art Peter, and upon this rock I will build my church; and the gates of hell shall not prevail against it. And I will give unto thee the keys of the kingdom of heaven: and whatsoever thou shalt bind on earth shall be bound in heaven: and whatsoever thou shalt loose on earth

shall be loosed in heaven. Then charged he his disciples that they should tell no man that he was Jesus the Christ" [Matthew 16:13 - 20]

Who do men say I am? If you know the answer, then keep it to yourself and get the key; continue to operate in that knowledge to secure your place with me in destiny (Christ reiterating). *"Then charged he his disciples that they should tell no man that he was Jesus the Christ"*. Let everyone who desires the release of virtues take the responsibility of finding out who I am! This is personal therefore, knowledge of who God is should be a personal desire.

With the adequate knowledge in place, let us explore some of the vital keys that help to cultivate values and enable the delivery of virtues as desired.

Genuine love for God

Love is the preserver of values and when values are well preserved, they generate great virtues. Your love for God is what defines your position in life. People who are experiencing daily outstanding progress in their endeavours in life can easily trace their success to the irresistible passion they exhibit for God and His kingdom. You can easily associate their progress to the level of their love for God. *"Then one of them, which was a lawyer, asked him a question, tempting him, and saying, Master, which is the great commandment in the law? Jesus said unto him, Thou shalt love the Lord thy God with all thy heart, and with all thy soul, and with all thy mind. This is the first and great commandment"* [Matthew 22: 35 - 38]. Your genuine love for God is what secures the delivery of the key to access virtues. David the king secured God's presence and backing all through his life simply by trading the key of genuine love for God and His kingdom. He chose to be abandoned by men and stand for God. In Psalms 69:7 – 9, he expressed his passion for God while he declared that: *"Because for thy sake I have borne reproach; shame hath covered my face. I am become a stranger unto my brethren, and an alien unto my mother's children. For the zeal of thine house hath eaten me up; and the reproaches of them that reproached thee are fallen upon me."*

Genuine love for God will exhilarate you to go extra miles for the promotion of His kingdom on earth. Genuine love will overwhelm you that death cannot stop you from standing for God. *"Set me as a seal upon thine heart, as a seal upon thine arm: for love is strong as death; jealousy is cruel as the grave: the coals thereof are coals of fire, which hath a most vehement flame"* [Song of Solomon 8:6]. When your love attains the level of being strong as death, you will start seeing yourself as being crucified already for the kingdom of God. Paul said in Galatians 2:*20 "I am crucified with Christ: nevertheless I live; yet not I, but Christ liveth in me: and the life which I now live in the flesh I live by the faith of the Son of God, who loved me, and gave himself for me."* His life had no meaning to himself because of the love he had for the kingdom of God. No wonder, he never struggled to command great virtues in his ministry. Wisdom became his daily bread, signs and wonders became his daily distribution simply by trading the key of genuine love for God. You count your loss to be great gain in celebrating God's worth, acknowledging and pleasing Him in all your ways.

Love makes you lay everything down to please God. Solomon loved the Lord and offered a thousand burnt offerings to the Lord and heaven opened upon him both in wisdom, riches, wealth, honour, dignity and above all security. *"And Solomon loved the Lord, walking in the statutes of David his father: only he sacrificed and burnt incense in high places. And the king went to Gibeon to sacrifice there; for that was the great high place: a thousand burnt offerings did Solomon offer upon that altar"* [1 Kings 3: 3 - 4] He laid all down at the altar without rethinking, because of his passion for God. Now, to define his kind of love, he was not doing this to secure protection, riches and or wealth, rather he showed his love for God in securing a heart of understanding to lead God's people in the way that would please God. He said to God, father I brought all these to you as my token simply because I love you. I just want to appreciate how you helped my father and also show my gratitude for counting me worthy to sit upon my father's throne. In case you want to respond to my sacrifice, this is my request: *"And now, O Lord my God, thou hast made thy servant king instead of David my father: and I am but a little child: I know not how to go out or come in. And thy servant is in the midst of thy people which thou hast chosen, a great people, that cannot be numbered nor counted for multitude. Give therefore thy servant an understanding heart to judge thy people, that I may discern between good and bad: for who is able to judge this thy so great a people? And the speech pleased the Lord, that Solomon had asked this thing.* [1 Kings 3: 7 - 10]. Yes, God was pleased because the sacrifice was raised out of pure heart of love. This type of genuine

     OLA JONES DUYILE   ◆

love will always provoke God's sovereignty for the release of great virtues beyond man's comprehension.

The Lord Jesus Christ called Peter thrice to confirm his genuine love for Him. Now when you love God, you supernaturally become the carrier of His power and naturally distribute His virtues to your generation. *"So when they had dined, Jesus saith to Simon Peter, Simon, son of Jonas, lovest thou me more than these? He saith unto him, Yea, Lord; thou knowest that I love thee. He saith unto him, Feed my lambs. He saith to him again the second time, Simon, son of Jonas, lovest thou me? He saith unto him, Yea, Lord; thou knowest that I love thee. He saith unto him, Feed my sheep. He saith unto him the third time, Simon, son of Jonas, lovest thou me? Peter was grieved because he said unto him the third time, Lovest thou me? And he said unto him, Lord, thou knowest all things; thou knowest that I love thee. Jesus saith unto him, Feed my sheep"* [John 21: 15 - 17]. Everyone who claims to love God is heartedly committed to feeding His sheep as the best way to demonstrate love for Him! You show God's worth to the world when you stand to represent Him in the field. If you are sold out to kingdom's promotion, you won't need to pray for virtues to be released upon your life, rather you will be turned to an agent of distribution of virtues.

In Deuteronomy 30:6 God committed Himself to ensure that our hearts are prepared for the level of love He desired from us. *"And the Lord thy God will circumcise thine heart, and the heart of thy seed, to love the Lord thy God with all thine heart, and with all thy soul, that thou mayest live."* Genuine love for God erases your sins and releases His grace (as virtues) to function in your life, for *"Hatred stirreth up strifes: but love covereth all sins"* [Proverbs 10:12]. I pray that your heart begins to pant for God in displaying genuine love for Him from this hour in Jesus name. When you hold this key, you are granted access to uncommon treasure houses that others who are faking it can't access.

The fear of God

The fear of God is the master key to the heart of God. The fear of God can be referred to as the consciousness of His omnipotence and by that operating an unequivocal sense of respect, awe, and total submission to the ethics, principles and personality of God. Making God first in your decision and considering the impact of your action on your relationship with God before executing it. Joseph appropriated his action with God's position in his life and would rather be sent to prison than jeopardizing his stand for God's values. He feared God and would not contravene God's ethics and principles, therefore he spilled upon the face of Potiphar's wife *"...how then can I do this great wickedness, and sin against God?"* He lost his coat of many colours and ended up in prison, but his decision (personal responsibility) to go for Godly fear brought him to the throne above Potiphar. His fear for God and his personal decision to take responsibility delivered the key needed to unravel the mysteries behind the king's dream. The secret of the king was made known to him on the platform of the operation of the key called the fear of the Lord! *"And Pharaoh said unto his servants, Can we find such a one as this is, a man in whom the Spirit of God is? And Pharaoh said unto Joseph, Forasmuch as God hath shewed thee all this, there is none so discreet and wise as thou art:"* [Genesis 39:9 and 41:38-39]

Wisdom is the principal driver of destiny, but wisdom has no value if it is not rooted in the fear of God. The fear of the Lord is the master key that secures the outpouring of divine wisdom to generate impact in life. It is the fear of God that guarantees quick understanding as emphasized in Isaiah 11:3 *"And shall make him of quick understanding in the fear of the Lord: and he shall not judge after the sight of his eyes, neither reprove after the hearing of his ears:"* Those who walk in the fear of God cheaply command ceaseless flow of virtues. This is the beginning of wisdom and it takes wisdom to make maximum impact in life. There are people who pray for the release of virtues and there are those who command virtues. Those who seek for the acts of God without godly fear always end up in frustration but those who discover God's way supernaturally command God's acts for the scriptures say *"He made known his ways unto Moses, his acts unto the children of Israel"* [Psalms 103:7].

Job was a man with a great heart of fear and reverence for God and this turned him to the envy of his generation. He dominated the financial affairs of the East in his time.

"There was a man in the land of Uz, whose name was Job; and that man was perfect and upright, and one that feared God, and eschewed evil. And there were born unto him seven sons and three daughters. His substance also was

As the greatest business merchant in the East, Job had the ample opportunity and personal choice to corrupt himself because of his affluence in the society, but he took the responsibility upon himself to walk in the fear of God. Job operated the key of Godly fear and became a threat to the kingdom of Satan. He became a 'No-Go' area for Satan and his devils. He walked in the fear of God to the extent that Satan had to give account of his persistence nature *"And the Lord said unto Satan, Hast thou considered my servant Job, that there is none like him in the earth, a perfect and an upright man, one that feareth God, and escheweth evil? Then Satan answered the Lord, and said, Doth Job fear God for nought? Hast not thou made an hedge about him, and about his house, and about all that he hath on every side? thou hast blessed the work of his hands, and his substance is increased in the land"* [Job 1: 8 - 10]. His household, properties, life and all that pertained to him were fully secured with the hedge of heaven built by God, simply because he walked in the fear of God. Friend, which virtue do you crave for from God that walking in the consciousness of His fear cannot deliver to you? Listen, you can love God with your life and not be fulfilled if your love is not genuinely rooted in the fear of God. Thus, until you learn how to walk in the fear of God, your love is fake and cannot draw virtues from God. Now let's quickly look at the distinctive factors of the fear of God in comparison with love.

Difference between Godly fear and love

Let me state here that it will take a heart full of wisdom and discretion to cultivate value and appreciate the worth of the vessels around you. Showing love is not enough to tap the virtues from the vessel. The fear of God must precede your love otherwise, its delivery will be of no effect. Love is sharable, love is transferable, love is quenchable, and love can wax cold, but FEAR is ultimate and indispensable, strong and sustained with proofs of its reality in manifestation. This is wisdom at work! The love you have for God can only draw His wisdom to work in your life, only your level of fear for God can determine the depth of wisdom you command. The fear of God is the foundation you lay for wisdom to dwell and the sustainability of wisdom is determined by the fear of God at work practically in your life.

Psalm 111: 10 says that *"The fear of the Lord is the beginning of wisdom: a good understanding have all they that do his commandments: his praise endureth for ever"* And Job declared in Job 28: 28 *"And unto man he said, Behold, the fear of the Lord, that is wisdom; and to depart from evil is understanding"*. It takes the fear of God and a genuine love rooted in godly fear to access the depth of riches in God.

Many people claim to love God but still rear their sacrifices in the upper altar and many love God but live contrary to God's principles! Yes, it is possible to love God and still operate in the foolishness of heart, because it is not love that builds values. Love draws wisdom and exposes value, only the fear of God establishes wisdom and generates values in our lives. Wisdom without the fear of God ends its carrier in the pool of foolishness making them the product of vanity upon vanity irrespective of their wealth and riches. The fear of God is what keeps His presence with us in any situation in life and as you all know that God's presence is His wisdom because it is His presence that makes the difference in our lives that men around us marvel at the product of our hands

And Solomon loved God… 1 Kings 3: 3 this drew wisdom, riches and wealth upon his life but there was a limit to the wisdom that Solomon could access and the virtues he could draw from God through his self-acclaimed love for God. You see, until you abide by His principles and pass all the conditions attached to them, the level of outpouring of virtues, either in capacity or provisional supply will be limited. Love is not enough, but it must be strengthened by walking practically in the fear of God

> *But king Solomon loved many strange women, together with the daughter of Pharaoh, women of the Moabites, Ammonites, Edomites, Zidonians, and Hittites; Of the nations concerning which the Lord said unto the children of Israel, Ye shall not go in to them, neither shall they come in unto you: for surely they will turn away your heart after their gods: Solomon clave unto these in love. And he had seven hundred wives, princesses, and three hundred concubines: and his wives turned away his heart. For it came to pass, when*

> Solomon was old, that his wives turned away his heart after other gods: and his heart was not perfect with the Lord his God, as was the heart of David his father. For Solomon went after Ashtoreth the goddess of the Zidonians, and after Milcom the abomination of the Ammonites. And Solomon did evil in the sight of the Lord, and went not fully after the Lord, as did David his father. Then did Solomon build an high place for Chemosh, the abomination of Moab, in the hill that is before Jerusalem, and for Molech, the abomination of the children of Ammon. And likewise did he for all his strange wives, which burnt incense and sacrificed unto their gods. And the Lord was angry with Solomon, because his heart was turned from the Lord God of Israel, which had appeared unto him twice, And had commanded him concerning this thing, that he should not go after other gods: but he kept not that which the Lord commanded. Wherefore the Lord said unto Solomon, Forasmuch as this is done of thee, and thou hast not kept my covenant and my statutes, which I have commanded thee, I will surely rend the kingdom from thee, and will give it to thy servant [1 kings 11: 1 - 11]

Solomon loved God, but he lacked the fear of God and he ended his wisdom in vanity upon vanity which in turn produced vanity for him! "*Vanity of vanities, saith the Preacher, vanity of vanities; all is vanity. What profit hath a man of all his labour which he taketh under the sun?*" [Ecclesiastes 1: 2 – 3] His love was in disobedience to the rules and principles laid down for him to enjoy full wisdom to the end – so he lost all! Understand therefore, that Solomon's level of wisdom is not the best one can get from God. There are higher levels of operation which if we strive to walk in the fear of God would be accessible to us. "*O the depth of the riches both of the wisdom and knowledge of God! how unsearchable are his judgments, and his ways past finding out!*" [Romans 11:33]. Hear the Saviour confirming the arrival of greater than Solomon on earth in Matthew 12:42 – "*The queen of the south shall rise up in the judgment with this generation, and shall condemn it: for she came from the uttermost parts of the earth to hear the wisdom of Solomon; and, behold, a greater than Solomon is here.*" Every wisdom built on the platform of mere love will crash, only those who walk in the fear of God can operate and manifest divine wisdom in its full capacity.

Now, see the men that prospered in the wisdom that was generated through godly fear and compare them to the one who claimed to love God:

> *"And it came to pass after these things, that his master's wife cast her eyes upon Joseph; and she said, Lie with me. But he refused, and said unto his master's wife, Behold, my master wotteth not what is with me in the house, and he hath committed all that he hath to my hand; There is none greater in this house than I; neither hath he kept back any thing from me but thee, because thou art his wife: how then can I do this great wickedness, and sin against God? And it came to pass, as she spake to Joseph day by day, that he hearkened not unto her, to lie by her, or to be with her. And it came to pass about this time, that Joseph went into the house to do his business; and there was none of the men of the house there within. And she caught him by his garment, saying, Lie with me: and he left his garment in her hand, and fled, and got him out. … (read through 13 – 19) And Joseph's master took him, and put him into the prison, a place where the king's prisoners were bound: and he was there in the prison. But the Lord was with Joseph, and shewed him mercy, and gave him favour in the sight of the keeper of the prison. And the keeper of the prison committed to Joseph's hand all the prisoners that were in the prison; and whatsoever they did there, he was the doer of it. The keeper of the prison looked not to any thing that was under his hand; because the Lord was with him, and that which he did, the Lord made it to prosper"* [Genesis 39: 7 – 23]

The fear of God shaped a new beginning for Joseph in the school of wisdom; he possessed the ability to depart from iniquity, so he gained mastery of understanding which made him an outstanding personality in bible history. Please walk in the fear of God and stop claiming this agape love for God. You cannot deceive God with your so-called agape, you can only deceive yourself. The modern age kind of love is deceptive – walk in the fear of God and He will count it as love for Himself and His kingdom

> *"Now there was a day when the sons of God came to present themselves before the Lord, and Satan came also among them. And the Lord said unto Satan, Whence comest thou? Then Satan answered the Lord, and said, From going*

to and fro in the earth, and from walking up and down in it. And the Lord said unto Satan, Hast thou considered my servant Job, that there is none like him in the earth, a perfect and an upright man, one that feareth God, and escheweth evil? Then Satan answered the Lord, and said, Doth Job fear God for nought? Hast not thou made an hedge about him, and about his house, and about all that he hath on every side? thou hast blessed the work of his hands, and his substance is increased in the land" [Job 1: 6 – 10]

It is the fear of God that provokes His acts and His acts are what we called the end products of divine wisdom.

This was the secret of our Saviour Jesus Christ, who never attempted any issue in life without the capital 'GO' ahead instruction from the Father. The fear of God gave Him *"quick understanding in the fear of the Lord:"* that He could *"not judge after the sight of his eyes, neither reprove after the hearing of his ears"* So, He ended up becoming the miracle machine of heaven on earth to the end that even 4-day old dead body that was buried and certified stinking came back to live (John 11 referred). His secret was the fear of God at work in His life. *"How God anointed Jesus of Nazareth with the Holy Ghost and with power: who went about doing good, and healing all that were oppressed of the devil; for God was with him"* [Acts 10: 38].

What is the fear of God?

...how then can I do this great wickedness, and sin against God?

i. Ability to do what please Him

ii. Sensible enough to align to His principles

iii. Submission to the kingdom rules while trembling at His instructions as may deem reflective in your daily endeavours

iv. Considering God first in all the steps you take, asking yourself whether it pleases God to take the step or not even before taken such step

v. Courage to take bold steps in reverencing God's word of instructions contrary to human seductive influence.

vi. Totally sold to Godly obedience with less consideration of human intimidating consequences

Obedience to instructions

A soul that detests instructions will lose taste of life and everyone who resists correction will be corrupted. An obedient heart is the breeding ground for miracles. Saul lost his throne to disobedience! He failed to hearken diligently to walk in the precept of and follow God's instructions and that cost him his throne, his family and eventually terminated his life in a disgraceful manner. *"And Samuel said, Hath the LORD as great delight in burnt offerings and sacrifices, as in obeying the voice of the LORD? Behold, to obey is better than sacrifice, and to hearken than the fat of rams"* [1 Samuel 15:22]. The key to all-round triumph in life is obedience; that is hearing what God says and doing what He instructs you to do without compromise or respect of persons. Obedience to instruction is what secures your place in the redemptive plan of God. Once you fail to hearken diligently to the instructions from God to do and walk in them, you naturally lose your place in His plan.

For instance, in the school of divine leading, security and guidance, our place in His plan is in obedience to His instructions. *"I will instruct thee and teach thee in the way which thou shalt go: I will guide thee with mine eye. Be ye not as the horse, or as the mule, which have no understanding: whose mouth must be held in with bit and bridle, lest they come near unto thee"* [Psalms 32: 8-9]. Also, *"And call upon me in the day of trouble: I will deliver thee, and thou shalt glorify me. But unto the wicked God saith, What hast thou to do to declare my statutes, or that thou shouldest take my covenant in thy mouth? Seeing thou hatest instruction, and castest my words behind thee"* [Psalms 50: 15 - 17].

The proof of your faith is in obedience to God's instruction and your height in life is determined by the level of your obedience. God does not desire sacrifice from you, for the silver and the gold belong to Him. All He desires from every one of us who aspires to see His glory is obedience.

> *"The proverbs of Solomon the son of David, king of Israel; To know wisdom and instruction; to perceive the words of understanding; To receive the instruction of wisdom, justice, and judgment, and equity; To give subtilty to the simple, to the young man knowledge and discretion. A wise man will hear, and will increase learning; and a man of understanding shall attain*

◆

unto wise counsels: To understand a proverb, and the interpretation; the words of the wise, and their dark sayings. The fear of the Lord is the beginning of knowledge: but fools despise wisdom and instruction. My son, hear the instruction of thy father, and forsake not the law of thy mother: For they shall be an ornament of grace unto thy head, and chains about thy neck" [Proverbs 1: 1- 9]

The chief of all wisdom is obedience; outside it is groaning in frustration for *"He openeth also their ear to discipline, and commandeth that they return from iniquity. If they obey and serve him, they shall spend their days in prosperity, and their years in pleasures. But if they obey not, they shall perish by the sword, and they shall die without knowledge"* [Job 36: 10 - 12]

"And it shall come to pass, if thou shalt hearken diligently unto the voice of the Lord thy God, to observe and to do all his commandments which I command thee this day, that the Lord thy God will set thee on high above all nations of the earth: And all these blessings shall come on thee, and overtake thee, if thou shalt hearken unto the voice of the Lord thy God" [Deuteronomy 28: 1-2] In some instances, God's instructions seem like rebuke to us, but they are not grievous and not meant for our destruction, rather they are for our repositioning. We need to build a heart of diligence, fear and reverence for Him and align our ways with His instructions in order to provoke the release of virtues from His throne of grace. *"Now no chastening for the present seemeth to be joyous, but grievous: nevertheless afterward it yieldeth the peaceable fruit of righteousness unto them which are exercised thereby. Wherefore lift up the hands which hang down, and the feeble knees; And make straight paths for your feet, lest that which is lame be turned out of the way; but let it rather be healed."* [Hebrews 12: 11- 13]

In Proverbs 1:23 we are instructed to *"Turn you at my reproof: behold, I will pour out my spirit unto you, I will make known my words unto you."* Turning in obedience is what turns us to be the envy of our world. There is an outpouring of His grace for our lifting when we turn to obey His commands.

Reverence to God and His vessels

Honouring God and His ordained vessels is another vital key to access the depth of virtues. The level of honour ascribed to God and His vessel determines the honour you receive back in form of virtues *"for them that honour me I will honour, and they that despise me shall be lightly esteemed."* [1 Samuel 2:30]. You can only enjoy virtues through honour. Elisha was just passing through a city when a woman took the responsibility with reverence and created a special room for him to stay whenever he was in town, a hospitality born out of reverence. Without discussing her plight with the vessel of God, there was a supernatural release of virtue to meet her dare need. Barrenness was terminated in her life and the siege of untimely death was destroyed. [2 Kings 4: 8 – 37]. Now, by the honour this Shunammite woman bestowed on Elisha, she received direction for her rescue from famine and returned to her land after seven years and all her substances were fully restored back to her by the order from the king. *"And it came to pass, as he was telling the king how he had restored a dead body to life, that, behold, the woman, whose son he had restored to life, cried to the king for her house and for her land. And Gehazi said, My lord, O king, this is the woman, and this is her son, whom Elisha restored to life. And when the king asked the woman, she told him. So the king appointed unto her a certain officer, saying, Restore all that was hers, and all the fruits of the field since the day that she left the land, even until now."* [read 2 Kings 8:1-6]. What a ceaseless privilege just by the reverence she showed! Whoever honours me will be honoured.

One of the ways to demonstrate your heart of reverence to God is to maintain consistent sweet fellowship both in service, praise and worship. This is an acceptable pattern for displaying your reverence for Him. Learn to minister unto the Lord through your worship, let your hands be lifted up, let your mouth be filled with praise and worship His Majesty with a heart of thanksgiving. This is the avenue for exploits in the school of faith, value and virtue.

Chapter 6

Resistance to Release

Why is this generation void of miracles, signs and wonders? Why are we not seeing the move of God? Where are the virtues of instance healings and deliverance? Well, they are still as fresh as they were in the beginning with God. God's light cannot go down! God's power can never diminish! His grace and mercy are everlasting, and His compassions fail not. They are new every morning: great is His faithfulness.

As earlier stated, when things are not right check yourself and your community and not God, because God is never a hindrance to the success of those who abide in His ways. His ways are not darkened, His commandments are not grievous, His instructions are not set to lead to oppression, our haughty and stubborn heart is the root cause of our failures and the resisting force to the release of unction.

"Hear, ye deaf; and look, ye blind, that ye may see. Who is blind, but my servant? or deaf, as my messenger that I sent? who is blind as he that is perfect, and blind as the Lord's servant? Seeing many things, but thou observest not; opening the ears, but he heareth not" [Isaiah 42: 18 - 20]

In this chapter, we shall be exploring seven (7) forces that are resisting the release of virtues in this generation. Also, we shall provide remedies for these cancerous resisting forces. Listen, in God's master plan, every redeemed is expected to stand as an agent of power and distributor of virtues. The redeemed are not re-positioned to be seeking for miracles, rather they are expected to be the miracle workers in the name of Jesus Christ. Among other **forces that resist the Release of Virtues** are:

Ignorance

Ignorance plays a major role in denial of virtues. It is the head of all principality and power in the school of resistance. What you are ignorant of cannot yield increase for you, your obliviousness is the resisting force behind the virtues you are expecting.

"They know not, neither will they understand; they walk on in darkness: all the foundations of the earth are out of course. I have said, Ye are gods; and all of you are children of the most High. But ye shall die like men, and fall like one of the princes" [Psalms 82:5 - 7]. Princes die like dogs because they know not who they are and the worth of the kingdom they belong to. Your entitlement to any welfare does not guarantee its delivery. It takes knowledge to possess your right in redemption. Until you come to term with knowledge of what Christ has purchased for you in redemption, life will continue to be a thing of struggle. Many blind people were in the same street with Bartimaeus, but none could come to the knowledge of the Healer and Restorer of destiny except Bartimaeus. He delivered himself by breaking the yoke of ignorance of who was passing his street and virtue was released for his liberty.

Arise, take the bold step of faith to destroy the yoke that keeps you in bondage! Ignorance is the name! Now, if God could heal the sick, raise the dead, restore eyes to the people who were born blind, wisdom demands that you settle in this understanding and light that He has not changed His agenda of healing and restoration. Your situation notwithstanding, if you believe, you will experience the performance of all that God has spoken. *"And blessed is she that believed: for there shall be a performance of those things which were told her from the Lord"* [Luke 1:45].

Complacency

In Deuteronomy 2:2-3, *"And the Lord spake unto me, saying, Ye have compassed this mountain long enough: turn you northward."* Arise, this is not your resting place! Don't be restricted to this level. Self-satisfaction is what limits the flow of virtues because God does not force greatness on man rather, He gives grace for everyone to determine his/her accomplishment in life. God is ever pleased

OLA JONES DUYILE

with your level as long as you are pleased to remain there. Life is a race and it is expected that everyone who desires the fullness and fulfilment of it must strive for accomplishment. The crown is waiting ahead, but only those who run the race to the end will be enthroned. Apostle Paul admonishing his son Timothy said *"Thou therefore endure hardness, as a good soldier of Jesus Christ. No man that warreth entangleth himself with the affairs of this life; that he may please him who hath chosen him to be a soldier. And if a man also strive for masteries, yet is he not crowned, except he strive lawfully. The husbandman that laboureth must be first partaker of the fruits. Consider what I say; and the Lord give thee understanding in all things."* [2 Timothy 2:3-7] Stop celebrating your achievement when there are still greater things to possess. Refuse to close your case when there is already a provision in redemption to turn the case to testimony. Destiny is limitless, progress has no end, only you have the power and authority to define and determine the end.

If a man also strives for masteries, yet is not crowned, except he strives lawfully; except he takes up the task and in desperation press for higher levels. The woman of the issue of blood that we studied in the previous chapters, had spent all she had on medication without any improvement. She was by nature expected to have given up looking for solution to her irrecoverable illness, yet she pressed for the virtues with the little energy remained in her and straightway, she was lifted from her terminal siege to total freedom. A crave for next level is what provokes the release of virtues, but self-satisfaction draws the curtain of limitation. Set a race in your spiritual life, rise up and make plan for the future in your career! Have a journey, make plan set a standard for yourself and stop celebrating or regretting your level when there is a greater future for you in Christ Jesus. It will shock you to know that heaven will not come down to make plans for you. You must present your reason before you can be justified. *"Produce your cause, saith the Lord; bring forth your strong reasons, saith the King of Jacob."* *"Put me in remembrance: let us plead together: declare thou, that thou mayest be justified."* That is how it works on this side of Jordan!

God already chose Jacob as the covenant child after the order of Abraham and Isaac, but that did not stop him from becoming a labourer in Laban's house. He was struggling for survival but refused to settle for his position under his uncle. He went after God for a change and suddenly virtue was released for his change. *"And Jacob was left alone; and there wrestled a man with him until the breaking of the day. And when he saw that he prevailed not against him, he touched the hollow of his thigh; and the hollow of Jacob's thigh was out of joint, as he wrestled with him. And he said, Let me go, for the day breaketh. And he said, I will not let thee go, except thou bless me. And he said unto him, What is thy name? And he said, Jacob. And he said, Thy name shall be called no more Jacob, but Israel: for as a prince hast thou power with God and with men, and hast prevailed"* [Genesis 32: 24 - 28] He prevailed by not being complacent. Complacency therefore is the breeding ground for stagnation and an enemy of impact. You can rise for your own change even now! and the virtues needed will be released upon you.

Pride

Pride is the resistance to the release of virtues! Every proud heart always assumes fulfilment and security without the knowledge of God as described in Psalms 73: 5 – 9 *"They are not in trouble as other men; neither are they plagued like other men. Therefore pride compasseth them about as a chain; violence covereth them as a garment. Their eyes stand out with fatness: they have more than heart could wish. They are corrupt, and speak wickedly concerning oppression: they speak loftily. They set their mouth against the heavens, and their tongue walketh through the earth."* And *"The wicked, through the pride of his countenance, will not seek after God: God is not in all his thoughts"* [Psalms 10:4] Virtues are resisted because pride has dominated the heart of men. It precedes denial and initiates destruction of virtues because it fails to recognize and appreciate the worth of the vessel. *"Pride goeth before destruction, and an haughty spirit before a fall"* [Proverbs 16:18]. So *"When pride cometh, then cometh shame: but with the lowly is wisdom"* And *"Only by pride cometh contention: but with the well advised is wisdom"* [Proverbs 11:2 and 13:10 respectively].

Pride strips its victim off the presence of God and stamps them with frustration and until they are clothed with humility, they are never allowed to experience God's manifold grace and mercy: *"for God resisteth the proud, and giveth grace to the humble."* Therefore, *"Hear ye, and give ear; be not proud: for the Lord hath spoken."* God has spoken once, and He wants you to humble yourself and hear it twice and believe that all power and authority needed for your freedom belong to Him. God is ever set to break the siege upon your life, but He requires your humility and submission to His Lordship. Until you bury your pride, the virtues needed for your lifting and liberty from that plague will never be released. God is interested in seeing you accomplish His purpose for your life, and He releases His grace to ensure your fulfilment. But he gives this grace more to the humbled and debase the proud *"But he giveth more grace. Wherefore he saith, God resisteth the proud, but giveth grace unto the humble."* [James 4:6]. Pride is the destroyer of destiny, but the choice is yours!

Lack of recognition

In this new age, God is hardly seen in the plan of man unlike the days of old when all that mattered to our forefathers was God and His commandments. People have lost their root to innovation and evolution. But until you recognize your root, you will never yield fruits. You cannot recognize your doctor as the final solution to the issues of your health and expect God to release the balm for your healings! You cannot exalt your bank for supply of credit for your financial needs and expect God to open the windows of heaven upon your life. *"Behold the voice of the cry of the daughter of my people because of them that dwell in a far country: Is not the Lord in Zion? is not her king in her? Why have they provoked me to anger with their graven images, and with strange vanities? The harvest is past, the summer is ended, and we are not saved. For the hurt of the daughter of my people am I hurt; I am black; astonishment hath taken hold on me. Is there no balm in Gilead; is there no physician there? why then is not the health of the daughter of my people recovered?"* [Jeremiah 8:19-22] The daughters no longer recognize the Balm in Gilead; they have lost sight of their Redeemer; they know not neither do they take it to heart to put God in their thought and recognize His Lordship.

Someone once confronted me after analyzing the terrorist activities going on all over the world and searching the scriptures to see what God is doing about it and he said to me what is going on? Is heaven no longer recognizing the earth as God's handiwork? My answer was that God has been forced to withdraw the host of Angels assigned to nations and individuals for their divine security because they have turned to the strength of their government. Nations now celebrate and boast of their military capability, while individuals are now too big to acknowledge divine security because they can acquire human and technology capabilities for their security. Friends, the secret of triumph in life is personal enlightenment about God and who He is to you. David found the truth about God and he enjoyed the flow of virtues all through his reign, both in terms of security, provision, grace, health among others. I am enjoying the same as I found all these in redemptive packages delivered to me by Christ Jesus and now I can declare with all understanding that '*My defence is of God, which saveth the upright in heart and Because of his strength will I wait upon Him: for God is my defence. Yea, the Almighty shall be my defence, and I shalt have plenty of silver*'.

To draw virtues from the vessel, there must be a genuine recognition and approbation of the vessel and with adequate reverence to match having understood His capabilities. Look therefore to the hole where you are hewn, recognize the source of your supply, that is the only way to generate value that draws virtues from the Vessel. "*For wisdom is a defence, and money is a defence: but the excellency of knowledge is, that wisdom giveth life to them that have it*" [Ecclesiastes 7:12]. Wisdom demands therefore that you recognize God as your hope in life otherwise you will keep struggling for life,

Lack of reverence

What you don't recognize you can't reverence and what you don't reverence will never yield increase for you. When the foundation of your faith is void of recognizing God as your hope and confidant, reverencing Him will be impossible. Virtues dried up because no one acknowledges and reverences God's capability to turn circumstance around. What draws from the strength of the king is the level of reverence, praise and honour ascribed to Him. What provokes virtues is the reverence to the carrier as declared by the Source of Virtues, the Lord Jesus in John 12:32 "*And I, if I be lifted up from the earth, will draw all men unto me.*" Every man is drawable on the platform of heartfelt, genuine veneration displayed in lifting the Drawer of destiny. But until this is exhibited, the virtues needed for the lifting of man will not be released. The Priests of old lifted their shoulders and began to appraise themselves for the great deeds they commanded in their priesthood offices. They forgot that God was the source of their strength, hence,

 OLA JONES DUYILE ◆

their blessings were turned to curses. *"And now, O ye priests, this commandment is for you. If ye will not hear, and if ye will not lay it to heart, to give glory unto my name, saith the Lord of hosts, I will even send a curse upon you, and I will curse your blessings: yea, I have cursed them already, because ye do not lay it to heart. Behold, I will corrupt your seed, and spread dung upon your faces, even the dung of your solemn feasts; and one shall take you away with it. And ye shall know that I have sent this commandment unto you, that my covenant might be with Levi, saith the Lord of hosts.* [Malachi 2: 1 - 4].

Self-centeredness

"And he spake a parable unto them, saying, The ground of a certain rich man brought forth plentifully: And he thought within himself, saying, What shall I do, because I have no room where to bestow my fruits? And he said, This will I do: I will pull down my barns, and build greater; and there will I bestow all my fruits and my goods. And I will say to my soul, Soul, thou hast much goods laid up for many years; take thine ease, eat, drink, and be merry. But God said unto him, Thou fool, this night thy soul shall be required of thee: then whose shall those things be, which thou hast provided? So is he that layeth up treasure for himself, and is not rich toward God" [Luke 12:16 - 21]

Whenever you see yourself as the only one that matters in life, you are denying yourself access to the grace of God. It is the 'me and me alone' mentality and lifestyle that dries the flow of virtues and erases destiny. Always remember that whatever is at your disposal is God's provision per time. No man has the capacity to provide his need without the help of God. In Deuteronomy 8:18, we are reminded thus: *"But thou shalt remember the Lord thy God: for it is he that giveth thee power to get wealth, that he may establish his covenant which he sware unto thy fathers, as it is this day"* When you fail to bring it to mind that whatever you have or whatever you are is as provided by God through His grace that separated you for the blessing. But when you start claiming that *"My power and the might of mine hand hath gotten me this wealth"* you are digging your grave without knowing. When the rich fool began to take stock of his wealth and achievement and attributed all to his own personal satisfaction, grace was withdrawn from him and his life was required. Self-centeredness delimits greatness and destroys the privilege to enjoy the fullness of God's riches and glory.

God's gifts are primarily given to us to impact others and not only ourselves; For *"the manifestation of the Spirit is given to every man to profit withal."* The gifts are released for our profiting through distribution and not for personal gain or self-allocation, but for impact on the society. God's provisions are made available for distribution and not meant to be stored for personal satisfaction. When you consider others, God will place into your hands what to use for yourself. This is the secret key that people misappropriate with riches, wealth, power and anointing. A widow had only one meal left for herself and her son, yet she thought more of what a stranger should eat and by that, virtue was released to sustain her for the entire famine in the land of Zarephath. *"And she went and did according to the saying of Elijah: and she, and he, and her house, did eat many days. And the barrel of meal wasted not, neither did the cruse of oil fail, according to the word of the Lord, which he spake by Elijah"* Her willingness to recognize and prioritize the need of others before her family gave her the full privilege of heaven's supply all through famine. Not only that, she was able to enjoy the virtue of restoration of life when her son fell sick and died. (Read 1 Kings 17: 8 – 24). Self-centeredness dries virtues and withdraws God's supplies.

Wrong influence

The release of virtues is a process and only those who go through the process will experience the delivery of the product. When you camp with people who stand to hinder the flow of virtue, the process will be jeopardized to the detriment of the product. What denies you of the product is wrong influence! Every defeat in life is traceable to wrong influence, either through counsel, advice, scheme, enticement and or enforcement. But *"Blessed is the man that walketh not in the counsel of the ungodly, nor standeth in the way of sinners, nor sitteth in the seat of the scornful. But his delight is in the law of the Lord; and in his law doth he meditate day and night* [Psalms 1:1-2]. Evil communication corrupts good initiative, destroys creation, quenches the fiery dart of faith and reduces its victim to a mere prey. Judas Iscariot was called by God according to divine election, but wrong influence terminated his destiny. While other disciples were busy finding out how their master carried out the kingdom tasks, Judas was busy negotiating with the scribes and the Pharisees until his destiny was trapped and his life burst asunder.

Please don't mistake anointing for discipline! Your charismatic and eloquent lifestyle cannot be substituted for personal awareness, which is spiritual discipline, your reasonable service. No matter your level of anointing and gifts. If you mingle with wrong people, your anointing will lose taste and men will trample it under their feet. So, *"Give not that which is holy unto the dogs, neither cast ye your pearls before swine, lest they trample them under their feet, and turn again and rend you."* Therefore, do not be deceived, evil communications will always corrupt good manners, wrong influence will hinder the flow of virtue. You cannot enhance your fear for God when you are keeping ungodly company. You cannot see any value in the things of God when all that surrounds you are ungodly people. As long as Israel remained in the company of people with strange habits, heaven remained closed and God's presence was not in view, but *"When Israel went out of Egypt, the house of Jacob from a people of strange language; Judah was his sanctuary, and Israel his dominion. The sea saw it, and fled: Jordan was driven back. The mountains skipped like rams, and the little hills like lambs. What ailed thee, O thou sea, that thou fleddest? thou Jordan, that thou wast driven back?"* [Psalm 114:1-5]. Awake to righteousness and be knowledgeable enough to preserve your faith in God: Wrong influence will turn your honour to shame and hinder the flow of virtues to your direction.

These seven principalities, among others are the forces that resist the flow of virtues! May knowledge bail you out of them in Jesus name.

ANTIDOTES TO RESISTANCE OF THE RELEASE OF VIRTUES

Glory be to God in the highest! God in His manifold wisdom has given us the privilege to make choices for our destiny. Nothing is impossible to change and as long as Christ is the way, there is always a way out of any ailing issue and predicament in life. However, the strongest opposition to the resisting forces of virtues is adequate knowledge. Majority don't know and once you lack the know-how of a thing, abuse is inevitable. So, the **antidote** to resistance of the release of virtue is **adequate knowledge** of who God is, what He can do and how much of the redemptive privilege available to us in connecting to His invincible capability. Knowledge and understanding of the ways of God positions you to the right path of life and secures the flow of virtues into your direction. Lack of knowledge is what makes people rebel against God's principles, ethics and sovereignty. Pharaoh lacked the knowledge of God and was turned to a beast and rebellious king. *"And Pharaoh said, Who is the Lord, that I should obey his voice to let Israel go? I know not the Lord, neither will I let Israel go"* [Exodus 5:2]. He could not humble himself because he did not know who God was. As long as you remain ignorant, the adversaries have the right to feast on you and ride upon your back, sweat and blood. It is knowledge that helps you to cultivate value for the vessel. Those who choose to be ignorant will live a life of indolence, if you are uninformed you will end up deformed and if you desire to be unacquainted you will remain a victim for life. Let knowledge reshape your life in God.

The Psalmist was full of knowledge and that gave him the edge over his adversaries. He prevailed at all levels because he knew his God and was proud to exclaim in Psalms 135:5 *"For I know that the Lord is great, and that our Lord is above all gods"* and *"I know that the Lord will maintain the cause of the afflicted, and the right of the poor"* [Psalms 140:12]. It is knowledge that secures a place for us in the sight of God and enables us to enjoy the fullness of His grace. Humble yourself therefore and seek for knowledge for it is knowledge that can stabilize you and make the strength of salvation available for your manifestation. The fear of the Lord is the treasure of knowledge. Knowledge transforms your complaints to compliments and draws strength out of your weakness. Knowledge changes your perspective about issues of life and enhances your insight with light, drawing new songs out of your depressed soul *"And in that day shall ye say, Praise the Lord, call upon his name, declare his doings among the people, make mention that his name is exalted. Sing unto the Lord; for he hath done excellent things: this is known in all the earth. Cry out and shout, thou inhabitant of Zion: for great is the Holy One of Israel in the midst of thee"*. [Isaiah 12: 4-6].

In addition to adequate knowledge, **Temperament and Simplicity of mind** also play an important role in drawing virtues from the vessel. Humility procures glory and attracts honour while character defines the state of opportunities. When your character is in the right order, capacity will be enhanced for greater release. It is the heart of flesh that gives way to the acts of God, when you embrace simplicity you will experience the supernatural flow of virtues. This is what guarantees your flight in the midst of hardship. When things are tough for others, you will keep smiling like someone living on another planet for *"When men are cast down, then thou shalt say, There is lifting up; and he shall save the humble person."* Cultivate the nature of Christ in humility, lowliness and singleness of eye with pure conscience and virtues will be flowing incessantly without end.

The Lord recommends that we should *"Take my yoke upon you, and learn of me; for I am meek and lowly in heart: and ye shall find rest unto your souls. For my yoke is easy, and my burden is light"* [Matthew 11:28-30]. His meekness and lowliness of heart secured the right hand of His father as His kingdom Headquarters. He possessed all the virtues of the father and was guided to the right hand of Majesty for eternal dominion over all principalities and powers. For *"The meek will he guide in judgment: and the meek will he teach his way"* [Psalms 25:9] and the beauty of salvation is only for the meek and lowly in heart *"For the Lord taketh pleasure in his people: he will beautify the meek with salvation"* [Psalms 149:4]. Lean on God for the renewal of strength. Build a nature of meekness and submit yourself under the power of God. Empty yourself that God might fill you up in grace and power. Your destiny shall not dry up in Jesus name.

Chapter 7

Discovering Value through Knowledge

Accomplishment in life does not begin with faith, for *faith is the substance of things hoped for, the evidence of things not seen.* It is the substance of what we expect to receive from the vessel and the evidence that it has been delivered even though we are yet to receive it in a physical form. This indicates that something must precede faith before it can function. Knowledge is what precedes faith! Therefore, accomplishment must begin with knowledge for faith to be built up and strengthened to deliver the expected substances. Values are cultivated through knowledge and faith is built by value. When faith is built upon knowledge, values are generated and understanding of the worth of the vessel is unveiled.

When faith is applied based on the worth and value of the vessel, virtues are supernaturally released to prove the strength of faith in action. No one values what he's not knowledgeable about and no one believes or exercises faith in what he does not value. Until knowledge is acquired, value is not cultivated, until there is understanding of the worth of a vessel, faith is not secured and until faith is secured virtues are not generated. So, the journey begins with knowledge! Knowledge of who the Vessel is, what the Vessel portrays or possesses and above all the omnipotence and capability of the vessel. Secondly, possessing the knowledge of who you are, what you are made of, your vantage (redemptive) position and privileged (divine) connection to the Vessel.

"I and my Father are one. Then the Jews took up stones again to stone him. Jesus answered them, Many good works have I shewed you from my Father; for which of those works do ye stone me? The Jews answered him, saying, For a

"I and my father are one!" What! This must be blasphemy of the highest order! You mean you are equal with God? Yes, said Jesus Christ! That is not pride or blasphemy, I am not trying to make myself equal with God, I am just bringing it to your knowledge that as He is, so I am; I am He and He is I! He is my father and I am His Son; that is what defines my values. Is it not written in your law, I said, Ye are gods? Is it not written in your law also that the son of a man is the heir and must bear the name of the man? "*If he called them gods, unto whom the word of God came, and the scripture cannot be broken; Say ye of him, whom the Father hath sanctified, and sent into the world, Thou blasphemest; because I said, I am the Son of God?*" Why then do you call yourself the seed of Abraham if you have no identity with Abraham?

Listen, for your information, I am the light of the world, I am the True Vine that springs up and directly connected to the Husbandman, "*Jesus saith unto him, I am the way, the truth, and the life: no man cometh unto the Father, but by me.* [John 14:6]. I am the Son of man and have the authority to forgive sins here on earth [Mark 2:10 *paraphrased*]. Listen, I am the Generator of virtues; I am the embodiment of all creations; my Father made all things by me and without me was not anything made that was made. In me is life and my life is the light you need for your survival. I have the custody of creations and the earlier you come to terms with this truth the better for you to enjoy the flow of virtues. Above all, my Father has handed over to me authority and power over all creations including death and hell "*For as the Father hath life in himself; so hath he given to the Son to have life in himself; And hath given him authority to execute judgment also, because he is the Son of man*" [John 5:26 – 27]

Hallelujah! That was the account of the Saviour of the world (Jesus Christ the Lord), to the people who were doubting and contending His Sonship! Knowledge lifted Him from the manger and set Him on the pinnacle of authority and dominion. He demonstrated His supremacy over every issue and was confirmed Rabbi, Master! He dominated His world by possessing full knowledge of who His Father was corresponding to His Sonship and *as he is, so are we in this world*. Knowledge is the master key that helps unlock the intrinsic value of man. You can never experience the fullness of God until you know who God is and it is impossible to have the fullness of your inheritance in God if you lack the knowledge of who you are and what you are made of. So, possessing the knowledge of who God is and your privileged position in Him will set you at the zenith of your fulfilment in life.

In this chapter, we shall be unveiling the mystery of knowledge both of God and your person in appropriating your fulfilment with His master plan for your life. Remember, that until knowledge is home, ignorance is effortlessly the crowned king of destiny and presumably, failure is permitted to rule over the affairs of life. *"They know not, neither will they understand; they walk on in darkness: all the foundations of the earth are out of course."* May your spirit mind wake up from slumber to receive the engrafted word of truth for your lifting this season.

WHAT IS KNOWLEDGE?

English Dictionary defines knowledge as "Facts, information, and skills acquired through experience or education; that is, the theoretical or practical understanding of a subject." It further states that knowledge is the "Awareness or familiarity gained by experience of a fact or situation." Scripturally, I define knowledge as the ability to possess God's mind regarding an issue. That is, knowing the intent of a thing and deriving light and understanding to appropriate your thinking and actions with its reality. Living by the insight and revelation to prove your know-how on the subject matter. Knowledge secures the wisdom and understanding to know what to do, and the strength to take necessary steps in actualizing God's purpose for your life. More importantly, possessing the capability to obtain and acquire practical and theoretical know-how of the issues of life and the steps to take to turn it to glory and honour.

Knowledge precedes understanding as you cannot claim to have full understanding of what you are not knowledgeable about. If knowledge is not in place, ignorance has the right to rule and irrespective of your expertise and competence, the level of understanding you claim to have is irrelevant outside knowledge.

WHAT ARE THE PRODUCTS OF KNOWLEDGE?

1. Knowledge produces strength

The first product of knowledge is strength; that is capacity to build faith, hope and the confidence needed to prevail and triumph. The strength to pursue after and draw virtues from the vessel. Knowledge makes for fulfilment and accomplishment of destiny. It takes knowledge of who God is to enjoy continuous ability and daily renewal of energy to excel in life. Among other things that knowledge procures is that it becomes the stability of your times and strength of salvation for your soul! In Isaiah 33: 5 – 8, the scripture reveals the supremacy of the Source of virtues and establishes knowledge and wisdom as the access to the Sources saying *"The Lord is exalted; for he dwelleth on high: he hath filled Zion with judgment and righteousness. And wisdom and knowledge shall be the stability of thy times, and strength of salvation: the fear of the Lord is his treasure. Behold, their valiant ones shall cry without: the ambassadors of peace shall weep bitterly. The highways lie waste, the wayfaring man ceaseth: he hath broken the covenant, he hath despised the cities, he regardeth no man."* It is not the physical strength that draws the virtues to our lives rather it is the knowledge we possess that gives us access to the virtues in the vessel.

2. Knowledge brings you out of the graves and dungeon of prison to take full command of territories

Your beginning and your passage in life notwithstanding, when knowledge is in place there will be a repositioning of status to secure your place in destiny. The account of Joseph depicts practical manifestation of the power of knowledge.

By knowledge, wisdom drew understanding and the prison gate was broken for his release.

> *"And it came to pass in the morning that his spirit was troubled; and he sent and called for all the magicians of Egypt, and all the wise men thereof: and Pharaoh told them his dream; but there was none that could interpret them unto Pharaoh. Then spake the chief butler unto Pharaoh, saying, I do remember my faults this day: Pharaoh was wroth with his servants, and put me in ward in the captain of the guard's house, both me and the chief baker: And we dreamed a dream in one night, I and he; we dreamed each man according to the interpretation of his dream. And there was there with us a young man, an Hebrew, servant to the captain of the guard; and we told him, and he interpreted to us our dreams; to each man according to his dream he did interpret. And it came to pass, as he interpreted to us, so it was; me he restored unto mine office, and him he hanged. Then Pharaoh sent and called Joseph, and they brought him hastily out of the dungeon: and he shaved himself, and changed his raiment, and came in unto Pharaoh"* [Genesis 41: 8 - 14]

Knowledge did not only bring him out of the dungeon of prison, knowledge repositioned him to take over the leadership of Egypt as a preserver of posterity and succourer of Israel.

"And Joseph said unto Pharaoh, The dream of Pharaoh is one: God hath shewed Pharaoh what he is about to do. The seven good kine are seven years; and the seven good ears are seven years: the dream is one. And the seven thin and ill favoured kine that came up after them are seven years; and the seven empty ears blasted with the east wind shall be seven years of famine... And Pharaoh said unto his servants, Can we find such a one as this is, a man in whom the Spirit of God is? And Pharaoh said unto Joseph, Forasmuch as God hath shewed thee all this, there is none so discreet and wise as thou art: Thou shalt be over my house, and according unto thy word shall all my people be ruled: only in the throne will I be greater than thou" [Genesis 41: 25 – 40]. Remember that the magicians, the astrologers and soothsayers of Egypt were people of wisdom and understanding of the tradition and rudiments of the land, yet none of them had the knowledge

to unravel the dream of the king. *"And it came to pass in the morning that his spirit was troubled; and he sent and called for all the magicians of Egypt, and all the wise men thereof: and Pharaoh told them his dream; but there was none that could interpret them unto Pharaoh."* [Genesis 41:8] Knowledge is the pillar that holds wisdom and understanding, until knowledge is in place, wisdom and understanding are eternally impotent.

3. Knowledge guides

Knowledge does not only lift from the prison; it also guides from bondage and give insight to the know-hows of what to do to take command of the situation around your life. The case of Jacob was an example of applied knowledge in the school of divine guide to release himself from Laban's scheme. He was enslaved until knowledge dawned on him. *"And he said unto him, Thou knowest how I have served thee, and how thy cattle was with me. For it was little which thou hadst before I came, and it is now increased unto a multitude; and the Lord hath blessed thee since my coming: and now when shall I provide for mine own house also?* A man that could not feed his family suddenly had a change of story by the efficacy of knowledge. *"And the man increased exceedingly, and had much cattle, and maidservants, and menservants, and camels, and asses."* [read Genesis 30: 25 – 43]. Knowledge guided him to a lasting solution and up he became great and exceedingly great to the extent that they began to envy him!

"And he heard the words of Laban's sons, saying, Jacob hath taken away all that was our father's; and of that which was our father's hath he gotten all this glory" [Genesis 31: 1]. I see knowledge bringing you out of slavery and setting you upon your throne in Jesus name

4. Knowledge justifies and releases your inheritance

"An hypocrite with his mouth destroyeth his neighbour: but through knowledge shall the just be delivered." [Proverbs 11:9]. You are justified through knowledge. The mystery of salvation was unveiled through knowledge. *"He shall see of the travail of his soul, and shall be satisfied: by his knowledge shall my righteous*

servant justify many; for he shall bear their iniquities" [Isaiah 53:11]. Grace and peace become your stability by the reason of the knowledge of God at your disposal. In 2 Peters 1:2 *"Grace and peace be multiplied unto you through the knowledge of God, and of Jesus our Lord,"* Above all, knowledge secures the delivery of your inheritance in God and fills your chambers with precious things *"And by knowledge shall the chambers be filled with all precious and pleasant riches* [Proverbs 24: 4]

5. Knowledge establishes and promotes

The depth of divine providence is a function of adequate knowledge and every high position is designed for the knowledgeable. Knowledge is what promotes and establishes a high throne for its possessor. Knowledge promotes through revelation and access to the secret things that are kept from common eyes. The knowhow of the deep things which are inaccessible by mere men are revealed to babes and suckling by the instrumentality of knowledge at their disposal. The leadership potentials of Joseph and Daniel were traceable to the knowledge they had in accessing the secret dreams which none of the principality and power of the nations and the kingdoms could fathom.

"The Chaldeans answered before the king, and said, There is not a man upon the earth that can shew the king's matter: therefore there is no king, lord, nor ruler, that asked such things at any magician, or astrologer, or Chaldean. And it is a rare thing that the king requireth, and there is none other that can shew it before the king, except the gods, whose dwelling is not with flesh." [Daniel 2:10-11] No flesh could know what the dream of the king was and the interpretation thereof but *"Then was the secret revealed unto Daniel in a night vision. Then Daniel blessed the God of heaven. Daniel answered and said, Blessed be the name of God for ever and ever: for wisdom and might are his: And he changeth the times and the seasons: he removeth kings, and setteth up kings: he giveth wisdom unto the wise, and knowledge to them that know understanding: He revealeth the deep and secret things: he knoweth what is in the darkness, and the light dwelleth with him. I thank thee, and praise thee,…"* [Daniel 2:19-23]

Daniel was a man of deep insight to kingdom mysteries. He possessed the knowledge of God and of Babylonian systems. He was preferred ten times better than all the sorcerers, astrologers, necromancers, soothsayers and the Chaldeans of the land simply by the depth of knowledge he possessed. Therefore *"It pleased Darius to set over the kingdom an hundred and twenty princes, which should be over the whole kingdom; And over these three presidents; of whom Daniel was first: that the princes might give accounts unto them, and the king should have no damage. Then this Daniel was preferred above the presidents and princes, because an excellent spirit was in him; and the king thought to set him over the whole realm."* [Daniel 6: 1 – 3] Knowledge set him over the whole realms of one hundred and twenty provinces, princes and three presidents! I see knowledge taking you from where you are now and placing you on your throne in Jesus' name.

6. Knowledge beget dominion (superiority)

Knowledge secures your dominion over all circumstances and places you above trials and oppositions. It takes knowledge to silence every force that is positioned to frustrate your ministry and career in life. Christ was in the wilderness teaching and healing the people and suddenly it occurred to Him that the people had nothing to eat. By knowledge He humiliated the shame and brought honour and joy to the camp. The scripture says He knew what He would do *"And this he said to prove him: for he himself knew what he would do."* [John 6:6]. Friend, every time you know what step to take in a certain issue, you naturally dominate.

Now the most crucial knowledge that needs to be sought for is the knowledge of who God (the Vessel) is. All the above listed products of knowledge are easily accomplished when you possess the knowledge of who your God is. Remember that it is only those who '**do**' know their God that can '**do**' great exploits in life. Apostle Paul said *"That I may know him, and the power of his resurrection, and the fellowship of his sufferings, being made conformable unto his death;* [Ephesian 3:10]. The question therefore is who is God and what do I need to know about Him?

WHO IS GOD?

> *"For this cause we also, since the day we heard it, do not cease to pray for you, and to desire that ye might be filled with the knowledge of his will in all wisdom and spiritual understanding; That ye might walk worthy of the Lord unto all pleasing, being fruitful in every good work, and increasing in the knowledge of God; Strengthened with all might, according to his glorious power, unto all patience and longsuffering with joyfulness; Giving thanks unto the Father, which hath made us meet to be partakers of the inheritance of the saints in light: Who hath delivered us from the power of darkness, and hath translated us into the kingdom of his dear Son: In whom we have redemption through his blood, even the forgiveness of sins: Who is the image of the invisible God, the firstborn of every creature: For by him were all things created, that are in heaven, and that are in earth, visible and invisible, whether they be thrones, or dominions, or principalities, or powers: all things were created by him, and for him: And he is before all things, and by him all things consist"* [Colossians 1:9 – 17]

The scriptures emphasized *"…that ye might be filled with the knowledge of his will in all wisdom and spiritual understanding"* There is the depth of God that man has not accessed, there are things of God that are yet to be revealed to man. Who knows the mind of God that he may teach us His ways?

You see, you can be praying and receiving answers to your prayers and yet don't know who God is. You can be talking with God and not even know who God is! Moses was a man with unusual insight and revelation, he spent time in the presence of God and upon the mount of God yet confessed that he does not know who God is. In Exodus 33: 12-13 *"And Moses said unto the Lord, See, thou sayest unto me, Bring up this people: and thou hast not let me know whom thou wilt send with me. Yet thou hast said, I know thee by name, and thou hast also found grace in my sight. Now therefore, I pray thee, if I have found grace in thy sight, shew me now thy way, that I may know thee, that I may find grace in thy sight: and consider that this nation is thy people."* (Read Exodus 33:11 – 19)

WHAT DO I NEED TO KNOW ABOUT GOD?

God is not just a Creator of heaven and earth and all that are therein, He is the sole Possessor of all things, living or nonliving, principalities and power, depth or height, all things are God's and He upholds all these things by the word of His power. His creative ability combined with His omnipotence, establish His place as God. God is a Supreme Being, the Source of power, authority and dominion, the Generator of virtues. He is the Alpha and the Omega of all issues of life. God describing Himself in Revelation 22:13 said *"I am Alpha and Omega, the beginning and the end, the first and the last"* and in Isaiah 48:12 *"Hearken unto me, O Jacob and Israel, my called; I am he; I am the first, I also am the last"* Hear me and know who I am for *"I am Alpha and Omega, the beginning and the ending, saith the Lord, which is, and which was, and which is to come, the Almighty"* [Revelation 1:8] *"And he said unto me, It is done. I am Alpha and Omega, the beginning and the end. I will give unto him that is athirst of the fountain of the water of life freely"* [Revelation 21:6]. He is invisible but omnipresent, unseen in the physical affairs of man but omniscient; the Invincible and unquestionable. He is the unchanging Changer, the Almighty God, the Everlasting Father!

One important aspect of God is His supremacy over all issues and circumstances. Everything answers to God and He does not answer to any. He possesses the capability to kill and to make alive and nothing can question His action. *"The Lord killeth, and maketh alive: he bringeth down to the grave, and bringeth up. The Lord maketh poor, and maketh rich: he bringeth low, and lifteth up."* [1 Samuel 2: 6 - 7] And in Deuteronomy 32: 39 *"See now that I, even I, am he, and there is no god with me: I kill, and I make alive; I wound, and I heal: neither is there any that can deliver out of my hand."* He has the final authority over issues and determines what becomes a vessel according to Romans 9:21 *"Hath not the potter power over the clay, of the same lump to make one vessel unto honour, and another unto dishonour?"* Now among others, you need to know the following about God:

1. **Know that God is the secret strength
   behind your continuity in life**

Psalms 118:14 -*The Lord is my strength and song, and is become my salvation.*

2. **Know that the embodiment of your strength is God**

Exodus 15:2 -*The Lord is my strength and song, and he is become my salvation: he is my God, and I will prepare him an habitation; my father's God, and I will exalt him.*

3. **Know that His revelation power is the strength for continuity**

2 Samuel 22:3- *The God of my rock; in him will I trust: he is my shield, and the horn of my salvation, my high tower, and my refuge, my saviour; thou savest me from violence.*

4. **Know that it is impossible to achieve
   anything in life without God**

John 15:5 - *I am the vine, ye are the branches: He that abideth in me, and I in him, the same bringeth forth much fruit: for without me ye can do nothing.*

5. **Know that all power belongs to God**

Psalms 62:11 - God hath spoken once; twice have I heard this; that power belongeth unto God. And in Psalms 95:4 – In his hand are the deep places of the earth: the strength of the hills is his also. The sea is his, and he made it: and his hands formed the dry land

6. **Know that His grace is the way out of weakness**

2 Corinthians 12:9 - And he said unto me, My grace is sufficient for thee: for my strength is made perfect in weakness. Most gladly therefore will I rather glory in my infirmities, that the power of Christ may rest upon me.

7. Know that He is too faithful to leave you in your state of weakness

It is a faithful saying: For if we be dead with him, we shall also live with him: If we suffer, we shall also reign with him: if we deny him, he also will deny us: If we believe not, yet he abideth faithful: he cannot deny himself. Of these things put them in remembrance, charging them before the Lord that they strive not about words to no profit, but to the subverting of the hearers. [2 Timothy 2: 11 – 14]

8. Know that He is the final answer to every situation

"This is the stone which was set at nought of you builders, which is become the head of the corner. Neither is there salvation in any other: for there is none other name under heaven given among men, whereby we must be saved." [Acts 4: 11 – 12]. You need to possess the knowledge and understand that God is God and cannot change according to Malachi 3:6 *"For I am the Lord, I change not; therefore ye sons of Jacob are not consumed"*

9. Know that God is the wall of defense for those who trust in Him

The enemies are aware of those whose defense is God. Job enjoyed this unique defense on his family and substances, Satan testifying of it to ascertain the reality. *"Then Satan answered the Lord, and said, Doth Job fear God for nought? Hast not thou made an hedge about him, and about his house, and about all that he hath on every side? thou hast blessed the work of his hands, and his substance is increased in the land"* [Job 1: b9 - 10] God is the wall of defense for His people who walk in His rules. *"He only is my rock and my salvation; he is my defence; I shall not be greatly moved."* [Psalms 62:2] Also, Psalms 62:6 says *"He only is my rock and my salvation: he is my defence; I shall not be moved."*

10. Know that God is LOVE

God is love and in Him is no hatred at all as stated in 1 John 4:8 – *"He that loveth not knoweth not God; for God is love"* Also, in 1 John 4:16, we are made to know that *"And we have known and believed the love that God hath to us. God is love; and he that dwelleth in love dwelleth in God, and God in him."* He re-purchased humanity back to Himself through His love. His love secured another chance for everyone to access Eden again and enjoy the fullness of His glory. *"For God so loved the world, that he gave his only begotten Son, that whosoever believeth in him should not perish, but have everlasting life. For God sent not his Son into the world to condemn the world; but that the world through him might be saved."* [John 3:16 - 17]

IDENTIFYING WITH THE TRUE PROTOTYPE

Your connection with God is such a unique privilege that He decided to make you in His image and fashioned you after His own likeness. God is your model, your archetype, who used Himself as a prototype for your making, meaning that as He is in heaven so are you expected to be. You share so much in common with your Maker that He does not wish to see any difference. However, you are what you paint yourself to be and until you discover the creator's intention for your life, you may keep struggling with your identity for life. In this section, I will be helping you to see the true you. I mean what you are made of and your originality as a child of God, an agent and the envy of heaven on earth. You are a seed of great value simply by the virtue of your making. You possess the virtues of life but what triggers these virtues is your ability to recognize and appreciate your value.

WHO ARE YOU?

This is the question that you need to ask yourself on daily basis until you discover who you are. Your worth in life is a subject of your identity. I have helped you to list some unique areas of your personality to help you appreciate your worth as a child of God. I decree your eyes be opened to see all these attributes in your personality in Jesus name.

1. The image and likeness of God:

"And God said, Let us make man in our image, after our likeness: and let them have dominion over the fish of the sea, and over the fowl of the air, and over the cattle, and over all the earth, and over every creeping thing that creepeth upon the earth. So God created man in his own image, in the image of God created he him; male and female created he them. And God blessed them..." [Genesis 1:26 - 28]. You are made in God's image and likeness and heaven recognizes you as the exact replica of the Supreme God.

2. A unique single product without duplicate

It will amaze you that of all the billions of humans that exist on the planet earth and innumerable creatures in creation, none looks like you and if any looks like you such cannot be you. You are such a unique creature with no duplicate other than the original Source (God). Your fingerprints, your eye colour, your personalities and your mission on earth are unique to meet the required purpose of creation.

3. A peculiar and holy nation

God created you as a showcase for His peculiarity on earth. You are not only unique, but delicately, wonderfully and fearfully made with all the peculiar nature and attributes of God. In 1 Peter 2:9, the scripture says that you are not only *loved "But ye are a chosen generation, a royal priesthood, an holy nation, a peculiar people; that ye should shew forth the praises of him who hath called you out of darkness into his marvellous light:* You and I are so peculiar that God delivered His only begotten Son *"Who gave himself for us, that he might redeem us from all iniquity, and purify unto himself a peculiar people, zealous of good works."* [Titus 2:14]. You have been loved, honoured and above all the Lord hath chosen you unto himself, as His new Israel and for His own peculiar treasure.

4. A god after the order of the Father God

Every species produces after its kind; therefore, God has deliberately created you after His own kind. That makes you god as your Father God. This was established before creation and confirmed by the scriptures that *"Ye are gods; and all of you are children of the most High."* It is not an understatement therefore to call yourself god because likes beget likes. Every time you wake up to the consciousness of this truth, you naturally dominate circumstances. God was about to send Moses back to Egypt *"And the Lord said unto Moses, See, I have made thee a god to Pharaoh: and Aaron thy brother shall be thy prophet. Thou shalt speak all that I command thee: and Aaron thy brother shall speak unto Pharaoh, that he send the children of Israel out of his land."* [Exodus 7:1 - 2] No wonder, when he cast his rod and the people saw the strange act *"Then the magicians said unto Pharaoh, This is the finger of God"* Every time you come to this level of knowledge, your fingers become the fingers of God; your utterance become God's utterance, your actions display God's supremacy over issues. In fact, you are God's mouthpiece, and ordained Ambassador of heaven on earth. *"And when the people saw what Paul had done, they lifted up their voices, saying in the speech of Lycaonia, The gods are come down to us in the likeness of men."* [Acts 14:11] Your acts must manifest God from this hour!

5. A covenant child

"And I, behold, I establish my covenant with you, and with your seed after you;" [Genesis 9:9] and *"My covenant will I not break, nor alter the thing that is gone out of my lips."* [Psalms 89:34] Every child of God is a covenant child. The covenant made with Abraham qualifies all the heirs of Abraham as covenant children and the covenant of the new testament which is the global covenant (made with the blood of the Saviour, Jesus Christ) adopts all the redeemed and engrafts them to the new covenant. As a redeemed of the Lord therefore all the benefits and the grace that can be found in the covenant are yours for possession as inheritance. Freedom from the pit, grace to salvation, healings, deliverances and what have you; all are now yours through the blood of the new covenant. As a child of God who has been bought with a price, there is a seal of the new covenant upon you which secures your place in God.

6. The light of the world, the salt of the earth and a city set on pinnacle that cannot be hid

You and I are created as the salt of the earth to season and preserve destiny from decadence. You are the light of God on earth and rightly positioned to brighten destinies. A city that is conspicuously set on a hill to give light and meaning to generations. *"Ye are the salt of the earth: but if the salt have lost his savour, wherewith shall it be salted? it is thenceforth good for nothing, but to be cast out, and to be trodden under foot of men. Ye are the light of the world. A city that is set on an hill cannot be hid. Neither do men light a candle, and put it under a bushel, but on a candlestick; and it giveth light unto all that are in the house. Let your light so shine before men, that they may see your good works, and glorify your Father which is in heaven." (Matthew 5:13 – 16).* That is your value on earth. You are a virtue carrier and an agent of impact on earth by the reason of your privileged sonship position. You are a pace setter in the realm of the supernatural and all that heaven expects from you is the manifestation of that shining light that will draw the gentiles to the knowledge of God through you.

7. Possessor of dominion over all creatures

You are created for dominion. Your root was dominion and authority, your scepter is the scepter of dominion and you are specially positioned to dominate all issues of life. In Psalms 8:2-6 the scripture recorded the privilege of all saints *"Out of the mouth of babes and sucklings hast thou ordained strength because of thine enemies, that thou mightest still the enemy and the avenger. When I consider thy heavens, the work of thy fingers, the moon and the stars, which thou hast ordained; What is man, that thou art mindful of him? and the son of man, that thou visitest him? For thou hast made him a little lower than the angels, and hast crowned him with glory and honour. Thou madest him to have dominion over the works of thy hands; thou hast put all things under his feet:"* Hallelujah! You are crowned with glory and honour and made to have dominion over all the works of God's hand. That was your initial scepter in creation according to Genesis 1:28 *"And God blessed them, and God said unto them, Be fruitful, and multiply, and replenish the earth, and subdue it: and have dominion over the fish of the sea, and over the fowl of the air, and over every living thing that moveth upon the earth"*

The Lord Jesus confirmed this in John 5: 26-27 *"For as the Father hath life in himself; so hath he given to the Son to have life in himself; And hath given him authority to execute judgment also, because he is the Son of man."* Friend, you are a man/woman to be envied on earth.

8. The battle axe of God and a weapon of war

"Thou art my battle axe and weapons of war: for with thee will I break in pieces the nations, and with thee will I destroy kingdoms; And with thee will I break in pieces the horse and his rider; and with thee will I break in pieces the chariot and his rider; With thee also will I break in pieces man and woman; and with thee will I break in pieces old and young; and with thee will I break in pieces the young man and the maid; I will also break in pieces with thee the shepherd and his flock; and with thee will I break in pieces the husbandman and his yoke of oxen; and with thee will I break in pieces captains and rulers."[Jeremiah 51:20 - 23]

I want you to be aware of the truth that nothing functions here on earth without your permission. God cannot execute any task without your permission. Also, the forces of hell have no audacity to operate on earth without the legal permission of man. No wonder each force strives to engage man in any activities purposely to penetrate the earth. Psalms 115:16 says *"The heaven, even the heavens, are the Lord's: but the earth hath he given to the children of men."* You and I are the legal owner of the earth and we stand as the agents for God to manifest His glory here on earth. God was about to rescue His own people out of Egypt but could not make any move until He employed Moses as His legal agent to carry out the task. Listen, you are the battle axe of God on earth and with you He will build, pull down, erect, and dismantle at the instance of your permission.

The judgment upon the earth shall be executed by you as the saint of God. Hear what the Lord Jesus said to all those who are His Disciples *"Then said Jesus to them again, Peace be unto you: as my Father hath sent me, even so send I you. And when he had said this, he breathed on them, and saith unto them, Receive ye the Holy Ghost: Whose soever sins ye remit, they are remitted unto them; and whose soever sins ye retain, they are retained.* [John 20:21 - 23]. May your place not be lost in this privileged and honourable position in Jesus name

9. Partaker of God's divine nature

"I and my Father are one. Then the Jews took up stones again to stone him. Jesus answered them, Many good works have I shewed you from my Father; for which of those works do ye stone me?" [John 10:30 - 32]. Every child of God possesses the same DNA with God by the privilege of creation in His image and after His likeness. We are the full copy of God and as a typical replica of God, we are called God's replication. As a carrier of His DNA replication, you share the same DNA with God both in nature, habit, character and conduct. You are designed to naturally partake of the divine nature of your father because you possess all that He possesses. You represent His personality here on earth and you carry the same genes. *"Whereby are given unto us exceeding great and precious promises: that by these ye might be partakers of the divine nature, having escaped the corruption that is in the world through lust."* [2 Peter 1:4] So, your escape from the corruption of the world has brought you to the realm of sharing the same nature with God through Christ Jesus. Among these divine natures are purity, truth, justice, love, peace, joy, holiness and godliness. All these combined nature gives you the opportunity to live a god-like lifestyle here on earth.

10. Carrier of God's glory and Spirit for manifestation

What a privilege! You are the carrier of God's glory on earth. In Isaiah 60: 1 – 8, the scripture commands your rising as the shining star of God that is set to reveal His glory to the world *"Arise, shine; for thy light is come, and the glory of the Lord is risen upon thee. For, behold, the darkness shall cover the earth, and gross darkness the people: but the Lord shall arise upon thee, and his glory shall be seen upon thee. And the Gentiles shall come to thy light, and kings to the brightness of thy rising. Lift up thine eyes round about, and see: all they gather themselves together, they come to thee: thy sons shall come from far, and thy daughters shall be nursed at thy side. Then thou shalt see, and flow together, and thine heart shall fear, and be enlarged; because the abundance of the sea shall be converted unto thee, the forces of the Gentiles shall come unto thee..."* And *"Who are these that fly as a cloud, and as the doves to their windows?"* They are the carriers of the glory of God! By redemption, you carry the glory of God on earth and it is this glory that distinguishes you among your peers. John 17: 22 says *"And the glory which thou gavest me I have given them; that they may be one, even as we are one:"* meaning that all the glory that Christ enjoyed here on earth are now yours for manifestation with greater influence on the society because greater works than this shall you do for the reason that Christ has returned to the Father.

11. The joy of God and the apple of God's eyes

You are cherished, nurtured and led as the apple of God's eye. In Deuteronomy 32:10 *"He found him in a desert land, and in the waste howling wilderness; he led him about, he instructed him, he kept him as the apple of his eye."* God rejoices having you as His vessel and peculiar child, His glory and blessing on earth. You are such a precious vessel that God cannot afford to lose sight of in care and love *"For thus saith the Lord of hosts; After the glory hath he sent me unto the nations which spoiled you: for he that toucheth you toucheth the apple of his eye"* [Zechariah 2:8] whoever touches you touches the apple of God's eye. In fact, the scripture describes you as the wife of God, the pure bride of the Lamb. *"Fear not; for thou shalt not be ashamed: neither be thou confounded; for thou shalt not be put to shame: for thou shalt forget the shame of thy youth, and shalt not remember the reproach of thy widowhood any more. For thy Maker is thine husband; the Lord of hosts is his name; and thy Redeemer the Holy One of Israel; The God of the whole earth shall he be called."* [Isaiah 54: 4-5]. Your Father, your Maker and your Husband: He dwells in you and rejoices over you in His love according to Zephaniah 3:17 *"The Lord thy God in the midst of thee is mighty; he will save, he will rejoice over thee with joy; he will rest in his love, he will joy over thee with singing."* You are a man/woman to be envied in your generation.

12. The pride of heaven on earth

You are the bedrock of the gospel of God on earth. You are the wing spread abroad to propagate the gospel of salvation to the earth. Heaven rejoices having you here on earth because you are an ambassador positioned to manifest the glory, virtues and pride of heaven here on earth. The honour of heaven is seen through you. Things are revealed to you for display here on earth. Remember, Jesus said in Matthew 11:25 *"At that time Jesus answered and said, I thank thee, O Father, Lord of heaven and earth, because thou hast hid these things from the wise and prudent, and hast revealed them unto babes."* You are the rock where the church of God is built *"And I say also unto thee, That thou art Peter, and upon this rock I will build my church; and the gates of hell shall not prevail against it. And I will give unto thee the keys of the kingdom of heaven: and whatsoever thou shalt bind on earth shall be bound in heaven: and whatsoever thou shalt loose on earth shall be loosed in heaven"* [Matthew 16:18-19]

13. King and Priest set apart to reign on earth

There are priests and prophets, there are kings and prophets, but we only have one King and Priest. The first king and priest was Melchizedek as recorded in Genesis 14:18 *"And Melchizedek king of Salem brought forth bread and wine: and he was the priest of the most high God."* And the scripture described this great priest and king as Christ who should later come to the earth to save God's people. *"For this Melchisedec, king of Salem, priest of the most high God, who met Abraham returning from the slaughter of the kings, and blessed him; To whom also Abraham gave a tenth part of all; first being by interpretation King of righteousness, and after that also King of Salem, which is, King of peace; Without father, without mother, without descent, having neither beginning of days, nor end of life; but made like unto the Son of God; abideth a priest continually."* [Hebrews 7:1 - 3]. And *"The Lord hath sworn, and will not repent, Thou art a priest for ever after the order of Melchizedek."* [Psalm 110:4] So Christ who appeared in the old testament as Melchizedek and later returned to the earth as the King and Priest is the only one who possess that enviable position.

But now Christ redeemed us from corruption and brought us to the envy of deity above priest and prophet, king and prophets, making us **king and priest** in the same likeness to Himself *"And hast made us unto our God kings and priests: and we shall reign on the earth"* [Revelation 5:10]. Indeed, you are a king and a priest; you possess the deity of the two principal forces with the scepter of authority to sit on your throne both as a king and a priest forever after the order of Christ the King of kings, the Lord over lords and the everlasting King and Priest. *"And hath made us kings and priests unto God and his Father; to him be glory and dominion for ever and ever. Amen."* [Revelation 1:6] You carry the scepter of a king and a priest to function in the office of Christ your Master.

14. The temple of the Spirit of God

You are bought as the sacred temple of the Spirit of God. You are the dwelling palace of the Holy Spirit. The price paid on you was to refine and turn you to the domicile of the Lord. God resides in you as His vessel. The scripture says *"What? know ye not that your body is the temple of the Holy Ghost which is in you, which ye have of God, and ye are not your own? For ye are bought with a price: therefore glorify God in your body, and in your spirit, which are God's. [1 Corinthians 6: 19-20]* and 1 Corinthians 3:16 confirms that *"Know ye not that ye are the temple of God, and that the Spirit of God dwelleth in you?"* The kingdom of God is within you. You are the carrier of His glory and virtues. *"And when he was demanded of the Pharisees, when the kingdom of God should come, he answered them and said, The kingdom of God cometh not with observation: Neither shall they say, Lo here! or, lo there! for, behold, the kingdom of God is within you"* [Luke 17:20 - 21]. Wake up to the knowledge of this and exercise your supremacy over all issues around you.

15. The friend of God

You are not just a child of God, you are the best friend of your father. Your master (Jesus Christ) said you are no longer a servant. He makes all things known to you, He develops your spirit as His candle. He keeps His Spirit in you to communicate with your spirit and bring to reality His will. You are granted access to secret things of heaven not as a child but as a friend. *"Henceforth I call you not servants; for the servant knoweth not what his lord doeth: but I have called you friends; for all things that I have heard of my Father I have made known unto you. Ye have not chosen me, but I have chosen you, and ordained you, that ye should go and bring forth fruit, and that your fruit should remain: that whatsoever ye shall ask of the Father in my name, he may give it you."* [John 15:15 - 16] You are now operating in the level of your progenitor, the patriarch Abraham the friend of God. What a privilege!

With all these clarifications, it is evident that you are a carrier of great values and a potential generator of greater virtues in life. You are not to be valued less than your worth as a refined precious child of God; you are not worth the measure of gold or silver, rather you are worth what heaven is worth on earth. I decree therefore that your worth begin to emerge in all areas of your life from this moment in Jesus name.

Remember when our Lord Jesus was here on earth, He declared *"I am the light of the world" "I am the door to the heart of the Father and no one comes to the Father except through me" "I and my Father are one"*:

> *"Then Pilate entered into the judgment hall again, and called Jesus, and said unto him, Art thou the King of the Jews? Jesus answered him, Sayest thou this thing of thyself, or did others tell it thee of me? Pilate answered, Am I a Jew? Thine own nation and the chief priests have delivered thee unto me: what hast thou done? Jesus answered, My kingdom is not of this world: if my kingdom were of this world, then would my servants fight, that I should not be delivered to the Jews: but now is my kingdom not from hence. Pilate therefore said unto him, Art thou a king then? Jesus answered, Thou sayest that I am a king. To this end was I born, and for this cause came I into the world, that I should bear witness unto the truth. Every one that is of the truth heareth my voice"* [John 18: 33 - 37]

And when He was about to ascend to His place of glory, He pronounced our values and worth, announcing to the Disciples thus: 'You are the light of the world. You are a city that is set on a hill which cannot be hidden. You are the salt of the earth sent forth to preserve destinies from decadence. You are designed to reveal the shining Light of heaven in the midst of darkness, so that men in darkness can see your good works and glorify your Father which is in heaven' *(Matthew 5:13 – 16 paraphrased and emphasized mine).* You are a man/woman to be envied in this world and not to be pitied by people.

YOUR WORTH AND POTENTIALS

"For whom he did foreknow, he also did predestinate to be conformed to the image of his Son, that he might be the firstborn among many brethren. Moreover whom he did predestinate, them he also called: and whom he called, them he also justified: and whom he justified, them he also glorified. [Romans 8: 29 - 30] If you have been redeemed by the blood of Jesus, then you have been re-born into the sonship fold as an heir (and a joint heir with Christ Jesus the First born) and are now a child of destiny. You are pre-destined for glory. I mean you are set apart to be glorified, I mean you are designed for higher flight in life. You are not a child of destitute but a child of destiny. You are not redeemed to be reduced but you are redeemed to show forth the praises of Him who hath called you into His own glory and virtue. For *"Grace and peace be multiplied unto you through the knowledge of God, and of Jesus our Lord, According as his divine power hath given unto us all things that pertain unto life and godliness, through the knowledge of him that hath called us to glory and virtue: Whereby are given unto us exceeding great and precious promises: that by these ye might be partakers of the divine nature, having escaped the corruption that is in the world through lust"* [2 Peter 1: 2 – 4]

As the redeemed of the Lord, you and I are the pride of God here on earth. We are His priests and Kings destined to reign on earth and not to be ruined by the system of the world (Revelation 5:10) So, you are too peculiar to be stranded in life. You are too distinct to be dumped as a nonentity in life. *"But ye are a chosen generation, a royal priesthood, an holy nation, a peculiar people; that ye should shew forth the praises of him who hath called you out of darkness into his marvellous light: Which in time past were not a people, but are now the people of God: which had not obtained mercy, but now have obtained mercy."* [1 Peter 2: 9 – 10] And as it is written, *"This people have I formed for myself; they shall shew forth my praise"* [Isaiah 43: 21] These two scriptures portray the precise identity of every redeemed of the Lord as:

- a chosen generation,
- a royal priesthood,
- an holy nation,
- a peculiar people;

You are purposely created to show forth the praises of him who hath called you out of darkness into his marvelous light. Hear what Christ said about your values on earth *"Ye are the light of the world. A city that is set on an hill cannot be hid. You are the salt of the earth: You are designed to reveal the shining Light of heaven in the midst of darkness, so that the men in darkness can see your good works, and glorify your Father which is in heaven"* (Matthew 5:13 – 16). These among others are your true identity and my true identity. By the virtue of this scriptural truth, you are destined for a higher dimension of the practical manifestation of heaven's glory as God's representative here on earth. In the school of virtues, you are not designed as an instrument for drawing virtues, but a vessel that generates and releases virtues to mankind. You are the vessel of God set apart for impact. Men should be thronging you to draw virtues from you as a sole representative of heaven on earth.

LET YOUR CHARACTER SPEAK YOUR VALUE

Your life pattern, your character and conduct, the steps you take in life, how you handle the issues of life and how you react to situations speak vividly who you are and what your worth is. Someone once said, 'character is the prophecy of the future' How you live your life shows the stuff you are made of. You cannot be made a king/queen and live a life of a slave. Being born with all these attributes does not guarantee an automatic possession. What establishes your quality and worth is your character.

How do you see yourself and how do you live to demonstrate (in a practical form) your true personality? This is what defines who you really are. For *"There is an evil which I have seen under the sun, as an error which proceedeth from the ruler: Folly is set in great dignity, and the rich sit in low place. I have seen servants upon horses, and princes walking as servants upon the earth"* [Ecclesiastes 10: 5 - 7]

Character is a choice born out of either ignorance, pride or deep knowledge of the truth. When your character is rooted in knowledge it will give a clear understanding of your worth and by the reason of your understanding, you possess the right mind to maintain, retain and demonstrate values. On the other hand, a choice born out of pure ignorance keeps the truth far away from you and enslaves you. Ignorance makes you live a life of destitute even though you were expected to live a palace-like lifestyle. People are kept in the dark because they lack the capacity to know who they are and what they possess in redemption. *"My people are destroyed for lack of knowledge: because thou hast rejected knowledge, I will also reject thee, that thou shalt be no priest to me: seeing thou hast forgotten the law of thy God, I will also forget thy children"* [Hosea 4:6] Ignorance keep its victim in perpetual captivity. *"Therefore my people are gone into captivity, because they have no knowledge: and their honourable men are famished, and their multitude dried up with thirst"* [Isaiah 5: 13]

If your character detests knowledge, failure will dominate you and if your habit hates knowledge, foolishness will take you for a ride. Above all, if you lack the habit of discipline in the knowledge of the things of God, most importantly, the fear of God, sin will dominate you. If you are ashamed to associate with God and His kingdom, you will be dislocated by the scheme of the devils. *"For I am not ashamed of the gospel of Christ: for it is the power of God unto salvation to every one that believeth; to the Jew first, and also to the Greek. For therein is the righteousness of God revealed from faith to faith: as it is written, The just shall live by faith. For the wrath of God is revealed from heaven against all ungodliness and unrighteousness of men, who hold the truth in unrighteousness; Because that which may be known of God is manifest in them; for God hath shewed it unto them. For the invisible things of him from the creation of the world are clearly seen, being understood by the things that are made, even his eternal power and Godhead; so that they are without excuse: Because that, when they knew God, they glorified him not as God, neither were thankful; but became vain in their imaginations, and their foolish heart was darkened. Professing themselves to be wise, they became fools, And changed the glory of the uncorruptible God into an image made like to corruptible man, and to birds, and fourfooted beasts, and creeping things. Wherefore God also gave them up to uncleanness through the lusts of their own hearts, to dishonour their own bodies between themselves"* [Romans 1: 16 - 24].

It is your character that aligns you to the knowledge of the principles and ethics of heaven to secure your place and enhance your values in life. Faith, value and virtue sorely depend on your habit because each of these three attributes functions at the mercy of your character. You shall not be displaced from God's virtues in Jesus name.

Chapter 8

Faith, Values and Virtues:
Their Great Demand

Every valuable item is at the mercy of contention and the more valuable the item the stronger the contention. It should equally be noted that valuable items are as costly as their values and delicately vulnerable by the level of the virtues they command. This is what defines the worth and price. The great demand for values and virtues therefore is a life of righteousness. There is the need for thorough purging and cleansing before our value can produce virtues. *If a man therefore purge himself from these, he shall be a vessel unto honour, sanctified, and meet for the master's use, and prepared unto every good work [2 Timothy 2:21]*

Every habitual sinner is a valueless entity and insignificant figure in the society. The soundness of mind is totally lost, and quality of values evaporate when one engages in sinful nature. Honour, glory and dignity are replaced with ignominy, shame and reproach because *"Righteousness exalteth a nation: but sin is a reproach to any people"* [Proverbs 14:34]. Additionally, when you engage in sin, your faith becomes fake, virtues are totally lost because values are turned to worthlessness, scornfulness, impertinence and inconsequential entities with no significance to associate with them.

CLEAN UP SO YOU CAN BE LIFTED UP!

One of the most dreadful ways of losing value is sin! Whenever sin strikes in a man's life, reproach replaces his value and his dignity is eroded while his shining light becomes indistinct because he is now defiled. The misery of defilement is that it extinguishes the values of man and replaces it with shame and reproach, leading to annihilation. The value we possess is the crown of God's glory which is our eternal covering on earth, and the only way to be stripped off that glory is through sinful living.

> *Know ye not that ye are the temple of God, and that the Spirit of God dwelleth in you? If any man defile the temple of God, him shall God destroy; for the temple of God is holy, which temple ye are. Let no man deceive himself. If any man among you seemeth to be wise in this world, let him become a fool, that he may be wise"* [1 Corinthians 3:16-18]

In this race, no one will help you to clean up. It is absolutely your responsibility to position yourself as a true branch of the Vine if you want to truly manifest the values of the Vine. God did not form you in His image to live a double life, rather, you were made in His image to possess His glory. You are not created as a fountain that yields both bitter and freshwater. You are not formed to be an entity of defilement and glory. You are created to maintain one single eye and that eye is the eye of God which connotes holiness.

> *"Doth a fountain send forth at the same place sweet water and bitter? Can the fig tree, my brethren, bear olive berries? either a vine, figs? so can no fountain both yield salt water and fresh. Who is a wise man and endued with knowledge among you? let him shew out of a good conversation his works with meekness of wisdom"* [James 3:11-13]

You cannot afford to live your life contrary to your divine personality. You need to clean up the mess, so you can portray and manifest the true values of God which are deposited in you. How can you be called the salt of the earth and yet not seasoning life? How can you be the light of the world and yet generating darkness to your society? How can you be made the temple of God and yet full of filthiness, immorality and ungodliness? This is absurd! But no one can change you except you, so rise, think and turn from every habit that robs you of dignity. Listen, every one of us has a mandate for greatness because every good and perfect thing comes from God, meaning that all that God created is perfect and primarily made for a specific purpose in life. Remember that *"Before I formed thee in the belly I knew thee; and before thou camest forth out of the womb I sanctified thee, and I ordained thee a prophet unto the nations"* *[Jeremiah 1:5]*. There is a prophetic mandate upon your life which is embedded within you to deliver your generation.

Nevertheless, God's plan for your life can be altered by the choice you make in life. Only those who are willing to reason with and walk in obedient to His plan will fulfil destiny. He is admonishing everyone to *"Come now, and let us reason together, saith the Lord: though your sins be as scarlet, they shall be as white as snow; though they be red like crimson, they shall be as wool. If ye be willing and obedient, ye shall eat the good of the land: But if ye refuse and rebel, ye shall be devoured with the sword: for the mouth of the Lord hath spoken it [Isaiah 1: 18 - 20]*. Your choice takes the preeminent over His plan, even though His plan looks good for you, it is left for you to accept, embrace and walk in it to maintain faith, value and generate virtues to your generation.

There was the case of a man called Samson, whose destiny was clearly defined by God and revealed to his parents for guidance, yet he gave himself to ungodliness and terminated his destiny prematurely. He lost values and his bowel burst out. *"And there was a certain man of Zorah, of the family of the Danites, whose name was Manoah; and his wife was barren, and bare not. And the angel of the Lord appeared unto the woman, and said unto her, Behold now, thou art barren, and bearest not: but thou shalt conceive, and bear a son. Now therefore beware, I pray thee, and drink not wine nor strong drink, and eat not any unclean thing: For, lo, thou shalt conceive, and bear a son; and no razor shall come on his head: for the child shall be a Nazarite unto God from the womb: and he shall begin to deliver Israel out of the hand of the Philistines"* *[Judges 13:2 - 5]*

Samson decided to lead his life in the opposite direction of God's plan. An agent sent to be the deliverer of Israel after the order of Moses, went after strange women. A man of valour and vigour went after whoredom and got trapped in his lust until his destiny was totally erased.

> *"And it came to pass afterward, that he loved a woman in the valley of Sorek, whose name was Delilah... And she said unto him, How canst thou say, I*

love thee, when thine heart is not with me? thou hast mocked me these three times, and hast not told me wherein thy great strength lieth. And it came to pass, when she pressed him daily with her words, and urged him, so that his soul was vexed unto death; That he told her all his heart, and said unto her, There hath not come a razor upon mine head; for I have been a Nazarite unto God from my mother's womb: if I be shaven, then my strength will go from me, and I shall become weak, and be like any other man. And when Delilah saw that he had told her all his heart, she sent and called for the lords of the Philistines, saying, Come up this once, for he hath shewed me all his heart. Then the lords of the Philistines came up unto her, and brought money in their hand. And she made him sleep upon her knees; and she called for a man, and she caused him to shave off the seven locks of his head; and she began to afflict him, and his strength went from him. And she said, The Philistines be upon thee, Samson. And he awoke out of his sleep, and said, I will go out as at other times before, and shake myself. And he wist not that the Lord was departed from him" [Judges 16: 4, 15 - 20

Oh, *"…he wist not that the Lord was departed from him!"* He lost his sense of reasoning and thought God will still be part of his ungodliness! Far be it from the Almighty God that He will behold iniquity!!! Please, get back and clean up before God departs from you in your sinful journey. Your future is not guaranteed if you continue in sin! Values are not in view for the ungodly! Wound, reproach and dishonour are the rewards and dead is the end result, *for the soul that sinneth shall die.* Why must you live as a destitute and die before your time when you have been deployed here on earth to live a fulfilled life as an ambassador of heaven?

As a precious seed, you are not sown in corruption, so wake up and stop swimming in defilement. You need to look at yourself in the mirror and speak the truth to yourself if that will help you. Listen, heaven is depending on you while the earth is earnestly expecting your manifestation as the true representative of God on earth. You cannot afford to continue the way you are now! There must be therefore, a desperate strive for transformation within you provoking you to manifest your true sonship. *"For the earnest expectation of the creature waiteth for the manifestation of the sons of God"* [Romans 8:19]. Stop creating another new testament episode of Samson, wake up and subscribe for purity; place a strong demand on yourself to go after righteousness. Your circumstance is not your problem, but your negligence and your complacency to uprightness. This is the simple reason why values are eroded in your life and around you. Wake up therefore and clean up the mess that the glory of God may find expression in your daily life.

Many times, we prove to be strong and think we can stand the power of defilement. Listen, the thief has three missions to kill, steal and to destroy. And you should understand that sin is the most pious thief of our time. If sin could succeed in stripping Adam of God's glory, I can assure you that anyone who compromises will be a victim. Wisdom demands therefore that you run from the camp of sinful influence to avoid being trapped by the thief. The scripture recommends that we run away from sins and what easily beset us and avoid fellowship with agents of sin.

> *"Flee fornication. Every sin that a man doeth is without the body; but he that committeth fornication sinneth against his own body. What? know ye not that your body is the temple of the Holy Ghost which is in you, which ye have of God, and ye are not your own? For ye are bought with a price: therefore glorify God in your body, and in your spirit, which are God's"* [1 Corinthians 6: 18-20]

Flee! Flee! Flee! Flee fornication! Flee youthful lust! Flee, flee, flee! That is scriptural recommendation to everyone who desires to be a vessel of honour, carrying the values of heaven to generate great virtues on earth. You have the greater part to play in this inevitable move. You have the major role to change your lifestyle. You are responsible for the change and until you make up your mind for this change, your values are not pronounced.

> *"Nevertheless the foundation of God standeth sure, having this seal, The Lord knoweth them that are his. And, Let every one that nameth the name of Christ depart from iniquity. But in a great house there are not only vessels of gold and of silver, but also of wood and of earth; and some to honour, and some to dishonour. If a man therefore purge himself from these, he shall be a*

> *vessel unto honour, sanctified, and meet for the master's use, and prepared unto every good work. Flee also youthful lusts: but follow righteousness, faith, charity, peace, with them that call on the Lord out of a pure heart. But foolish and unlearned questions avoid, knowing that they do gender strifes"* [2 Timothy 2: 19-23]

Let everyone that names the name of Christ depart from iniquity. Let them flee from the lust of the flesh, eyes and the pride of life. Let them embrace righteousness, strive for holiness, stretch for uprightness and run after the fear of God so that the glory of God can be expressively pronounced in their lives.

SIN SHALL NOT HAVE DOMINION OVER YOU

As a precious seed with great value and inexplicable worth, every saint is susceptible to defilement. However, the scripture has made it clear that we all have power to destroy sin and the nature of sin if we so desire to be free from its entanglement. God was speaking with Cain while he was wroth with his brother on the account that his sacrifice was not accepted and God warned him that *"If thou doest well, shalt thou not be accepted? and if thou doest not well, sin lieth at the door. And unto thee shall be his desire, and thou shalt rule over him"* [Genesis 4:7]. Though sin seems to be knocking at the door of our heart, it will only come in when we give it the chance to come into our life. That is, by carelessly choosing a wrong path to walk in, sin will effortlessly creep in, but if you resist it, it will not have dominion over you.

> *Likewise reckon ye also yourselves to be dead indeed unto sin, but alive unto God through Jesus Christ our Lord. Let not sin therefore reign in your mortal body, that ye should obey it in the lusts thereof. Neither yield ye your members as instruments of unrighteousness unto sin: but yield yourselves unto God, as those that are alive from the dead, and your members as instruments of righteousness unto God. For sin shall not have dominion over you: for ye are not under the law, but under grace. What then? shall we sin, because we are not under the law, but under grace? God forbid. Know ye not, that to whom ye yield yourselves servants to obey, his servants ye are to whom ye obey; whether*

Yes, *sin shall not have dominion over you* because you have been made free from sin and now have become the seed of righteousness. Therefore, align with the Spirit of righteousness in order to quench the fiery dart of sin around your life. If you allow your steps to be ordered by the word of God, sin will not destroy your value. In Psalms 119:133, the Psalmist says, *"Order my steps in thy word: and let not any iniquity have dominion over me."* Also, in Psalms 19:13 *"Keep back thy servant also from presumptuous sins; let them not have dominion over me: then shall I be upright, and I shall be innocent from the great transgression."* All this has to do with you finding God's way and aligning yourself to walking therein with consciousness of your mind and total dependency on the Spirit of God for help.

Friend, sin does not only destroy value, it destroys destiny forever! Cain became a beast and a vagabond in life, Solomon a man of wisdom became a man of vanity simply by giving in to sin. Samson the deliverer became a subject of ridicule in his generation. The children of Israel lost all capacity to confront the smallest nation Ai because an Achan was in their congregation. Sin corrupts creation! Sin destroys destiny, sin erases value and replaces it with reproach, wound and dishonor! Sin corrupts mentality, only righteousness can quicken our mental soundness and generate adequate value that will help us command respect in society.

What sin does is to drive God far away from us because His eyes are so holy that He cannot behold iniquity. When sin has succeeded in keeping us out of God's site, values are lost, and we are opened to all vulnerabilities. Remember that it takes God's presence for man to generate values and when God is not there, values are replaced with contemptuousness.

RIGHTEOUSNESS - THE GREAT DEMAND FOR FAITH, VALUES AND VIRTUES

The price for values must be fully paid with the consciousness of mind and action on our part to desist from ungodliness and seek for purity with clear conscience. If we truly belong to the kingdom, then wisdom demands that we live by the principles of the kingdom and righteousness is the key! If we are children of God and the seed of Abraham through redemption, then we must walk in the path of righteousness for our values to be spoken of. We are responsible for keeping ourselves pure since *"We know that whosoever is born of God sinneth not; but he that is begotten of God keepeth himself, and that wicked one toucheth him not* [1 John 5:18].

Christ Jesus exemplified the life of righteousness all through His life here on earth. His life was perfect amidst a corrupt, defiled and un-regenerated community. He called everyone together and asked *"Which of you convinceth me of sin? And if I say the truth, why do ye not believe me?"* [John 8:46] The response was overwhelmingly None! 'Not a single' person, because He lived to please the Father and that helped Him to manifest the Father in an inexplicable but humbling way which no man has ever experienced. Righteousness was His girdle; purity, holiness, uprightness and the fear of God were His daily steps. His values spoke for Him and men who believed in His worth enjoyed tremendous virtues that were released through impact. See what the Psalmist wrote concerning Him:

> *"And in thy majesty ride prosperously because of truth and meekness and righteousness; and thy right hand shall teach thee terrible things. Thine arrows are sharp in the heart of the king's enemies; whereby the people fall under thee. Thy throne, O God, is for ever and ever: the sceptre of thy kingdom is a right sceptre. Thou lovest righteousness, and hatest wickedness: therefore God, thy God, hath anointed thee with the oil of gladness above thy fellows. All thy garments smell of myrrh, and aloes, and cassia, out of the ivory palaces, whereby they have made thee glad. Kings' daughters were among thy honourable women: upon thy right hand did stand the queen in gold of Ophir"* [Psalms 45: 4 - 9]

He did not consider Himself Lord and God but humbled Himself in the sight of His Father and among men, walking in the fear of God. He paid the price of righteousness for values and He generated great virtues to all generations; even until tomorrow, the fruits of His righteousness are still manifesting.

Joseph took it upon himself to live a life of purity in Egypt and we all know how he ended. This young man had all the privileges to be corrupt like Samson, but he exclaimed in the room of temptation *"how then can I do this great wickedness, and sin against God?"* 'I'd rather be in jail forever than to sell my destiny to immorality.' That was the price he paid, wherefore God hath highly elevated Joseph and placed him above all ministers and citizens of Egypt. The choice of righteousness turned a slave and a prisoner to the father of the king of the land. Righteousness exalts, purity elevates, holiness promotes, and the fear of God enthrone. The price must be consciously paid! Righteousness is the price for value!

SEPARATE FROM SIN BEFORE IT SEPARATES YOU FROM GOD!

"When Israel went out of Egypt, the house of Jacob from a people of strange language; Judah was his sanctuary, and Israel his dominion. The sea saw it, and fled: Jordan was driven back. The mountains skipped like rams, and the little hills like lambs. What ailed thee, O thou sea, that thou fleddest? thou Jordan, that thou wast driven back? Ye mountains, that ye skipped like rams; and ye little hills, like lambs? Tremble, thou earth, at the presence of the Lord, at the presence of the God of Jacob; Which turned the rock into a standing water, the flint into a fountain of waters" [Psalm 114:1-8]

There are people around you who are part of your life, and are the initiators of evil steps, ungodly thoughts and wrong decisions you make. I will adjure you right now in the name of God to rise up and cast them out of your sight and write them off your destiny before they succeed in writing you off God's book of life. As long as you harbour Achan in your camp, or you continue to dwell in the midst of scornful, values will be out of sight and your faith will be unproductive. Get yourself together and clear off the debris in your camp so that the glory of God might be revealed in you and values might glow. The children of Israel could not lift up their head until they departed from the camp of strange people whose ways were contrary to the ways designed for Israel. People of strange language; idol worshipers and abusers of mankind. But after their departure, the glory of God descended upon them and their values began to generate great virtues. Sin keeps God far away from the camp of men, only righteousness attracts His presence.

The target of sin is the values you possess and when care is not taken, sin will succeed in stripping off the values and render you a victim of shame and reproach. So, arise, and take violent action *"Casting down imaginations, and every high thing that exalteth itself against the knowledge of God, and bringing into captivity every thought to the obedience of Christ;"* Sin has nothing to lose but has all capacity to destroy precious souls. Sin is a thief and *"The thief cometh not, but for to steal, and to kill, and to destroy."* Awake therefore and understand that all agents of sins around you have nothing to lose and if you compromise with them now, they will cast you down forever. *"Wherefore come out from among them, and be ye separate, saith the Lord, and touch not the unclean thing; and I will receive you, And will be a Father unto you, and ye shall be my sons and daughters, saith the Lord Almighty"* [2 Corinthians 6:17 - 18]. Your sonship is a function of your separation from the camp of sinners. Separate from every sinful nature and the Lord will crown you with honour and dignity, you will be valuable in the society!

Your value is in your level of purity, but sin is the defect in it; *"and it* shall *come to pass when thou shalt* have *the dominion, that thou shalt break his yoke from off thy neck*! You already have the dominion through redemption therefore arise, break the yoke of sin from your neck and be pure! Be ye *therefore* perfect, *even as your Father which is in heaven is perfect.* This is the strength of your faith and the secret pool where your values can be drawn. We are not talking about your personal sin alone, but your contribution to other people's sins and your acceptance or compromise with sinners. Apostle Paul wrote to his son Timothy in 1 Timothy 5:22 and warned him to *"Lay hands suddenly on no man, neither be partaker of other men's sins: keep thyself pure."* And *"Who knowing the judgment of God, that they which commit such things are worthy of death, not only do the same, but have pleasure in them that do them."* [Romans 1: 32] Purity is what beget value, therefore keep yourself pure for *"Unto the pure all things are pure: but unto them that are defiled, and unbelieving is nothing pure; but even their mind and conscience is defiled"* [Titus 1:15].

Now, one of the values that we possess which helps us to generate virtues to our generation is the wisdom from above. I mean the wisdom for creativity, the depth of riches that gives us command over the affairs of life. However, this value has its root in purity, righteousness, holiness and the fear of God to function and generate virtues. Solomon was filled with wisdom and that gave him his place in the kingdom of his father until sin came into his life and stripped him of wisdom to function effectively. Sin corrupted his value and ultimately terminated his virtues; while immorality reduced his wisdom to mere vanity. God's righteousness is near; His salvation is gone forth, and His arms will judge the people; the isles shall wait upon Him, and on His arm shall they trust. I want you therefore to look unto Abraham your father, and unto Sarah that 'bare' you: and learn how God called him alone, and blessed him, and increased him on the platform of righteousness.

Prepare yourself by making your choice to seek for the right way of life in obedience and the fear of God; "*Let not sin therefore reign in your mortal body, that ye should obey it in the lusts thereof. Neither yield ye your members as instruments of unrighteousness unto sin: but yield yourselves unto God, as those that are alive from the dead, and your members as instruments of righteousness unto God.*" Make the right choice to live a valuable life "*For the mystery of iniquity doth already work: only he who now letteth will let, until he be taken out of the way*" [2 Thessalonians 2:7]. Refuse to make your life miserable when God has designed you to be a wonder to your generation. God's wisdom for possessing value that culminates in generating greater virtues is coming your way right now in Jesus name.

Chapter 9

Generating Value Through Divine Wisdom

"My son, eat thou honey, because it is good; and the honeycomb, which is sweet to thy taste: So shall the knowledge of wisdom be unto thy soul: when thou hast found it, then there shall be a reward, and thy expectation shall not be cut off" [Proverbs 24:13 - 14]. Every release of virtue is traceable to the wisdom at work in a man. Wisdom strengthens, wisdom enhances and promotes destiny. Knowledge enlightens, understanding makes you stand out but it is wisdom that establishes, builds, justifies and stabilizes destiny.

Proverbs 4:7 declares wisdom as the principal thing which must be the earnest desire of every redeemed because *"Through wisdom is an house builded; and by understanding it is established: And by knowledge shall the chambers be filled with all precious and pleasant riches. A wise man is strong; yea, a man of knowledge increaseth strength. For by wise counsel thou shalt make thy war: and in multitude of counsellors there is safety."* [Proverbs 24:3 - 6]. Every deed of man is as provoked by the wisdom (irrespective of the kind) at work. For *"The Lord by wisdom hath founded the earth; by understanding hath he established the heavens."* [Proverbs 3:19] and Psalms 136:5 confirmed that *"To him that by wisdom made the heavens: for his mercy endureth for ever."*

WHAT IS WISDOM?

Wisdom is an exceptional gift endowed through Godly fear and reverence. Jack Wellman wrote in one of his articles on wisdom that 'Wisdom isn't simply intelligence or knowledge or even understanding. It is the ability to use these to think and act in such a way that common sense prevails, and choices are beneficial and productive.' He continued to expose the source and origin of wisdom that 'Wisdom begins and ends with the fear of the Lord' and further explained that this kind of fear is 'a deep, abiding, holy reverence and respect for the Lord and for His Word, the Bible'. Proverbs 1:7 says *"The fear of the Lord is the beginning of knowledge: but fools despise wisdom and instruction."* and walking in this wisdom *"Then shalt thou understand the fear of the Lord, and find the knowledge of God."* [Proverbs 2:5]

Wisdom is knowing the will of God, understanding His ways and subscribing to its demand, walking in the path with fear and reverence. Putting God's thought first, abiding by His ethics and principles. Possessing the understanding of His worth and acknowledging His value, receiving instructions from Him and maintaining unswerving obedience to His commands. *"Give instruction to a wise man, and he will be yet wiser: teach a just man, and he will increase in learning. The fear of the Lord is the beginning of wisdom: and the knowledge of the holy is understanding. For by me thy days shall be multiplied, and the years of thy life shall be increased."* [Proverbs 9:9 - 11]

Wisdom is not about knowing better than other people but the application of knowledge to the benefit of God ordained course. It is the 'ability to judge correctly and to follow the best course of action, based on knowledge and understanding'[10] in the fear of God.

While Godly wisdom finds its root in the fear of God, other kinds of wisdom derive their strength from their own roots. *"The fear of the Lord is the instruction of wisdom; and before honour is humility"* [Proverbs 15:33].

The price of wisdom is not in the materialistic or common sagacity displayed by men in this generation. It is beyond the ability to think and act using common sense and insight such as knowledge, experience, understanding, influence, *et cetera*. It is more costly than affluence and mere commonsense. *"Wherefore is there a price in the hand of a fool to get wisdom, seeing he hath no heart to it?"* [Proverbs 17:16]. Most people believe that riches and wealth are the primary need for the procurement of wisdom. Listen, riches and wealth cannot

---

[10] *(Lockyer p. 1103).*

buy wisdom. Wisdom is an endowment, a gift that needs to be sought for. The scripture says, 'get wisdom!' *"Get wisdom, get understanding: forget it not; neither decline from the words of my mouth"* [Proverbs 4:5]. And in Proverbs 4:7, *"Wisdom is the principal thing; therefore get wisdom: and with all thy getting get understanding."* Hence, *"How much better is it to get wisdom than gold! and to get understanding rather to be chosen than silver!"* [Proverbs 16:16]. Just as riches and wealth do not naturally procure blessing because you can be rich and not be blessed, so it is to the paradigm of wisdom; riches and wealth cannot procure wisdom. Equally speaking, as you cannot be blessed and not be supernaturally rich and wealthy so also when wisdom is in place, it naturally creates avenues for riches and wealth.

Not every wisdom has its root in God as only the wisdom generated through Godly fear is directly connected to God. Yes, money cannot procure wisdom, however, people who thought they could acquire wisdom with money or through fame might be right, after all it has to do with the kind of wisdom they aspire to possess. Solomon was endowed with wisdom through his love for God and was operating practical wisdom across the world until he came to the conclusion that *"A feast is made for laughter, and wine maketh merry: but money answereth all things"* [Ecclesiastes 10:19]. He lost wisdom and was returned to vanity. Money cannot buy Godly wisdom!

WHAT ARE THE VARIOUS KINDS OF WISDOM?

"Who is a wise man and endued with knowledge among you? let him shew out of a good conversation his works with meekness of wisdom. But if ye have bitter envying and strife in your hearts, glory not, and lie not against the truth. This wisdom descendeth not from above, but is earthly, sensual, devilish. For where envying and strife is, there is confusion and every evil work. But the wisdom that is from above is first pure, then peaceable, gentle, and easy to be intreated, full of mercy and good fruits, without partiality, and without hypocrisy. And the fruit of righteousness is sown in peace of them that make peace" [James 3: 13 - 18]

Briefly, there are four (4) kinds of wisdom at operation under the heaven as depicted in the above scripture:[11]

Earthly wisdom: This is common knowledge operated by everyone for common results but is limited in capacity to handle complex situations. It is the usual kind of wisdom where children grow up to know that the mouth is used for eating, and legs are used for walking. Everyone naturally grows to know this because it is inherent in our personality as humans.

Sensual or intellectual wisdom: This is academic acquisition which is scientifically proved to be strong and agile in handling academic issues but limited in ability to handle spiritual issues of life.

Devilish wisdom: This is diabolical wisdom devised by the forces of darkness to manipulate its victims in life. This is demonic, satanic and produces regrettable results which cause its victims to mourn at the last, when their flesh and body are consumed in hell. Even though this kind of wisdom looks attractive and seems to command speedy answers to issues, it is the subtlest and most deceptive way of scheming people out of God's will and entangling them into eternal darkness. It is also weak in the face of tough issues since it's an act of deception which has no solid foundation in the truth.

DIVINE WISDOM

This is the wisdom of God at work on earth to promote and enhance man's capacity to function rightly and productively. It is an indescribable kind of wisdom that generates inexplicable results at all levels and in all phases making men marvel by the mighty works which are manifested through the hand of its carrier! There was an account of the manifestation of divine wisdom at operation in the life of our Saviour Jesus Christ:

> *"And when the sabbath day was come, he began to teach in the synagogue: and many hearing him were astonished, saying, From whence hath this man these things? and what wisdom is this which is given unto him, that even such*

---

[11] *For more on the subject of Wisdom watch out for the following books authored by me: Accessing the well of Wisdom and Keys to Divine Wisdom*

Our major focus in this book is divine wisdom which is able to guide you and deliver to you effective and meaningful, stress-free strategies for all-round triumph and dominion in your kingdom. It leads you to the well of grace where virtues can easily be drawn with the cord of values.

WHAT IS DIVINE WISDOM AND HOW DOES IT OPERATE IN THE SCHOOL OF FAITH, VALUE AND VIRTUE?

"But the wisdom that is from above is first pure, then peaceable, gentle, and easy to be intreated, full of mercy and good fruits, without partiality, and without hypocrisy. And the fruit of righteousness is sown in peace of them that make peace" [James 3: 17 – 18]

Divine wisdom is the master builder of destiny. It is the breath of God that triggers the spirit man in you to function with productive capacity that cannot be described.

Wisdom is operating divine ideas for the fulfilment of God's mandate for our lives. Divine wisdom is an insight triggered through the breath of God to command revolution. We are talking about a heavenly deposit that culminates in inexplicable revelation for productive impact in its delivery. *"But there is a spirit in man: and the inspiration of the Almighty giveth them understanding."*

Divine wisdom is the application of kingdom strategies in possessing and demonstrating kingdom glory on earth. Divine wisdom is the artefact of divine visitation that produces inexplicable revelation. And revelation gives you mastery over issues of life since it carries the virtue that promotes slave above kings of the land. *"Then the king Nebuchadnezzar fell upon his face, and worshipped Daniel, and commanded that they should offer an oblation and sweet odours unto him. The king answered unto Daniel, and said, Of a truth it is, that your God is a God of gods, and a Lord of kings, and a revealer of secrets, seeing thou couldest reveal this secret. Then the king made Daniel a great man, and gave him many great gifts, and made him ruler over the whole province of Babylon, and chief of the governors over all the wise men of Babylon"* [Daniel 2: 46 – 48]

WHAT ARE THE MYSTERIES OF THIS KIND OF WISDOM?

Wisdom is a mystery that delivers outside human psychological thought and imagination but is driven by the force of faith to accomplish its deliveries. The woman of the issue of blood operated wisdom to draw virtues against all medical belief systems. Among others, wisdom commands the following mysteries as great virtues:

- Unfathomable proofs in its delivery even when men least expected
- Possession of the spirit of understanding beyond human expression
- Generates immeasurable productive capability
- Possesses leadership capability that cannot be marched and or measured
- Delivery of heavenly calculated strategies for resolving complex issues in life
- Commands peace and stability by providing solution to seemingly impossible circumstance and breathe calmness in a turbulent situation

WHERE CAN THIS TYPE OF WISDOM BE FOUND?

Now, wisdom is the deep thing that is kept beyond the common eye, but when discovered delivers unparalleled results. Wisdom is the secret of heaven unraveled to man for profiting. *"O the depth of the riches both of the <u>wisdom</u> and knowledge of God! how unsearchable are his judgments, and his ways past finding out!"* [Romans 11:33]. It is a virtue in another dimension. It is a hidden treasure that demands for thorough search on the part of those who desire to be endowed with it, for...

"There is a path which no fowl knoweth, and which the vulture's eye hath not seen: The lion's whelps have not trodden it, nor the fierce lion passed by it. He putteth forth his hand upon the rock; he overturneth the mountains

by the roots. He cutteth out rivers among the rocks; and his eye seeth every precious thing. He bindeth the floods from overflowing; and the thing that is hid bringeth he forth to light. But where shall wisdom be found? and where is the place of understanding? Man knoweth not the price thereof; neither is it found in the land of the living. The depth saith, It is not in me: and the sea saith, It is not with me. It cannot be gotten for gold, neither shall silver be weighed for the price thereof. It cannot be valued with the gold of Ophir, with the precious onyx, or the sapphire. The gold and the crystal cannot equal it: and the exchange of it shall not be for jewels of fine gold. No mention shall be made of coral, or of pearls: for the price of wisdom is above rubies. The topaz of Ethiopia shall not equal it, neither shall it be valued with pure gold. Whence then cometh wisdom? and where is the place of understanding? Seeing it is hid from the eyes of all living, and kept close from the fowls of the air. Destruction and death say, We have heard the fame thereof with our ears. God understandeth the way thereof, and he knoweth the place thereof. For he looketh to the ends of the earth, and seeth under the whole heaven" [Job 28: 7 - 24]

Divine wisdom is kept in the book of life called the Bible and this can only be accessed through the knowledge of the fear of the Lord. The bible is the collection of God's thoughts, acts and will, which is collectively referred to as 'God's wisdom in print'. God's word is the pool of wisdom; the word of God is wisdom bank gathered and organized by the Spirit of God. It takes the fear of God to access the deep things of God and it takes the Spirit of God to possess a quick understanding of the things of God. *"And shall make him of quick understanding in the fear of the Lord: and he shall not judge after the sight of his eyes, neither reprove after the hearing of his ears:"*

What is the word of God?

"And they were all amazed, and spake among themselves, saying, What a word is this! for with authority and power he commandeth the unclean spirits, and they come out." [Luke 4:36] Yes what a word? He has gained access to the Word of life and wisdom is now manifesting through Him as a Vessel of the Word. Virtues

are now released to meet the needs of the people just by the operation of divine wisdom which is the direct product of God's word.

The word of God is the container of the thoughts of God. God's word is God's thought and God's thought is God's wisdom. According to 2 Timothy 3:16 *"All scripture is given by inspiration of God, and is profitable for doctrine, for reproof, for correction, for instruction in righteousness:"* In Isaiah [14: 24,26 & 27] *"The Lord of hosts hath sworn, saying, Surely as I have thought, so shall it come to pass; and as I have purposed, so shall it stand: This is the purpose that is purposed upon the whole earth: and this is the hand that is stretched out upon all the nations. For the Lord of hosts hath purposed, and who shall disannul it? and his hand is stretched out, and who shall turn it back?"*

The word of God is the secret of God and as someone said, 'the secret of a man is inside his story' God's word reveals God's secret.

Secondly, **the word of God is the force behind creation**. By wisdom, God put His thought which is equally His word into use and then creation emerged. *"In the beginning God created the heaven and the earth. And the earth was without form, and void; and darkness was upon the face of the deep. And the Spirit of God moved upon the face of the waters. And God said, Let there be light: and there was light. And God saw the light, that it was good: and God divided the light from the darkness"* [Genesis 1: 1 - 4]

So, the word of God is the wisdom, strength, capability and the integrity of God for the building of all things.

> *"Happy is the man that findeth wisdom, and the man that getteth understanding. For the merchandise of it is better than the merchandise of silver, and the gain thereof than fine gold. She is more precious than rubies: and all the things thou canst desire are not to be compared unto her. Length of days is in her right hand; and in her left hand riches and honour. Her ways are ways of pleasantness, and all her paths are peace. She is a tree of life to them that lay hold upon her: and happy is every one that retaineth her. The Lord by wisdom hath founded the earth; by understanding hath he established the heavens. By his knowledge the depths are broken up, and the clouds drop down the dew. My son, let not them depart from thine eyes: keep sound wisdom and discretion: So shall they be life unto thy soul, and grace to thy neck. Then shalt*

thou walk in thy way safely, and thy foot shall not stumble. When thou liest down, thou shalt not be afraid: yea, thou shalt lie down, and thy sleep shall be sweet. Be not afraid of sudden fear, neither of the desolation of the wicked, when it cometh. For the Lord shall be thy confidence, and shall keep thy foot from being taken" [Proverbs 3: 13 - 26]

And *"Through wisdom is an house builded; and by understanding it is established: And by knowledge shall the chambers be filled with all precious and pleasant riches. A wise man is strong; yea, a man of knowledge increaseth strength. For by wise counsel thou shalt make thy war: and in multitude of counsellors there is safety"* [Proverbs 24:3 – 6].

God's word is therefore the source of wisdom and strength for the redeemed. It is the secret stronghold behind creativity, innovation and ideas. It opens our heart to discover new things and enables us to gain access to the thoughts and plans of God even before it is unraveled to the world. Behold I do a new thing, shall you not know it? Before it happens, I will make it known to you through my word. *"Behold, the former things are come to pass, and new things do I declare: before they spring forth I tell you of them"* [Isaiah 42:9].

Thirdly, God's word is the **wisdom bank** for the purchase of all the necessities of life and everyone that invests in it gains mastery of the hiding treasures of wealth. The more your investment the greater your insight. I mean investment of time to explore until it begins to manifest in a practical form. In Proverbs 24: 13 – 14, the scriptures say, *"My son, eat thou honey, because it is good; and the honeycomb, which is sweet to thy taste: So shall the knowledge of wisdom be unto thy soul: when thou hast found it, then there shall be a reward, and thy expectation shall not be cut off."* Ultimately, the word of God is the honey of life and it gives life for everyone who desires to live. It is worth spending time and resources on. The Word Himself (Jesus Christ) revealed the secret of the word to us and admonished us to *"Search the scriptures; for in them ye think ye have eternal life: and they are they which testify of me"* [John 5: 39]

In Joshua 1:8, God admonished Joshua to keep the book as the master light to his path on daily living saying, *"This book of the law shall not depart out of thy mouth; but thou shalt meditate therein day and night, that thou mayest observe to do according to all that is written therein: for then thou shalt make thy way prosperous, and then thou shalt have good success."* Oh, this is sweeter than honey! The Word of God is the wisdom for creating wealth, riches, prosperity and good success.

> *"Jesus answered and said unto her, If thou knewest the gift of God, and who it is that saith to thee, Give me to drink; thou wouldest have asked of him, and he would have given thee living water. The woman saith unto him, Sir, thou hast nothing to draw with, and the well is deep: from whence then hast thou that living water?"* [John 4: 10-11]

The word of God is the depth of wisdom. It carries the hiding treasures of life that generate values for man and produces virtues to our generation. There is the price to pay to get wisdom that turns our lives into valuable entities in our community and society at large. *"O the depth of the riches both of the wisdom and knowledge of God! how unsearchable are his judgments, and his ways past finding out! For who hath known the mind of the Lord? or who hath been his counsellor? Or who hath first given to him, and it shall be recompensed unto him again? For of him, and through him, and to him, are all things: to whom be glory for ever. Amen. [Romans 11: 33 - 36]*

A dedicated search! This is not for the lazy, as it is too deep and will require dedicated search to access the depth of it. *"The woman saith unto him, Sir, thou hast nothing to draw with, and the well is deep: from whence then hast thou that living water?"* [John 4:11] I see you gaining access to this depth of riches in Jesus name.

Fourthly, **the word of God is light** because the entrance of His words illuminates and opens destinies to deep insight, revelation and understanding. *"And the light shineth in darkness; and the darkness comprehended it not."* God's word is the **light** that cannot be overpowered by darkness. It is the light that generates such forces of release to the earth.

> *"In the beginning was the Word, and the Word was with God, and the Word was God. The same was in the beginning with God. All things were made by him; and without him was not any thing made that was made. In him was life; and the life was the light of men. And the light shineth in darkness; and the*

Nothing happens without the word of God at work – as nothing can be achieved outside wisdom. Jesus went about displaying kingdom signs and wonders by the spoken word to the end that people marveled saying – *what a word?* It is the word that lightens our world, making us shine as light to the world. *"The entrance of thy words giveth light; it giveth understanding unto the simple" [Psalm 119:130].* The entrance of His word turns us to light and unveils deep secrets and hiding things to us for our manifestation as signs and wonders. How does the word become part of our life? We imbibe and inoculate ourselves with the word by eating it daily, making it our daily menu. Jeremiah 15:16 says *"Thy words were found, and I did eat them; and thy word was unto me the joy and rejoicing of mine heart: for I am called by thy name, O Lord God of hosts."* This indicates that when God's word gains access into our being, it creates the joy needed to fulfil destiny and becomes the rejoicing of our soul. Remember that it takes joy to draw water from the well of salvation. God's word produces that joy needed to draw virtues from the vessel.

Finally, **the word of God is a refiner's fire and a hammer, the breaker of stones**

"Is not my word like as a fire? saith the Lord; and like a hammer that breaketh the rock in pieces?" [Jeremiah 23: 29]. The word is the refiner and purifier of everyone that turns to God for a change of heart. *"But who may abide the day of his coming? and who shall stand when he appeareth? for he is like a*

The word of God establishes life to the redeemed and keeps us spiritually minded in sustaining the body because *"It is the spirit that quickeneth; the flesh profiteth nothing: the words that I speak unto you, they are spirit, and they are life."* [John 6:63]

Now, it has been concluded that there is nothing new under the sun and all that makes for life and godliness are as contained in the word of God which is the Bible: *"The thing that hath been, it is that which shall be; and that which is done is that which shall be done: and there is no new thing under the sun. Is there any thing whereof it may be said, See, this is new? it hath been already of old time, which was before us."* [Ecclesiastes 1: 9 – 10]

However, every deep thing is kept in the deep places of God and only those who possess the mind of God can access this depth of *riches. "For who hath known the mind of the Lord, that he may instruct him? But we have the mind of Christ."* We are expected to operate the same mind of Christ as the redeemed of the Lord, which is the mind full of wisdom divine! God still declares new things and when we possess this mind of Christ, we will secure access to the new things, making them known to us before they spring forth.

But Seeing (this kind of wisdom), it is hiding from the eyes of all living, and kept close from the fowls of the air. This indicates that divine wisdom MUST be sought for and acquired with all sense of desperation. It must be coveted after as the best gift from God because it is the only stronghold that secures a great future for the redeemed. Wisdom enables you to see and appreciate God's value and His worth in your life and this is the platform for the release of virtues to your direction. Wisdom produces and promotes your worth in the society. You are rated by the level of wisdom at work and how much impact you can make in life.

Notably speaking, your worth in the society is defined by the level of wisdom at work in your life. Your wisdom is measured by the way you conduct yourself, the way you react to things and the way you handle the affairs of life either in your relationship with people and or your conduct during conflict. Now if you are the type who reacts in anger and your reactions are reflective in the words you utter in your angry state, mark it that you will soon lose value, because anger lies in the bosom of a fool and words are strong, they never die, but live to represent you in the future. So, what comes out of your mouth defines your worth and your character expresses who you are.

Nabal was a very rich man, he was rich in cattle and in all things yet his habitual nature, his untamed tongue and his abusive character tagged him a fool. (Read 1 Samuel 25). And his wife said, *"Let not my lord, I pray thee, regard this man of Belial, even Nabal: for as his name is, so is he; Nabal is his name, and folly is with him:"* With all his riches and wealth, Nabal worth nothing both in his household and the society at large. He died mysteriously, because he was a fool.

> *"But it came to pass in the morning, when the wine was gone out of Nabal, and his wife had told him these things, that his heart died within him, and he became as a stone. And it came to pass about ten days after, that the Lord smote Nabal, that he died. And when David heard that Nabal was dead, he said, Blessed be the Lord, that hath pleaded the cause of my reproach from the hand of Nabal, and hath kept his servant from evil: for the Lord hath returned the wickedness of Nabal upon his own head. And David sent and communed with Abigail, to take her to him to wife"* [1 Samuel 25: 37 - 39]

It takes wisdom to preserve life. Those who lack it will die miserable death, even though they possess riches and wealth. When life is void of wisdom, it gives foolishness the full fledge capacity to rule and when foolishness rules it causes untimely death just as depicted in Ecclesiastes 7:17: *"Be not over much wicked, neither be thou foolish: why shouldest thou die before thy time?"* Get wisdom and get understanding to know how to handle the affairs of life around you! I decree that your life shall not be a waste in your generation for lack of wisdom! You shall not end your life like Nabal in Jesus name.

OPERATING DIVINE WISDOM FOR VALUES

"But the wisdom that is from above is first pure, then peaceable, gentle, and easy to be entreated, full of mercy and good fruits, without partiality, and without hypocrisy"

[James 3:17]. Divine wisdom is from above and it is released upon those who diligently seek for it. This kind of wisdom surpasses all other wisdom put together because it is from above and whatever is from above is above all. This divine wisdom is the operational knowledge of heaven that gets things done in line with God's plan, principles and purpose. This kind of wisdom is divinely established as the factory where values are supernaturally created. It is therefore not procured but diligently sought for and bestowed on man for use in securing God's plan and purpose for mankind. *"If any of you lack wisdom, let him ask of God, that giveth to all men liberally, and upbraideth not; and it shall be given him."* *[James 1:5]*

Moreover, in the school of wisdom, there is the seeking phase, there is the possessing stage and there is the operational stage. Wisdom does not speak by mere possession, wisdom generates impacts through engagement. It manifests through practical operational activities in the field. Divine wisdom is given to us purposely to serve mankind and to represent God's kingdom here on earth. It is not for puffing, it is not for display of talent which has become the arrogant nature of most people these days, most especially in the church. Everyone who is privileged to be endowed with divine wisdom has the task of serving his/her generation, creating values and generating greater impact on the society. Solomon sought for wisdom to serve God's people and lead them in line with God's principles. Hear what he said:

> *"And now, O Lord my God, thou hast made thy servant king instead of David my father: and I am but a little child: I know not how to go out or come in. And thy servant is in the midst of thy people which thou hast chosen, a great people, that cannot be numbered nor counted for multitude. Give therefore thy servant an understanding heart to judge thy people, that I may discern between good and bad: for who is able to judge this thy so great a people? And the speech pleased the Lord, that Solomon had asked this thing."* *[1 Kings 3: 7 – 10]*

If you are endowed with wisdom and all you could deliver is puffing, bragging and show-casing, then your worth and value are not reckoned with because your human dignity is abysmally questionable. *"Now some are puffed up, as though I would not come to you. But I will come to you shortly, if the Lord will, and will know, not the speech of them which are puffed up, but the power. For the kingdom of God is not in word, but in power"* *[1 Corinthians 4:18 - 20]*.

Your worth is not in the show off, your puffing does not reveal your value. Your value only speaks through your action, mostly in the field while reaching out to mankind to prove your ambassadorial status.

Most importantly, wisdom is designed to enhance value and give meaning to human personality. However, you may succeed in procuring some level of value and increase your worth, but the question is how do you sustain, preserve and retain this level of value and worth all through your life? How do you ensure that your generation derives benefit from your value and generations after you are still drawing virtues from your worth?

HOW TO SUSTAIN, PRESERVE AND RETAIN VALUES

One of the vital truths that everyone needs to embrace and align with is the reality that every individual's life is predominantly designed for service. We are deliberately formed and or created to serve, remember *"let my people go that they may **serve** me"*. Serving God and serving humanity is the core purpose of human existence. Divine wisdom is unleashed on us primarily for service. Christ (the Wisdom pool) came and at the age of twelve, He was able to spell out His mission on earth 'going after His Father's business'; that is, engaging heavenly deposited wisdom in a practical form serving humanity to enhance and articulate the worth and value of His father's kingdom. *"And he said unto them, How is it that ye sought me? wist ye not that I must be about my Father's business?"* [Luke 2:49]

He spent the first 30 years developing, observing, preparing and engaging in divers' community workshops (read Luke 2: 40-52); carrying out feasibility studies to understand the strategies to adopt in launching the kingdom business here on earth. He spent enough time to appropriate His mission with God's plan, building upon the fear of God which is the root of wisdom.

Though, nothing was said about His worth and value during this time, but when He was anointed and officially launched to the field, His fame went abroad, His values were revealed, and His worth burst forth in an explosive form. He began to reach out to people, bringing the word of life to the dead, reviving the lame, strengthening the weak, getting the feeble back on their feet. And the people began to proclaim His worth and values *"And when the sabbath day was come, he began to teach in the synagogue: and many hearing him were astonished, saying, From whence hath* this *man these things? and what wisdom is this which is given unto him, that even such mighty works are wrought by his hands?"* [Mark 6:2]. Repeatedly, *in* Luke 4: 14 – 44, we read in verse 36 through to 37, that the people were unbelievably shocked with the potential He displayed, and the compassion released toward the suffering community *"And they were all amazed, and spake among themselves, saying, What a word is this! for with authority and power he commandeth the unclean spirits, and they come out. And the fame of him went out into every place of the country round about."* He wrought mighty works among the people through the instrumentality of divine wisdom given to Him by the Father and His worth and values were preserved, retained and sustained across generations.

Joseph appeared before king Pharaoh and as soon as he was re-positioned, he took his journey to the field to serve humanity and preserve posterity. *"And Joseph was thirty years old when he stood before Pharaoh king of Egypt. And Joseph went out from the presence of Pharaoh and went throughout all the land of Egypt"* [Genesis 41:46]. The disciples echoed *in Acts 6:2 – 4 "Then the twelve called the multitude of the disciples unto them, and said, It is not reason that we should leave the word of God, and serve tables. Wherefore, brethren, look ye out among you seven men of honest report, full of the Holy Ghost and wisdom, whom we may appoint over this business. But we will give ourselves continually to prayer, and to the ministry of the word."* So, life is all about services, we are designed to render services at every level as long as we carry the breath of the Almighty God in us. Our best is revealed in us through service. This is where we demonstrate the God-likeness in us, sharing the passion and love of the kingdom to others. Most interestingly, heartfelt, kingdom inclined service is the preserver of human value and retainer of human worth.

Our services reveal our conducts, characters and habits which corroborate our value and worth. Service is a privilege with the expectation that we maintain passionate spirit, serving and treating others fairly with a mindset of kingdom fulfilment. That is, seeing our service not only in relation to man but God, doing it with fear and reverence to God the rewarder of those who diligently serve in line with the kingdom guidelines, rules and ethics. It is your habit that defines your worth and value to your world even as Apostle Paul admonished his son Timothy *"Let no man despise thy youth; but be thou an example of the believers, in word, in conversation, in charity, in spirit, in faith, in purity"* [1 Timothy 4:12]. Therefore, you need to conduct yourself in your various services (both for the kingdom promotion and to mankind at large) in such a way that your values and worth will be pronounced, respected, preserved and sustained.

Value is preserved not because of the magnificent level of talents and or gifts you possess or display, but by your character, conduct and ethical discipline. Doing the right things and acting the right way are the golden platforms that help to secure, preserve and protect values. Values feed on trust while behaviour exposes your worth to the outside world. Your behaviour and how you handle your daily routine display to others how much you appreciate your roles and responsibilities which may include different perspectives of ethical conduct. You are therefore responsible for the roles you play in the society which will correspond to the reaction you receive as feedback from the society.

You cannot be an abuser of rules and laws, basic principles of life and societal ethics and think people will appreciate your value. But if your daily obligation is directed towards enhancing other people's living and the environment you live in, people will naturally be part of your life and appreciate your worth. The centurion in Capernaum had this testimony from his community which gave him an honourable attention from Jesus our Saviour, God approved of his honour by his activities in his own community.

"And when they came to Jesus, they besought him instantly, saying, That he was worthy for whom he should do this: For he loveth our nation, and he hath built us a synagogue." [Luke 7: 3 - 5]. His conduct, his input and charity to his community pronounced his worth and value to Christ and that brought salvation and healing to his home.

Value is all about how you conduct yourself. In Colossians 4:6, the word of God admonishes that you *"Let your speech be always with grace, seasoned with salt, that ye may know how ye ought to answer every man."* Remember that our Saviour went about doing good and healing with passion and compassion, carrying other people's burden and bearing their pains; releasing them from chains and launching them to a new life full of hope and assurance (Acts 10:38). No wonder, His worth and values are still speaking for Him after over 2000 years here on earth. Friends, character is likened to vapour, there is no way you can prevent it from evaporating and revealing its true colour and our worth and values are kept in our character. I pray that your worth and value shall not smell evil savour to your generation in Jesus name.

Let your communication be clearly furnished with truth as a brand ambassador that represents the kingdom of God here on earth. Let your life be a guide for others to follow, stop engaging in deliberate deceptive activities that will end up labelling you as a misrepresentative of the truth.

You owe yourself the right to live a life worthy of emulation. Make a positive impact and let your yea be yea and your nay be nay. That is how to sustain, maintain and retain honour and respect in the society.

EQUALITY IN DEALING AND TREATMENT (James 2: 1 - 10)

What made the ministry of Christ unique was His ability to carry everyone along without compromise or upbraiding. He attended to sinners with wisdom and gained them back to God without condemnation. He equally helped the religiously - acclaimed righteous people in the society by aligning them to the true path of righteousness as against their self-acclaimed righteousness, bringing balance and equality to both parties irrespective of their different state. His equality in dealing without respect for a person unquestionably gave way to such tremendous awareness of His Lordship over all issues of life. Everything was subject to Him, including principalities and power because He was not partial in judgment, but strictly and without partiality operated by the principles of His father. *"For there is no respect of persons with God"* [Romans 2:11].

"Then Peter opened his mouth, and said, Of a truth I perceive that God is no respecter of persons: But in every nation he that feareth him, and worketh righteousness, is accepted with him" [Acts 10: 34 - 35] There is the need to treat people equally, though there are occasion where some people enjoy more grace in our sight than other, but there is the need to discipline ourselves in ensuring balance in our handling issues relating to people of different class.

POSSESSING THINKING CAPACITY

You will agree with me that wisdom is the master generator of value. Getting wisdom must be paramount in your needs. Your yearning therefore must be earnestly and desperately seek for wisdom and ensure you get it with proof.

One of the most vital keys to access wisdom is right thinking. The level of your thinking ability is what defines the level of success and or failure you experience. You can never outlive your thinking because the depth of your thinking is what defines the level of your operation and manifestation. Your values are derived from your thinking. Your worth is the product of your thinking and your personality is visibly revealed through your thought.

> *"Labour not to be rich: cease from thine own wisdom. Wilt thou set thine eyes upon that which is not? for riches certainly make themselves wings; they fly away as an eagle toward heaven. Eat thou not the bread of him that hath an evil eye, neither desire thou his dainty meats: For as he thinketh in his heart, so is he: Eat and drink, saith he to thee; but his heart is not with thee. The morsel which thou hast eaten shalt thou vomit up, and lose thy sweet words."* [Proverbs 23: 4 – 8]

Thinkers are rulers, those who think wisely ultimately become great leaders in the society. Their secret is that they have been able to pound the word in their heart and all that needs to be analyzed have been completed in their thinking faculty – and they produce good results after their thorough evaluation. Thinking mind is the pool (well of wisdom) where wisdom-generated insights and revelations are manufactured for impart. When you are able to create time to think, you will access deep things that are not commonly revealed to people. This is the stronghold of wisdom that generates worth and gives value to life.

Proverbs 20:27 states that *"The spirit of man is the candle of the Lord, searching all the inward parts of the belly."* Your spirit is not created dormant, but it's created to be active always. Your spirit is to at all times communicate with the Spirit of the Lord in order to search the inward part of the belly as it is written *"Deep calleth unto deep at the noise of thy waterspouts: all thy waves and thy billows are gone over me"* [Psalms 42:7]. Engaging your spirit in the school of right thinking gets you connected to the Spirit of God to provoke divine wisdom which makes tremendous power available for insight and revelation. God deals principally with the heart of man and in most cases the thought that goes on in the heart of man is as important to God as the soul of man. God expects the spirit of man to receive inspiration from Him to function in line with His primary purpose for the earth.

　　OLA JONES DUYILE　　◆

Elihu exposed the secret of quietness in the school of debate and helped us to understand that talk of the lips tends to dispute when he engaged his spirit mind in thinking about the plight of Job and the manipulative strategies of his friends.

> *"So these three men ceased to answer Job, because he was righteous in his own eyes. Then was kindled the wrath of Elihu the son of Barachel the Buzite, of the kindred of Ram: against Job was his wrath kindled, because he justified himself rather than God. Also against his three friends was his wrath kindled, because they had found no answer, and yet had condemned Job. Now Elihu had waited till Job had spoken, because they were elder than he. When Elihu saw that there was no answer in the mouth of these three men, then his wrath was kindled. And Elihu the son of Barachel the Buzite answered and said, I am young, and ye are very old; wherefore I was afraid, and durst not shew you mine opinion. I said, Days should speak, and multitude of years should teach wisdom. But there is a spirit in man: and the inspiration of the Almighty giveth them understanding. Great men are not always wise: neither do the aged understand judgment. Therefore I said, Hearken to me; I also will shew mine opinion. Behold, I waited for your words; I gave ear to your reasons, whilst ye searched out what to say. Yea, I attended unto you, and, behold, there was none of you that convinced Job, or that answered his words: Lest ye should say, We have found out wisdom: God thrusteth him down, not man."* [Job 32: 1 – 13]

"Then was kindled the wrath of Elihu the son of Barachel" because Elihu has been engaging his thinking mind to analyze the happenings around Job and all the pressures from his friends that compounded Job's situation. You see, *Great men are not always wise: neither do the aged understand judgment.* It has to do with how much everyone makes use of his/her mind in the school of thinking. It's all about how much you are able to pound on those issues, looking at it with the mirror of the word of God and finding the right path in line with God's will for that issue. Nothing changes until we can view it with the mirror of God's word and this demands for thinking.

The scripture says *"Nevertheless, when it shall turn to the Lord, the veil shall be taken away. Now the Lord is that Spirit: and where the Spirit of the Lord is, there is liberty. But we all, with open face beholding as in a glass the glory of the Lord, are changed into the same image from glory to glory, even as by the Spirit of the Lord."* [2 Corinthians 3: 16 - 18]

This indicates that when we return to the thinking room, then the veil shall be taken away and as we engage our spirit with the Spirit of liberty, we will gain access to the mysteries of the kingdom. Additionally, while we behold the mysteries through the mirror of His word, there is a radical change of the seemingly impossible situation. We experience breakthrough by gaining mastery of the mind of God regarding the issue. Then, hope and expectations are turned from the present level of glory to the higher, and brighter glory. All these happen simply by engaging our mind in line with God's mind in the school of thinking.

Thinkers are operators of insight and the revealer of the depth of wisdom secret. They are easily tagged valuable in the society because they, through their thinking capacity, have answers to the hard algorithms of the world. Get to the thinking room and think over that issue until your light breaks forth. You rush into conclusion easily that is why wisdom is not functioning the way it should. Every question of life requires an insightful thought for an accurate answer. They brought a woman who was caught in the act to the Lord Jesus for judgment and He thought it over, He *"stooped down, and with his finger wrote on the ground, as though he heard them not. So when they continued asking him, he lifted up himself, and said unto them, He that is without sin among you, let him first cast a stone at her. And again he stooped down, and wrote on the ground. And they which heard it, being convicted by their own conscience, went out one by one, beginning at the eldest, even unto the last: and Jesus was left alone, and the woman standing in the midst."* [Read John 8: 1 - 12] His thinking faculty connected Him to the source of inspiration and the answer to the accusation and temptation was delivered to humiliate the tempters and the accusers.

Someone asked my father in faith Bishop Oyedepo what he does with his time and he replied, "I read, and I think". On another occasion, one of his friends in the ministry came around and when they were showing him round the house, he saw one quiet, lighted room and asked what that room was for and Bishop replied, 'that is my thinking room' and the friend marvelled that someone can create a room for thinking. No wonder, his value is felt everywhere in his generation. Please wake up and get your spirit mind together. God is looking for people who will use their right mind to figure out what heaven is planning next. God said in His word *"Behold, the former things are come to pass, and new things do I declare: before they spring forth I tell you of them."* [Isaiah 42:9]. And in Isaiah 43:19 He said *"Behold, I will do a new thing; now it shall spring forth; shall ye not know it? I will even make a way in the wilderness, and rivers in the desert."* So, if we can think in His direction, all these secrets will be unraveled to us before manifesting to the public. God is waiting for every one of us to engage our mind to find out His plans, purposes and His next move for the earth. Arise therefore and engage your mind in right thinking, so you can be valuable in His master plan for your generation.

Hear what He said in Jeremiah 29:13 *"And ye shall seek me, and find me, when ye shall search for me with all your heart."* And verse 14 says *"And I will be found of you, saith the Lord"* I will be found of you when you create room for thinking and reasoning with my plan. In the school of inquiry, we don't spend time harassing God in prayers. Though, we separate ourselves in fasting and prayers, yet we spend valuable time to think along with His will concerning what we are praying about. We ask questions and wait for answers to know what He would say concerning the issues. That is why He said, *"Call unto me, and I will answer thee, and shew thee great and mighty things, which thou knowest not."* *[Jeremiah 33:3].* Engage more in thinking through the truth instead of harassing Him in the school of prayer. Your value is revealed by your depth of reasoning with God. Build a quiet closet for thinking, prepare to reason with God in that situation; that is the only guaranteed access to the good of the land including your total justification from condemnation. *"Come now, and let us reason together, saith the Lord: though your sins be as scarlet, they shall be as white as snow; though they be red like crimson, they shall be as wool. If ye be willing and obedient, ye shall eat the good of the land:"* [Isaiah 1:18 -19]

ENGAGING THE ACT OF MEDITATION

Again, *"This book of the law shall not depart out of thy mouth; but thou shalt meditate therein day and night, that thou mayest observe to do according to all that is written therein: for then thou shalt make thy way prosperous, and then thou shalt have good success."* [Joshua 1:8] Meditation is the ability to assimilate the truth, by pounding on it in the heart, analyze and conclude that it is the truth. It is an engagement for accessing the deep things of God for man's repositioning and alignment to the right path of life. It is the secret answer to the delivery of all expectations. The truth of God's word is accessed through meditation. Wisdom manifests by thinking through and filtering answers out of complex questions through the act of meditation. Ability to meditate on things gives you control over circumstances and makes you operate in wisdom that produces answers in a complex situation.

> *"Let no man despise thy youth; but be thou an example of the believers, in word, in conversation, in charity, in spirit, in faith, in purity. Till I come, give attendance to reading, to exhortation, to doctrine. Neglect not the gift that is in thee, which was given thee by prophecy, with the laying on of the hands of the presbytery. Meditate upon these things; give thyself wholly to them; that thy profiting may appear to all. Take heed unto thyself, and unto the doctrine; continue in them: for in doing this thou shalt both save thyself, and them that hear thee."* [1Timothy 4: 12 - 16]

The Psalmist exclaimed in Psalm 19: 14 *"Let the words of my mouth, and the meditation of my heart, be acceptable in thy sight, O Lord, my strength, and my redeemer."* That is, Lord, grant me the grace to access your plan for my life in this specific area. In Genesis 24:63, we learnt that, *"And Isaac went out to meditate in the field at the eventide: and he lifted up his eyes, and saw, and, behold, the camels were coming."* His ability to meditate on his expected future brought instant answers to his desired marital settlement while at the same time ended his mourning for *"Isaac was comforted after his mother's death".* When you are able to think through, you will supernaturally experience breakthrough which is the product of your worth in life.

THE MIND AND SPIRIT OF PATIENCE

Wisdom is operative in patience and not anxiety. Patience is the master key to the world of divine wisdom. Lack of patience is the manifestation of foolishness. *"Therefore being justified by faith, we have peace with God through our Lord Jesus*

Christ: By whom also we have access by faith into this grace wherein we stand, and rejoice in hope of the glory of God. And not only so, but we glory in tribulations also: knowing that tribulation worketh patience; And patience, experience; and experience, hope: And hope maketh not ashamed; because the love of God is shed abroad in our hearts by the Holy Ghost which is given unto us." [Romans 5:1 – 5]

In your patience, you possess your soul, so it takes patience to access divine wisdom. It takes patience to operate divine wisdom. It takes patience to walk with God in His wisdom and it takes patience to receive from God.

THE PLACE OF THE HOLY SPIRIT AS THE WISDOM OF GOD IN THE NEW TESTAMENT DISPENSATION

All the above-mentioned keys are held by the Holy Spirit and only Him can guarantee our access to divine wisdom. The Spirit of God is the wisdom of God at work in this New Testament age. The last day ministry of Jesus Christ is the ministry built on the platform of wisdom, and the Holy Spirit is the Actor and Operator of this wisdom. *"But this is that which was spoken by the prophet Joel; And it shall come to pass in the last days, saith God, I will pour out of my Spirit upon all flesh: and your sons and your daughters shall prophesy, and your young men shall see visions, and your old men shall dream dreams: And on my servants and on my handmaidens I will pour out in those days of my Spirit; and they shall prophesy: And I will shew wonders in heaven above, and signs in the earth beneath; blood, and fire, and vapour of smoke: The sun shall be turned into darkness, and the moon into blood, before that great and notable day of the Lord come: And it shall come to pass, that whosoever shall call on the name of the Lord shall be saved."* [Acts 2: 16 - 21]

The Holy Spirit plays the overall role in securing our values and worth in life. The virtues we generate are His impacts and without Him we can achieve nothing in life. He is the only Ordained Helper assigned by Jesus Christ the Saviour to help mankind, teaching us the truth, showing us things to come and securing a glorious future for us in God. *"But the Comforter, which is the Holy Ghost, whom the Father will send in my name, he shall teach you all things, and bring all things to your remembrance, whatsoever I have said unto you."* [John 14:26]. He is equally ascribed the responsibility to guide us through the truth as depicted in *John 16: 13 – 14; "Howbeit when he, the Spirit of truth, is come, he will guide you into all truth: for he shall not speak of himself; but whatsoever he shall hear, that shall he speak: and he will shew you things to come. He shall glorify me: for he shall receive of mine, and shall shew it unto you."* Our encounter with Him is what enlists us as the candidate and instrument for his manifestation.

The anointing and indwelling power of the Holy Spirit in us is one of the vital channels through which we encounter the mystery of wisdom and insight to function. And in conclusion, wisdom is needed to enhance our values in life, most importantly in our field of endeavours. Wisdom is the generator of virtues which helps procure values for its carrier. Wisdom is power, and it is the gift of the Spirit, therefore I command the spirit of wisdom to fall upon you this hour for your values to be revealed in Jesus name. Amen

Chapter 10

The Power of Humility

In the school of value, humility is the baseline for generating virtues. Your worth is measured by your level of humility in delivering results. Everyone who generates virtues of great impact on the society is commonly identified with a lifestyle of humility. Leadership is determined by the level of humility and not competence, though the latter plays a vital role in leading others but competence without humility is like a house built without foundation. Heaven only reckon with the humbled, the meek and lowly in heart as it is written *"Blessed are the* meek: *for they shall inherit the earth."* The meek always have a place with God and they naturally occupy the leadership position.

"At the same time came the disciples unto Jesus, saying, Who is the greatest in the kingdom of heaven? And Jesus called a little child unto him, and set him in the midst of them, And said, Verily I say unto you, Except ye be converted, and become as little children, ye shall not enter into the kingdom of heaven. Whosoever therefore shall humble himself as this little child, the same is greatest in the kingdom of heaven." [Matthew 18:1-4]

Your leadership capacity is simply measured by your lifestyle of humility. Pride is the destroyer of values and when there is no value, virtues naturally lose flavor and when virtues have lost its savour impact cannot be felt in the society. Thus, at the root of 'virtue-lessness' lies the deficiency of humility, which produces value that helps generate virtues. Men are easily brought down by the pride in them. *"And whosoever shall exalt himself shall be abased; and he that shall humble himself shall be exalted. [Matthew 23:12];* Furthermore, grace is always available for the humbled in heart *"But he giveth more grace. Wherefore he saith, God resisteth the proud, but giveth grace unto the humble"* *[James 4:6]*

Humility should be seen as part of our daily lifestyle and it is expected to be demonstrated at various levels in our daily dealing. It portrays our character in expression, thought and action. Many possess the great leadership potentials but lack the humility required to maintain the leadership quality; thus, they are more of a threat in the society than blessing. It was once said by a man of wisdom that 'Leadership is a function of capacity and character,' unfortunately 'many possess the capacity to deliver but lack the character to match.' The character connotes humility being practically displayed in conversation, in conduct, in operating faith, in charity, in leading and being led. This implies therefore that values are bound to be eroded without humility, the magnitude of your leadership potential and capacity notwithstanding!

Age has nothing to do with humility! It is a habit that must be cultivated in the heart and demonstrated through our daily activities. Josiah was eight years old when he began reigning in Israel and regardless of his age, he maintained his integrity to please God by doing that which was right. While he was still young, he began to seek after the God of David his father; he embraced the fear of God, walking in the ways of David his father, and declined neither to the right hand, nor to the left. Now when they found the book in the house of God during renovation under his reign, they brought the book to his palace and read it to him. This young man trembled before God's word and rented his royal garments when he found out that the people were not living in line with God's ordinances. Now he went to enquire from the Lord what must be done, and the prophetess spoke of the wrath of God that is coming upon the land but spoke differently and kindly about the king:

> *"And as for the king of Judah, who sent you to enquire of the Lord, so shall ye say unto him, Thus saith the Lord God of Israel concerning the words which thou hast heard; Because thine heart was tender, and thou didst humble thyself before God, when thou heardest his words against this place, and against the inhabitants thereof, and humbledst thyself before me, and didst*

He humbled himself and God preserved his life, promoted him and the impact of his kingdom was felt across the land of Israel. He generated such tremendous virtues of sanity and the fear of God through his humbled spirit. He humbled himself in the sight of God and succeeded in restoring Israel back to God. Not only did he restore sanity back to Israel, he also made sure that the whole land walked in the laws of God all through his reign. *"And Josiah took away all the abominations out of all the countries that pertained to the children of Israel, and made all that were present in Israel to serve, even to serve the Lord their God. And all his days they departed not from following the Lord, the God of their fathers."* His humble nature established his value and his worth was pronounced across many nations. Friend, humility preserves, promotes and establishes honour and dignity for those who possess it, both before God and man.

Become a child

A child is born and by the virtue of his lowliness and meekness, he is nurtured to become a son. Humility brings us to the level of a child who always takes the least in a row, counted as the least among family, yet being cared for by all as the carrier of the glory of the family and an heir of the kingdom. Humility creates an avenue that portrays a man with the quality of having a modest or low view of his importance than others even though his position assumes him more important. It is the principle of demonstrating a lifestyle of low estimate of our own importance either in social, administrative, spiritual or political designation. Rather than living the standard of our position, we lowly demonstrate the dimension that portrays our unprivileged background even though it's not the reality.

Humility cannot be achieved in us until we allow the mind of Christ to dominate us. He was God but refused to live in that form, rather He humbled

Himself to become an ordinary man amidst humanity, serving mankind like a selfless servant; became poor against His rich status simply to make mankind rich in their poor state.

> *"Let nothing be done through strife or vainglory; but in lowliness of mind let each esteem other better than themselves. Look not every man on his own things, but every man also on the things of others. Let this mind be in you, which was also in Christ Jesus: Who, being in the form of God, thought it not robbery to be equal with God: But made himself of no reputation, and took upon him the form of a servant, and was made in the likeness of men: And being found in fashion as a man, he humbled himself, and became obedient unto death, even the death of the cross. Wherefore God also hath highly exalted him, and given him a name which is above every name: That at the name of Jesus every knee should bow, of things in heaven, and things in earth, and things under the earth; And that every tongue should confess that Jesus Christ is Lord, to the glory of God the Father." [Philippians 2: 3 - 11]*

That He humbled Himself did not make Him less in authority and power, rather, His humility enhanced His capacity to manifest in full-fledged, the manifold glory of His Father. God anointed Him (Christ) with the oil of gladness *above* His fellows because of His humility, His love for righteousness, and passionate abhorrence for wickedness. He was anointed beyond measure, showing that humility is not synonymous with stupidity, rather it connotes access to Godliness. It accommodates and demonstrates the spirit of tolerance while upbraiding pride and arrogance within the framework of relationship and social practices. Humility demands for positive self-regard with conscious mindset and having an awareness of your strengths and weaknesses. This helps you to concentrate on what you are good at, and how best you can present your input to the society in a respectable manner.

> *"And it came to pass, that after three days they found him in the temple, sitting in the midst of the doctors, both hearing them, and asking them questions. And all that heard him were astonished at his understanding and answers." [Luke 2: 46-47]*

He was sent as the Saviour of the world and at twelve years old, was found humbly seated in the midst of elites of His time, learning and contributing to the affairs of life. At twelve, we didn't hear that He had started school! Humility schooled Him to a place of honour and dignity. He became Wonderful, Counsellor, the mighty God, the everlasting Father, the Prince of Peace" and the government was laid upon His shoulder because He was a man of humility, trusted by God to deliver heaven's vision on earth.

Humility is making contributions based on your areas of strength, in helping people realize and benefit from your servanthood privilege. Submitting to the demand of humility and lowliness of heart in your endeavour would enable people around you to define and appreciate your worth. But dwelling on your privilege, power and position will enhance pride, promote abuse of opportunities and reveal your weakness instead of your strength. There is the need for you therefore, to understand your vision and model your way toward your worth. You need to be clear about your values and define your philosophy that would help direct your contribution and dictate your action in the society in such a humble and acceptable way. This will enable you to be accepted with respect and in turn create a platform for your virtues to be released to mankind in your community and your generation at large.

Christ Jesus was anointed with the Holy Ghost and with power in such a dimension that no man had ever witnessed. Despite this unfathomable power and authority, He was simply going about healing and delivering people from the oppression of the devils. He was not discussing and arguing religion to show that He was sent as a Son of God, rather He was given to service with humility, reaching every low-estate people in the community with the strength, power and authority made available to Him by the Father. Then people realized His worth and they embraced Him with all honour and respect. You see values are derived from services and when services are delivered on the platform of humility it generates honour and dignity. Therefore, let this mind of a child be in you to enhance your growth to a son for unto us a child *is* born, unto us a son *is* given: and the *government* shall be *upon* the shoulder of the son who was once a child but exhibited humility of heart to grow to a son. Children are born but sons are raised in humility that they might take responsibility and become assets to their world.

THE PLACE OF MEEKNESS

Humility is the power generator; it is therefore impossible to be endued with power from on high if we lack the spirit of humility. The power needed to generate virtues comes from God and not from our intellect, rigorous services, expertise, influence and or affluence. It takes a humbled and meek heart to receive such power and authority to impart our society in line with God's plan. The virtues we produce are the direct correspondence of the revelation we receive from God through His teaching and guidance and only meekness qualifies us to be taught and be guided by God. *"The meek will he guide in judgment: and the meek will he teach his way"* [Psalms 25:9]. Also, *"Blessed are the meek: for they shall inherit the earth"* [Matthew 5:5]. And in the area of upliftment, *"The Lord lifteth up the meek: he casteth the wicked down to the ground"* [Psalms 147:6]

Regrettably speaking, the supernatural is lost in our generation today because humility is lost in our daily lifestyle and pride has been allowed to dominate the hearts. The first miracles that I ever witnessed in my Christian journey happened when I was in one of the Scandinavian countries for village evangelism with one of the notable churches in the city. We got to the village at night and were directly led to the crusade. I was the least among the twelve people in the team as some were Senior Pastors, some well-known and self-acclaimed evangelists, prophets and healers. In fact, I felt low and less privileged in the team, but I was persuaded that God would not need my title to perfect His will and use me as His vessel to carry out His ordained assignment. We got to the crusade and were ushered to the podium to pray for the sick and the afflicted. I was scared to my bone and cried Jesus, help me for I am not worthy to do this! My team members were professionals in the field, so they confidently walked in and started demonstrating with their tenacity and exerting human energy to pull the lame up to walk by force. I was scared to touch anyone and suddenly the Lord spoke to me to move forward and He pointed at a woman with a big goitre, (a swelling of the neck as a result of an enlargement of the thyroid gland), and instructed me saying *"because you have humbled yourself in my sight, I am ready to manifest myself through you, touch that woman in my name"* I went forward trembling and shaking touched the woman and screamed in Jesus name! Suddenly the big goitre disappeared.

While my professional team members were still struggling to get the lame man to walk, the Lord instructed me to go forward again and this time He said *"hold that man's hand and command in my name to come forth and be the same as the other hand"* I looked at the man, his left hand was shorter than the right, about half shorter and I held the short hand and cried 'hand grow out in the name of Jesus' the hand came out immediately and was the same size as the other. Then the crusade started in a very heated dimension. Humility worked it out and Christ Jesus began to manifest through His Precious Holy Spirit.

When my team members saw what was happening, they stopped their mechanization and psychological manipulation, came to me and started asking how did you do that? I responded, 'we are sent by the Master and we can only manifest by the Master and not by our power or energy' Humility is the key sir. I want you to know that virtues are the products of humility and not ability. Awake from your pride and allow Christ the Owner of power and authority to manifest through you less you become an empty barrel and a good for nothing noise making vessel. Understand that the kingdom of God is not in word, mechanization and or psychological manipulation, but in power and this power is only accessible by the humbled in heart.

Equally speaking, our inheritance is delivered on the platform of the meekness of our heart. Pride disqualifies us from receiving our inheritance in God *"But the meek shall inherit the earth; and shall delight themselves in the abundance of peace"* [Psalms 37:11]. This is where we need to come out of our closet and embrace the spirit of meekness so that God can use us to accomplish His purpose and plan for our community and our generation. When your meekness graduates to humility, grace is naturally released for your greatness. Moses enjoyed the fullness of God's presence and practically displayed the authority and power of heaven on earth by the instrument of meekness. He was the only living who had access to God's presence and literally saw God, talking face to face with God even as a man spoke with his friend as recorded in Exodus 33:11 *"And the Lord spake unto Moses face to face, as a man speaketh unto his friend. And he turned again into the camp: but his servant Joshua, the son of Nun, a young man, departed not out of the tabernacle."* His secret was found in Numbers 12:3, *"(Now the man Moses was very meek, above all the men which were upon the face of the earth.)"* His meek nature launched him to greatness.

God is responsible for the defense of the meek and humbled. Through meekness, the man Moses enjoyed the full backing of God at every level, even when his brother and sister rose against him in ministry. *"And Miriam and Aaron spake against Moses because of the Ethiopian woman whom he had married: for he had married an Ethiopian woman. And they said, Hath the Lord indeed spoken only by Moses? hath he not spoken also by us? And the Lord heard it. (Now the man Moses was very meek, above all the men which were upon the face of the earth.) And the Lord spake suddenly unto Moses, and unto Aaron, and unto Miriam, Come out ye three unto the tabernacle of the congregation. And they three came out. And the Lord came down in the pillar of the cloud, and stood in the door of the tabernacle, and called Aaron and Miriam: and they both came forth. And he said, Hear now my words: If there be a prophet among you, I the Lord will make myself known unto him in a vision, and will speak unto him in a dream. My servant Moses is not so, who is faithful in all mine house. With him will I speak mouth to mouth, even apparently, and not in dark speeches; and the similitude of the Lord shall he behold: wherefore then were ye not afraid to speak against my servant Moses? And the anger of the Lord was kindled against them; and he departed. And the cloud departed from off the tabernacle; and, behold, Miriam became leprous, white as snow: and Aaron looked upon Miriam, and, behold, she was leprous. And Aaron said unto Moses, Alas, my lord, I beseech thee, lay not the sin upon us, wherein we have done foolishly, and wherein we have sinned."* [Numbers 12: 1 - 11]

Korah, Dathan and Abiram rose against him in Numbers chapter 16 and God gave him authority and dominion over them to determine how the three agents should be wiped out of the congregation of Israel. *"And it came to pass, as he had made an end of speaking all these words, that the ground clave asunder that was under them: And the earth opened her mouth, and swallowed them up, and their houses, and all the men that appertained unto Korah, and all their goods. They, and all that appertained to them, went down alive into the pit, and the earth closed upon them: and they perished from among the congregation."* [Numbers 16:31 - 33] He spoke, and God confirmed immediately. When meekness finds its way in your life, God's power and presence will be made available and accessible for you.

Abraham's meekness brought him to the realm of blessing and direct access to God. He became the friend of God because he was meek enough to be guided

OLA JONES DUYILE

and taught by God, following God without questioning His authority. Above all, the Saviour, our Mirror (Jesus Christ the Son of God) said, *"I am meek and lowly in heart"* meaning that if you come after me in this frequency you will enhance your value, generate virtues and more importantly, *"ye shall find rest unto your souls"*.

Your problem isn't that you are not fasting and praying enough, your problem is that you lack the meek heart to be guided. Your pride has overwhelmed you, turning your heart to an unteachable one. Please brace up and embrace a new heart, a heart of flesh, a heart of meekness so that your worth will be pronounced and the great virtues of God in you will be released to bless your generation.

Humility Provokes Virtues

In Proverbs 29:23, the word of God states clearly that *"A man's pride shall bring him low: but honour shall uphold the humble in spirit."* And James 4:10 admonished that you should *"Humble yourselves in the sight of the Lord, and he shall lift you up"* The story of the Centurion clearly revealed that God honours people based on the level of their humility and not their position in the society. *"Then Jesus went with them. And when he was now not far from the house, the centurion sent friends to him, saying unto him, Lord, trouble not thyself: for I am not worthy that thou shouldest enter under my roof: Wherefore neither thought I myself worthy to come unto thee: but say in a word, and my servant shall be healed. For I also am a man set under authority, having under me soldiers, and I say unto one, Go, and he goeth; and to another, Come, and he cometh; and to my servant, Do this, and he doeth it. When Jesus heard these things, he marvelled at him, and turned him about, and said unto the people that followed him, I say unto you, I have not found so great faith, no, not in Israel. And they that were sent, returning to the house, found the servant whole that had been sick."* [Luke 7: 6 – 10]

Every act of God is triggered by the humility of the people who desire to experience it. Our humility and conduct in demonstrating meekness are what commit God to manifest His sovereignty through the release of virtues to meet our needs. *"If I shut up heaven that there be no rain, or if I command the locusts to devour the land, or if I send pestilence among my people; If my people, which are called by my name, shall humble themselves, and pray, and seek my face, and turn from their wicked ways; then will I hear from heaven, and will forgive their sin, and will heal their land"* [2 Chronicles 7: 13 - 14]. Not only that, our value is a function of our humility therefore humble yourself both in the sight of God and man that your worth may be spoken about. Your worth shall not turn worthless because of pride and your values shall not be erased in your generation due to pride and arrogance in the mighty name of Jesus. I decree that through your humbled nature, God shall position you as a vessel to distribute His virtues to your generation in Jesus name.

GRACE YOUR ACCESS TO HUMILITY

Pride is commonly the nature of man because of the environment and the pattern of upbringing. But one of the ways to get rid of it is to consciously embrace grace to enjoy help for your spirit. Whatever grows in grace becomes naturally humbled with the understanding that all that is available are the products of grace and not efforts. In Luke 2:40, it was recorded that Jesus grew in grace, no wonder He became eternally the meekest Lord of all. *"And the child grew, and waxed strong in spirit, filled with wisdom: and the grace of God was upon him"* He was the Carrier of the grace of God and that gave Him direct access to all that the Father has in His possession. Grace generated humility in Him which enabled Him to execute the Father's agenda without thinking about His own life. *"And being found in fashion as a man, he humbled himself, and became obedient unto death, even the death of the cross."* Grace humbled Him even to the cross, grace went with Him to the grave, He triumphed through grace, was brought out of the grave and ushered to eternal glory through the power of grace.

Apostle Paul, a man with such unusual insight and revelations of the mysteries of God attributed his greatness to God's grace made available for him to explore the unexplorable. He counted his proficiency and self-pride as loss for the grace of God and the excellency of the knowledge of Christ that secures productivity in human endeavours. *"But by the grace of God I am what I am: and his grace which was bestowed upon me was not in vain; but I laboured more abundantly than they all: yet not I, but the grace of God which was with me"* [1 Corinthians 15:10]. While writing to the church in Philippi, he reiterated *"Yea doubtless, and I count all things but loss for the excellency of the knowledge of*

Christ Jesus my Lord: for whom I have suffered the loss of all things, and do count them but dung, that I may win Christ" [Philippians 3:8]. How did he attain this virtue-generated and enviable height in the ministry? Simply by losing pride and embracing God's grace as revealed in verse seven of the same Philippians chapter three *"But what things were gain to me, those I counted loss for Christ."*

Grace helps us to cast our acclaimed capability upon God's ability bringing about divine help in time of need. I define grace as God's ability in man's inability to enhance man's capacity to take 'untakeable' steps, act the 'unactable' and dare the 'undareable', thereby generating inexplicable results. Also, grace enables us to handle issues with Godly fear which end up in the release of virtues without struggle. 1 Peter 4:10 states that *"As every man hath received the gift, even so minister the same one to another, as good stewards of the manifold grace of God"* let us therefore come boldly to the throne of grace that we might obtain the help required to maintain a humbled spirit that will enable us to produce great values in life. *"Looking diligently lest any man fail of the grace of God; lest any root of bitterness springing up trouble you, and thereby many be defiled"* [Hebrews 12:15]

When pride is at home, values are erased, worth becomes insignificant and virtues are completely lost. Humility is what generates values and distinguishes us among men. Our worth therefore is not in the throne we occupy, but in the level of meekness and humility we exhibit. Nebuchadnezzar was a man that enjoyed full blessing during his reign as a king. Power and authority were given to him by God to rule over nations and provinces. In fact, he was referred to as 'king of kings' during his time as stated in Daniel 2: 37-38; *"Thou, O king, art a king of kings: for the God of heaven hath given thee a kingdom, power, and strength, and glory. And wheresoever the children of men dwell, the beasts of the field and the fowls of the heaven hath he given into thine hand, and hath made thee ruler over them all. Thou art this head of gold."* Unfortunately, pride stripped him of all the honour and glory! His pride and arrogance reduced him to a mere grass eating beast and he began to eat grass because he forgot that God demotes the pride in heart and exalts the humbled. Please understand that *"the most High ruleth in the kingdom of men, and giveth it to whomsoever he will"* therefore, handle that privileged position with humility and deal with people in the fear of God if you don't want to turn your glory to shame and reproach.

> *"This is the interpretation, O king, and this is the decree of the most High, which is come upon my lord the king: That they shall drive thee from men, and thy dwelling shall be with the beasts of the field, and they shall make thee to eat grass as oxen, and they shall wet thee with the dew of heaven, and seven times shall pass over thee, till thou know that the most High ruleth in the kingdom of men, and giveth it to whomsoever he will."* [Daniel 4:24 - 25]

While humility elevates to the throne, pride brings down to the pit. *"Humble yourselves in the sight of the Lord, and he shall lift you up"* [James 4:10]. All things lay bare before Him and He delivers the keys of the kingdom to whosoever He will. Nevertheless, the humbled in heart shall possess the keys, therefore, humble yourselves under the mighty hand of God, that he may exalt you in due time. You shall be elevated in your field this season and by the virtue of your humility, your generation shall enjoy the blessings of God released through you to the world in the mighty name of Jesus.

Chapter 11

Provoking Virtues through the Mysteries of Praise and Sacrifice

God's virtues are provoked by the acts and the move of men, most importantly with earnest heartfelt, desperate moves of faith. Everyone desires to see and experience God's move, but we fail to recall that failure is the end-product of any aspiration that is void of action. We do not just aspire to see God's greatness; we act to provoke His greatness and some of the ways to get this done is through practical and conscious engagement in heartfelt praise and covenant-driven sacrifice. In this chapter, we shall be unveiling the mysteries behind these two forces that provoke the presence of God and the release of His virtues in a strange dimension.

ACCESSING HIS PRESENCE

I need to establish this basic truth here that murmuring is the breeding ground for mourning and complaining about everything will excessively complicate your situation. Every time you complain about your situation you deprive yourself of the access needed to draw virtues from the Vessel. It takes the cord of praise to break into His presence where we are privileged to draw strength for triumph. *"Enter into his gates with thanksgiving, and into his courts with praise: be thankful unto him, and bless his name" [Psalms 100:4].* The best of the King resides in His presence! The precious goodies are kept in the treasure house of the king and always at the right side, for *"Thou wilt shew me the path of life: in thy presence is fulness of joy; at thy right hand there are pleasures for evermore"* [Psalms 16:11]. However, this treasure house can only be accessed through praise and adoration. The wealth, honour, glory, strength and capability of the king are revealed through the mystery of praise.

One of the ways to practically show the magnitude of the value we place on God is through the power of praise. Praise is the only ordained and recognized key that guarantees our direct access to the glorious presence of God. Praise becomes the habitation of God and it is comely to Him, propelling His immeasurable sovereignty to act in unusual capacity on behalf of man.

If it takes praise to access the presence of the king and praise is needed as the key to unlock the treasure house of the king, then **what is praise?**

Praise is the expression of your respect, warm approval, awe-inspiring admiration and gratitude to God as an act of worship. The Middle English defines praise as 'setting a price on, attaching value to' and with great admiration expressing boundless respect and gratitude 'equivalent in value' towards a deity. In Ezra 3:11, the people saw the deed of God and were overwhelmed by His grace and help in securing the foundation of His house to be laid after several years of persecution. *"And they sang together by course in praising and giving thanks unto the Lord; because he is good, for his mercy endureth for ever toward Israel. And all the people shouted with a great shout, when they praised the Lord, because the foundation of the house of the Lord was laid."* They exhibited the act of demonstrating their gratitude, honour and respect to the God of Israel for this huge achievement. They lifted up their voices and *"Give thanks unto the Lord, call upon his name, make known his deeds among the people"* [1 Chronicles 16:8]

Our fulfilment in life is a function of the fruit of our lips as stated in Proverbs 18:20 *"A man's belly shall be satisfied with the fruit of his mouth; and with the increase of his lips shall he be filled."* But the key to this fulfilment is the ability to render our sacrifice to God with our lips. Hebrews 13:15 states that *"By him therefore let us offer the sacrifice of praise to God continually, that is, the fruit of our lips giving thanks to his name."* The virtues of God are simply provoked by the application of our lips to release the fruits in the form of praise, thanksgiving and worship to the King of kings who makes all things beautiful in His own time for us. Giving thanks to God as a prove of our trust, confidence and hope in *"the living God, who giveth us richly all things to enjoy;"*

Now, the earth holds the wealth of every nation as well as individual blessings. You will agree with me that every treasure that people, nations and or kingdoms are dying to acquire is derived from the earth; talking about gold, silver, iron, petroleum *et cetera*. Nations are devising different means to explore the riches of the earth but failed to realize that God ordained access to the womb of the earth is praise. Praise is the key to unlock the womb of the earth for the exploration of great virtues that culminate in greatness. *"Let the people praise thee, O God; let all the people praise thee. Then shall the earth yield her increase; and God, even our own God, shall bless us. God shall bless us; and all the ends of the earth shall fear him"* [Psalm 67:5 -7].

Praise provokes the presence of God which is the path of life that secures the fullness of joy and eternal pleasure for the saints. Prayer of the saints commits God's integrity and provokes His sovereignty to manifest His power and display His God-ability. But praise provokes His presence which in turn generates virtues for the release of man from chain and chuckles of life, and in addition, the release of earnest desires and needs.

In prayer, we are limited to moving our mountains through our faith and declaration, *"For verily I say unto you, That whosoever shall say unto this mountain, Be thou removed, and be thou cast into the sea; and shall not doubt in his heart, but shall believe that those things which he saith shall come to pass; he shall have whatsoever he saith"* [Mark 11:23] but in praise mountains are dissolved and valleys are filled up.

When we engage in praise to the Almighty God, we compel His presence to our situation and when He arrives, mountains melt, and valleys are filled at the instance of His fearful presence. As it is written: *"Oh that thou wouldest rend the heavens, that thou wouldest come down, that the mountains might flow down at thy presence, As when the melting fire burneth, the fire causeth the waters to boil, to make thy name known to thine adversaries, that the nations may tremble at thy presence! When thou didst terrible things which we looked not for, thou camest down, the mountains flowed down at thy presence. For since the beginning of the world men have not heard, nor perceived by the ear, neither hath the eye seen, O God, beside thee, what he hath prepared for him that waiteth for him"* [Isaiah 64: 1 - 4].

Whatever will take God will require praise! Judah was under the siege of the children of Ammon, Moab, and mount Seir, with zero military capability to confront them. Their king cried to God for rescue and God responded with a demand, Praise me! *"Ye shall not need to fight in this battle: set yourselves, stand ye still, and see the salvation of the Lord with you, O Judah and Jerusalem: fear not, nor be dismayed; to morrow go out against them: for the Lord will be with you. And Jehoshaphat bowed his head with his face to the ground: and all Judah and the inhabitants of Jerusalem fell before the Lord, worshipping the Lord. And the Levites, of the children of the Kohathites, and of the children of the Korhites, stood up to praise the Lord God of Israel with a loud voice on high"* Then, the prophet instructed Jehoshaphat the king to gather all the singers, musicians and players of instruments and let them praise God in the beauty of holiness. *"And when he had consulted with the people, he appointed singers unto the Lord, and that should praise the beauty of holiness, as they went out before the army, and to say, Praise the Lord; for his mercy endureth for ever."* This is the only force that can get God to step into your situation and when He does, virtues are released, and vengeance is poured out to silence oppositions and consume all adversaries.

"And when they began to sing and to praise, the Lord set ambushments against the children of Ammon, Moab, and mount Seir, which were come against Judah; and they were smitten. For the children of Ammon and Moab stood up against the inhabitants of mount Seir, utterly to slay and destroy them: and when they had made an end of the inhabitants of Seir, every one helped to destroy another. And when Judah came toward the watch tower in the wilderness, they looked unto the multitude, and, behold, they were dead bodies fallen to the earth, and none escaped. And when Jehoshaphat and his people came to take away the spoil of them, they found among them in abundance both riches with the dead bodies, and precious jewels, which they stripped off for themselves, more than they could carry away: and they were three days in gathering of the spoil, it was so much. And on the fourth day they assembled themselves in the valley of Berachah; for there they blessed the Lord: therefore the name of the same place was called, The valley of Berachah, unto this day. Then they returned, every man of Judah and Jerusalem, and Jehoshaphat in the forefront of them, to go again to Jerusalem with joy; for the Lord had made them to rejoice over their enemies." [read 2 Chronicles 20: 1 - 30]. Praise provoked God's presence as the battle axe for Judah and launched them to their abundance of substances, granting them an all-round rest, causing their fear and dread to fall upon all the neighbouring countries around them. What a defense!

In *[Psalms 68:1-4]*, the Psalmist revealed the secret of God's presence in man's situation *"Let God arise, let his enemies be scattered: let them also that hate him flee before him. As smoke is driven away, so drive them away: as wax melteth before the fire, so let the wicked perish at the presence of God."* When He arises, every opposition to His will and purpose are dealt with and His presence will cause the saints to rejoice over their adversaries as depicted in verse 3 *"But let the righteous be glad; let them rejoice before God: yea, let them exceedingly rejoice"* But how do we invoke His rising? Verse 4 says *"Sing unto God, sing praises to his name: extol him that rideth upon the heavens by his name Jah, and rejoice before him"* So, the cord that draws God's attention and move Him to a standing action is praise and it is the expectation that we continually render praises to God without season *"lifting up holy hands, without wrath and doubting"* building up our most holy faith in admonition, praising God and *"Giving thanks always for all things unto God and the Father in the name of our Lord Jesus Christ;"* [Ephesians 5:20].

Praising God does not only strengthen faith, it equally energizes hope and stabilizes the heart of confidence and spirit of trust in the efficacy of God's response to issues. Abraham's faith was strengthened, and his hope was secured with full assurance and confidence in the promise of God regarding the expected covenant seed. *"But he did not doubt or waver in unbelief concerning the promise of God, but he grew strong and empowered by faith, giving glory to God, being fully convinced that God had the power to do what He had promised."* [Romans 4: 20-21 AMP]. He was empowered by faith and began giving glory to God until his praise drew Isaac the resulting virtue. The key to that closed door of your life is simply praise. Let the people praise Him if they desire to see His greatness.

THE MYSTERY OF SACRIFICE

The best of God is kept in His secret treasure house because *"The secret things belong unto the Lord our God"* However, people who understand God's immeasurable value make unusual sacrifices to access the secret things that are yet to be revealed to humanity. For *"those things which are revealed belong unto us and to our children for ever, that we may do all the words of this law"* [Deuteronomy 29:29] People who experience the best of God are the people who take time to discover the secret things of God. Moreover, they did not only discover them but equally apply their findings in practical form and engage them to secure the best of God.

Sacrifice is one of the vital ways to secure access to the secret treasure of God's manifold virtues. The word of God declares thus *"Gather my saints together unto me; those that have made a covenant with me by sacrifice. And the heavens shall declare his righteousness: for God is judge himself" [Psalms 50:5-6].* Those who understand the mystery of sacrifice are supernaturally given access to the secret place of the Most High God. They inherit the untapped virtues of God and manifest it physically to their world to prove the authenticity of the efficacy of sacrificial offerings. When sacrifice is laid down upon the right altar and the sweet smelling savour ascend to God, it supernaturally commands an opened check from God for men to fill whatever they desire from Him *"And Solomon loved the Lord, walking in the statutes of David his father: only he sacrificed and burnt incense in high places. And the king went to Gibeon to sacrifice there; for that was the great high place: a thousand burnt offerings did Solomon offer upon that altar. In Gibeon the Lord appeared to Solomon in a dream by night: and God said, Ask what I shall give thee" [1 Kings 3:3-5].* A heart of love, obedience and passion for God coupled with costly sacrifice engender an open check for generational wealth, riches, wisdom, liberty and eternal dominion!

Friends, this is too heavy for human acclimatization because our human nature is logically adaptable to cheap and free stuff just as a wise man once said. But I can assure you that sacrifice is the costliest of all services. *"And the king said unto Araunah, Nay; but I will surely buy it of thee at a price: neither will I offer burnt offerings unto the Lord my God of that which doth cost me nothing. So David bought the threshing floor and the oxen for fifty shekels of silver" [2 Samuel 24:24].* Sacrifice demands for the best of you in terms of resources, commitment and what have you, and only those who are ready to pay the price will enjoy the unusual harvest of virtues from above. The true meaning of sacrifice is in its cost! It must cost you something otherwise it does not attract God's release. That's why the English Dictionary helps us to define it as 'An act of giving up something valued for the sake of something else regarded as more important or worthy' Absolutely, you 'Give up (something valued) for the sake of other considerations[12]' Definitely, it has to be valuable but with the understanding that God's worth is more valuable to us and the resulting virtues are more precious than what we have laid down as sacrifice to provoke His incredible virtues to our life.

Christ Jesus is certified as eternal Lord of lords and King of kings through self-sacrifice. He became the Sacrificial Lamb for the redemption and restoration of mankind as portrayed in John 1:29 *"… Behold the Lamb of God, which taketh away the sin of the world"*, and that gave Him His place for eternity. He did not come to the world to destroy the mystery of sacrifice, rather He came to open the door for all the saints to understand and engage in it. For He said *"Unto you it is given to know the mystery of the kingdom of God: but unto them that are without, all these things are done in parables"* [Mark 4:11]. He equally established this mystery when He revealed to us that sacrifice is part of the commandments He came to establish and fulfil. *"Therefore doth my Father love me, because I lay down my life, that I might take it again. No man taketh it from me, but I lay it down of myself. I have power to lay it down, and I have power to take it again. This commandment have I received of my Father"* [John 10:17-18]. This is the force that distinguishes the saints among the acclaimed believers and gathers those who have made covenant to serve God with sacrifice. No wonder the scriptures admonish us in Hebrew 12:2 that we should strive to emulate Christ by earnestly *"Looking unto Jesus the author and finisher of our faith; who for the joy that was set before him endured the cross, despising the shame, and is set down at the right hand of the throne of God."* Who for the greater virtue submitted Himself to be made a sacrificial Lamb and propitiation for the sins of the world! This was the price He paid for His greater and eternal enthronement.

ALTAR OF UNUSUAL SACRIFICE FOR SECURING THE COVENANT OF SAFETY

The first sacrifice in human history was a great risk and costliest of all! Now God instructed Noah to select animals in this pattern, a male and a female to preserve the species after the flood that destroyed the whole earth. Then the

---

[12] *https://en.oxforddictionaries.com/definition/sacrifice*

flood ended, and the entire earth was wiped out, and Noah came forth with a seal of sacrifice to appease God and to re-establish the covenant of indestructible safety for humanity. He demonstrated his value for God through sacrifice and heaven responded with an everlasting covenant.

> *And Noah builded an altar unto the Lord; and took of every clean beast, and of every clean fowl, and offered burnt offerings on the altar. And the Lord smelled a sweet savour; and the Lord said in his heart, I will not again curse the ground any more for man's sake; for the imagination of man's heart is evil from his youth; neither will I again smite any more every thing living, as I have done. While the earth remaineth, seedtime and harvest, and cold and heat, and summer and winter, and day and night shall not cease. [Genesis 8:20-22]*

By sacrifice, God re-visited the covenant and established a new one with Noah with eternal vow never to destroy humanity by flood.

It took Abraham twenty-five years of waiting upon the promise of God to get his only covenant son Isaac. And God walked to him in the cool of the day to tempt him with the costliest and most valuable treasure of his life: *"And it came to pass after these things, that God did tempt Abraham, and said unto him, Abraham: and he said, Behold, here I am. And he said, Take now thy son, thine only son Isaac, whom thou lovest, and get thee into the land of Moriah; and offer him there for a burnt offering upon one of the mountains which I will tell thee of."* [Genesis 22: 1 - 2]

And Abraham, without hesitation, took Isaac his beloved son and journeyed for three days to the said mountain to sacrifice Isaac to the Lord as instructed by God. *"And Abraham rose up early in the morning, and saddled his ass, and took two of his young men with him, and Isaac his son, and clave the wood for the burnt offering, and rose up, and went unto the place of which God had told him. Then on the third day Abraham lifted up his eyes, and saw the place afar off"* [Genesis 22: 3 - 4]. I need to emphasize here that what makes sacrifice acceptable to God, is neither the volume nor the eagerness, but obedience to His instruction. Whatever He tells you to do must be done in line with His instruction. This is what provokes His integrity to act beyond our expectation. You need to also understand that God is not in need and will never be in need of whatever you think you are laying down as sacrifices. God just wants to move you out of your present state to another level of envy and glory. Abraham understood this, and he had no problem obeying God and presenting Isaac as a sacrificial lamb. He knew that God would never allow Isaac to be slain. Hear what he said to the lad after he located the mountain and the son, Isaac perceived there was no lamb for the sacrifice:

> *"And Abraham said unto his young men, Abide ye here with the ass; and I and the lad will go yonder and worship, and come again to you. And Abraham took the wood of the burnt offering, and laid it upon Isaac his son; and he took the fire in his hand, and a knife; and they went both of them together. And Isaac spake unto Abraham his father, and said, My father: and he said, Here am I, my son. And he said, Behold the fire and the wood: but where is the lamb for a burnt offering? And Abraham said, My son, God will provide himself a lamb for a burnt offering: so they went both of them together"* [Genesis 22: 5 - 8]

Mostly, sacrifice is a means of attesting the stability of your faith. It is an act of demonstrating your confidence and trust in God and a step consciously taken in actualizing your divine elevation to your desired level in life.

THE PLATFORM OF SACRIFICE

Every genuine sacrifice must be preceded with the rearing of an altar. The altar of purity of heart, the altar of grace and supplication, the altar of divine connection and 'engraced' fellowship, the altar of faith and expectation. The most significant part of the acts of men who made acceptable sacrifice was the building of the altar. *"And Noah builded an altar unto the Lord"* It was also recorded that *"Abraham built an altar"* to the Lord where he laid Isaac his sacrificial seed. Solomon went to the high place at *"Gibeon to sacrifice there; for that was the great high place: a thousand burnt offerings did Solomon offer upon that altar."* The impact of the sacrifice is not in the volume but in the preparation of the altar for the Lord. Your altar is the platform for your sacrifice and until the altar is rightly positioned, sacrifice might become an abomination to the Lord.

The fire of God will only be released upon the sacrifice rendered on the altar of purity. The virtues of God which is the consuming fire for our sacrifice is only attracted by the pureness of the altar which connotes our heart. Every tangible manifestation of the acts of God is provoked by the pureness of the heart of man. Christ Jesus made His body a living sacrifice, holy acceptable to God both in righteousness, purity, holiness and the fear of God as His reasonable service. He was accepted as the overall Sacrificial Lamb of God on the platform of purity. He subjected Himself to a lifestyle of purity and became the Lamb without blemish, sanctified and approved for eternal redemption as the propitiation for the sins of the world through sacrifice. By the pureness of this Sacrificial Lamb, the fire of salvation was released and it's still burning all over the world till this present time. So, put the wood in order before you place your sacrifice. Let it be reared out of purity, obedience and sanctity, it will convincingly attract the fire!

"And they came to the place which God had told him of; and Abraham built an altar there, and laid the wood in order" Sacrifice raised out of a heart of obedience, coupled with passionate love, fear, reverence and value for God provokes God's capability to manifest His glory and virtues. Sacrifice provokes oath and causes God to swear by Himself on your behalf. Sacrifice causes God to go beyond His reach and take the responsibility for your destiny. It is the generator of greater and inexplicable virtues! It draws the line between the covenant practitioners and the mere believers, celebrating followers or addicted religious practitioners.

The virtues of irrevocable blessings were released upon Abraham to the end that generations after him are still swimming in the blessings. Up till this present generation, Abraham's seed are still possessing the gates of their enemies across the earth. Their secret is not in the modern machineries and sophisticated IT technology they have been able to build, but their secret is the costliest sacrifice made by their progenitor, the patriarch Abraham. It takes sacrifice to be certified by God! Your eternal certification in the realm of blessings hangs on your level of sacrifice. Get on board therefore and stir heaven with your sacrifice! Provoke the rain of heaven upon your life by drawing the cord that holds the blessings through sacrifice. Approach God with your costliest sacrifice and watch the heavens declaring his righteousness on your behalf as God justifies you. Generations after you shall continue to reap the fruit of the sacrifice you made in your own lifetime in Jesus name.

Some years back, as a student, I was busy doing menial jobs to support myself and my family. But one unique day, I was in a meeting and I heard a testimony of a young lady of about seventeen (17) years old who was bedridden due to a very strange ailment. According to her, she had been prayed for by all available men and women of God, including the presiding Bishop but there was no improvement, neither was she healed of any. She decided to raise an altar of sacrifice for her release from the siege of strange terminal disease. She woke up one early morning and gathered all that she had in terms of cash and headed to the tabernacle (church auditorium). It was not a normal service day, she went alone to engage in the mystery of sacrifice for her release. According to her testimony, she got to the altar of the Lord and cried. 'Lord Jesus, I am here to lay all down at your feet as a sacrifice for my release. You made me from the beginning, Lord re-make me; take away this stranger in my body and restore health to me according to your tender mercy and love. Thank you, Lord! Amen' She laid the sacrifice upon the altar and turned back. Immediately a hand reached out to her and she got her liberty from that selfsame hour.

As soon as I heard this testimony, my spirit stirred within me, I was provoked! I said to God; 'Lord, I am tired of doing menial job for sustenance, even if I am the dullest of all in the IT world, I believe your wisdom can change my story. Lord Jesus, if you can settle this little girl by her sacrifice, you can change my status too by sacrifice because you are not a respecter of person.' I went ahead and gathered all that was available against the month's budget and I said 'Lord, I am in my first year as an IT student (Masters' degree level), I am confident in your divine wisdom in my life that I have some knowledge in this field, therefore I am due for market. I desire a change of level in my career Lord and I therefore lay this sacrifice for a change of position' As soon as I made the transfer to the store house, a strange message popped up in my email box and that settled me forever. People keep claiming that I had luck to have been launched into the market before I could complete my education, but I kept telling them that it was not luck that came my way, but the light of the truth that led me to take an 'untakeable' step in securing the impossible. Friends, kingdom sacrifice, works, most importantly, when it is from the heart and is tangibly costly. It is an avenue for the release of greater virtues for prompt transformation of destiny.

Significantly, and above all, let your sacrifice be costly and meaningfully raised and let it be from the heart! David raised a costly sacrifice to avert plague in the land. He "...*built an altar unto the Lord and offered burnt offerings and peace offerings. So the Lord was entreated for the land, and the plague was stayed from Israel*" (2 Samuel 24:24 - 25). The virtues needed to stop the plagues in your life and family can be provoked and invoked by sacrifice. Just lay it down upon the altar at the feet of Christ the Saviour and the plague shall be averted. Solomon reared an altar of sacrifice for the release of unusual wealth, riches and wisdom (1 Kings 3). His father David fought all through his 53 years reign as a king, but Solomon broke the generational curses of battles in his family by sacrifice because the scripture recorded that he had peace all through his kingdom until his heart was turned away from God. You can also stop that generational curses and ancestral influences that have been feasting on you and reaping your family apart by simply raise an altar of sacrifice and lay all the curses at the feet of Jesus the One who already took all curses out of the way and nailed them to His cross.

TYPES OF SACRIFICE

There are two distinct types of sacrifice; **instructional** and **willing**. Instructional sacrifice is that type of sacrifice instructed or commanded by God in testing the stability of our faith and to prove the quality of our walk with Him. This was the case of our father Abraham as it was recorded that God did tempt him. "*And it came to pass after these things, that God did tempt Abraham, and said unto him, Abraham: and he said, Behold, here I am. And he said, Take now thy son, thine only son Isaac, whom thou lovest, and get thee into the land of Moriah; and offer him there for a burnt offering upon one of the mountains which I will tell thee of*" *[Genesis 22: 1 - 2]*. This type of sacrifice comes with instruction and guidelines which must be strictly followed in obedience and reverence to God. The criteria for pass or fail is in obedience to the instructions. You do not determine the measure, place and time, all these are dictated by God and made known to you through the instructions. In the same proportion with the instructions, the virtues that would be released are not what you can imagine. God determines the measure of the sacrifice in accordance with the magnitude of the releases.

I had two notable occasions for this type of sacrifice; one was the sacrifice of time. God instructed me to take one week off from my office and dedicate it to His kingdom tasks without engaging in any other things. I agreed with Him, signed off from the office and gave myself to the tasks He apportioned to me for that specific time. That same week, someone walked to me and gave me the exact amount of money I should have received in my one-week invoice as a consultant, raw cash without tax to be paid. Secondly, God said to me one early morning 'I want you to call my servant (He mentioned the name to me) and ask him to go price the car he likes, and you pay for it' I did and by His grace and provision paid for the car for that His servant. Few months later, I was to buy my own first car and the Lord rewarded me with the exact amount I paid for His servant's car. I already paid for my car when the dealer called me and apologized for taking too much for the car and later returned some thousands back to my account. On checking the refund, it was exactly same amount I paid for God's servant's car. God is a faithful God.

Secondly, a **willing** sacrifice reared based on a specific desire. A willing sacrifice is such a personal and deliberate sacrifice with the desire to reach to God's grace and sovereignty in securing the new level we crave for in life. Solomon engaged in deliberate sacrifice to the Lord to draw wisdom, riches, wealth and security in his kingdom. The Saviour (our Lord Jesus Christ) openly spoke concerning His deliberate and willing sacrifice and said: *"Therefore doth my Father love me, because I lay down my life, that I might take it again. No man taketh it from me, but I lay it down of myself. I have power to lay it down, and I have power to take it again. This commandment have I received of my Father"* *[John 10:17-18]*. He called it power to lay down without being enforced against our intention. When this power is in place it always precedes the power to receive and it naturally secures God's attention.

I am not talking about this modern-day charismatic style of professional stealing and systematic robbery of the innocent. They prophesy to people in their greed instructing the innocent worshippers to read Psalms 121 three times and make a sacrificial seed of 121 Dollars and the curses on their life and family shall be broken! That is mechanized robbery orchestrated through religious covetousness and psychological manipulation to feast on the innocent but ignorant believers. I am talking about the self-motivated, kingdom acceptable sacrifice provoked by the truth and having God's word as the foundation with unshaking faith as the anchor cord. Apostle Paul admonished that we should emulate the church in Macedonia who exemplified this when they made the costliest sacrifice with their willing heart.

It has to be from a willing heart! Christ Jesus deliberately made Himself a sacrificial lamb for the sins of the world by the will of God. His power to lay down preceded all expectations, wherefore God's virtue has raised Him to be King over all heavens and earth and beneath. His willing sacrifice brought Him to the place of Lordship over all creatures and the entire planets including heaven of heavens. *"And being found in fashion as a man, he humbled himself, and became obedient unto death, even the death of the cross. Wherefore God also hath highly exalted him, and given him a name which is above every name: That at the name of Jesus every knee should bow, of things in heaven, and things in earth, and things under the earth; And that every tongue should confess that Jesus Christ is Lord, to the glory of God the Father"* [Philippians 2:8 - 11].

Bear in mind that a willing sacrifice could be monetary, assets and properties, time and services but the greatest of all is self. When we willingly make ourselves a living sacrifice to God and for the promotion of His kingdom, we supernaturally ascend to God's presence as the smoke of sweet savour, well pleasing to God. *"For if there be first a willing mind, it is accepted according to that a man hath, and not according to that he hath not"* [2 Corinthians 8:12]. We can only access the best of God when we make ourselves sacrificial lamb for the promotion of His kingdom (our mind and actions become a reasonable sacrifice).

Remember it does not imply killing of goats and bulls or turtle doves to sacrifice to God. Jesus already took the place of that sort of sacrifice. He became the Lamb and was slain for us all. But I am talking about your commitment to kingdom elevation through your time, resources and substances. I entered into a covenant of sacrifice, where I made myself and all that associate with me a seed unto God since September 1999. A living sacrifice both in service, conduct and in giving and ever since then the rain of His grace, strength for continuity and provision has never ceased from falling upon my life. Though, I have been through many challenges, but the challenges only succeeded in helping me to channel my ways in His will. Trials have become the established force for my triumph and persecution remain the simulating force that keep enhancing my promotion and elevation.

Your sacrifice becomes irrevocably established and sealed with an oath when you are able to declare as Apostle Paul did in Galatians 2:20 *"I am crucified with Christ: nevertheless I live; yet not I, but Christ liveth in me: and the life which I now live in the flesh I live by the faith of the Son of God, who loved me, and gave himself for me"*. Do you want to really experience the greater virtues of God? Then make your life a seed to Him and the course of His kingdom. If these two-notable kingdom-reckoning forces (that is, heartfelt continued praise and sacrifice) become part of your daily lifestyle, then God's best will naturally become your inheritance for life. You are due for the next levels in Jesus name.

Chapter 12

Pulling Virtues through the Force of Prayer

> *"And he spake a parable unto them to this end, that men ought always to pray, and not to faint; Saying, There was in a city a judge, which feared not God, neither regarded man: And there was a widow in that city; and she came unto him, saying, Avenge me of mine adversary. And he would not for a while: but afterward he said within himself, Though I fear not God, nor regard man; Yet because this widow troubleth me, I will avenge her, lest by her continual coming she weary me. And the Lord said, Hear what the unjust judge saith. And shall not God avenge his own elect, which cry day and night unto him, though he bear long with them? I tell you that he will avenge them speedily. Nevertheless when the Son of man cometh, shall he find faith on the earth?"*
> *[Luke 18:1-8]*

Man's ability is not weighed by the amount of physical energy he has but by the level of his insight to spiritual matters and the effectiveness of his spirit man to obtain and deliver spiritual products. Every tangible delivery is traceable to the power exercised on the mount of prayer. We engage in prayer to combat situations (hindrances, obstructions, stumbling blocks on our way, oppositions to our breakthrough, accusers of our life *et cetera*). We engage in prayer to secure divine backing; we engage in prayer to possess our possession and to secure our peace and rest. Most significant of all, we pray purposely to pull virtues out of the Vessel for our all-round settlement. Prayer stands as the weapon for securing heaven's attention for our undeniable victory in spiritual issues of life. It is the pivot weapon for securing our destiny for *"When I cry unto thee, then shall mine enemies turn back: this I know; for God is for me."* [Psalms 56:9] and *"If my people, which are called by my name, shall humble themselves, and pray, and seek my face, and turn from their wicked ways; then will I hear from heaven, and will forgive their sin, and will heal their land"* [2 Chronicles 7: 14].

The power of every child of God is exercised through prayer, meaning that your prayer life is what measures your spiritual ability to secure heaven's support for your victory and triumph in the race of life. Everyone that strives in prayer ultimately strives for a great mastery of the crown of glory and triumph. While praise get God to you, prayer gets you to God *"Then shalt thou call, and the Lord shall answer; thou shalt cry, and he shall say, Here I am"* It takes prayer to get at God, it takes prayer to present our requests, it takes prayer to move mountain and stumbling blocks on our ways to fulfilment of destiny. Even faith is expressed through prayers. Hope is measured through our persistent lifespan in the school of prayer. In fact, what defines our total dependence on God is the level of our commitment to prayer as a communication channel for engaging in daily conversation with God. Ultimately, Power is secured through prayer as it is the channel through which we exercise authority to secure our dominion over every issue in our life.

> *"If ye have faith as a grain of mustard seed, ye shall say unto this mountain, Remove hence to yonder place; and it shall remove; and nothing shall be impossible unto you."* [Matthew 17:20] And *"Verily I say unto you, If ye have faith, and doubt not, ye shall not only do this which is done to the fig tree, but also if ye shall say unto this mountain, Be thou removed, and be thou cast into the sea; it shall be done."* [Matthew 21:21] Faith is exercised through prayer to secure our victory *"For whatsoever is born of God overcometh the world: and this is the victory that overcometh the world, even our faith."* [1 John 5:4].

It takes prayer to secure your place in destiny. Christ Jesus was sent to the world to accomplish an eternally defined mission, but until He was driven to the wilderness for intensive prayer He could not gain full access to the center of God's ordained mandate for His life. *"And Jesus being full of the Holy Ghost returned from Jordan, and was led by the Spirit into the wilderness,* (to engage in intensive prayer and fasting) *Being forty days* (in ceaseless prayer seeking to know the Father's will, afterward) *tempted of the devil. And in those days he did eat nothing:* (but fastened His eye on the word and submitting His flesh to be prepared for the task ahead) *and when they were ended,* (with full assurance of direction to God's plan for His life*) he afterward hungered"* [Luke 4:1-2 paraphrased]. He went after God in prayer for the delivery of the sceptre of authority and dominion for the actualization of His purpose on earth. He prevailed against Satan and returned with authority to dominate His world and to fulfil God's mandate for His life. *"And Jesus returned* (from the mount of prayer) *in the power of the Spirit into Galilee: and* (having received through prayer the guide and understood the steps to take in fulfilling God's mandate and taking those steps) *there went out a fame of him through all the region round about"* [Luke 4:14 paraphrased].

Nothing works outside prayer and supplication. Listen, in John 20:21, the same Saviour revealed to us when He said *"…Peace be unto you: as my Father hath sent me, even so send I you."* If we are sent even as the Father hath sent Him, then wisdom demands that we should take the same step He took to discover and accomplish the Father's mandate for our life. He took the step of prayer to secure His place in God's agenda for His life. He drew virtues from heaven by the force of prayer *"Now when all the people were baptized, it came to pass, that Jesus also being baptized, and **praying**, the heaven was opened, And the Holy Ghost descended in a bodily shape like a dove upon him, and a voice came from heaven, which said, Thou art my beloved Son; in thee I am well pleased. [Luke 3:21-22]* His heaven was opened by the weapon of prayer. He pulled virtues from the throne of grace and became God's grace here on earth and forever more, Amen! Prayer changed His status from Jesus to Rabbi, Master and Christ the Saviour. No wonder, He is the Way, the Truth and the Life! Anyone can bear the name Jesus, but no one has ever attained the level of Christ except the King of Kings and the Lord of lords Himself, who secured His unique position through the weapon of prayer.

Prayer compels the release of virtues because it is usually done through faith and believe. We pray because we believe in God's worth, integrity and sovereignty to answer and resolve our problems with His invaluable mercy, grace, power and authority. We esteem His value so much that we confidently approach Him with all our desires and equally expect the delivery of the same. *"And this is the confidence that we have in him, that, if we ask any thing according to his will, he heareth us: And if we know that he hear us, whatsoever we ask, we know that we have the petitions that we desired of him"* [1 John 5: 14 – 15]

The promises of the Father can be appropriated with the force of fasting and prayer to bring them to accomplishment. That you received the promises by prophetic declaration does not connote the reality of its actualization and delivery. There is the demand for effectual fervent prayer to draw the promises and produce tremendous power for actualization. Now Christ came to His Disciples and promised to fill them with the power required for their great manifestation in the ministry. *"And, behold, I send the promise of my Father upon you: but tarry ye in the city of Jerusalem, until ye be endued with power from on high"* [Luke 24:49]. To confirm this, He said to them in Acts 1: 8 *"But ye shall receive power, after that the Holy Ghost is come upon you: and ye shall be witnesses unto me both in Jerusalem, and in all Judaea, and in Samaria, and unto the uttermost part of the earth."* Thus, they went to Jerusalem and camped themselves at the upper room, fasting and praying with earnest expectation of the release of power as promised.

> *"And when the day of Pentecost was fully come, they were all with one accord in one place. And suddenly there came a sound from heaven as of a rushing mighty wind, and it filled all the house where they were sitting. And there appeared unto them cloven tongues like as of fire, and it sat upon each of them. And they were all filled with the Holy Ghost, and began to speak with other tongues, as the Spirit gave them utterance."* [Acts 2: 1 - 4]

WHAT IS PRAYER

"Let my prayer be set forth before thee as incense; and the lifting up of my hands as the evening sacrifice" [Psalms 141:2]. Prayer is the spiritual incense that proceeds from the heart of a believer to the throne of grace (God) as supplication for divine intervention. It is a weapon of change and transformation. Jabez was conceived in sorrow, born in sorrow and named sorrow, but through prayer, he was turned to

the most honourable man among his brethren. *"And Jabez was more honourable than his brethren: and his mother called his name Jabez, saying, Because I bare him with sorrow. And Jabez called on the God of Israel, saying, Oh that thou wouldest bless me indeed, and enlarge my coast, and that thine hand might be with me, and that thou wouldest keep me from evil, that it may not grieve me! And God granted him that which he requested"* [1 Chronicles 4: 9 – 10].

Prayer turned his status around and delivered his inheritance to him as a seed of Abraham. Prayer is the weapon for supernatural turnaround of events and circumstances. In Genesis 25:21 it was recorded that Isaac sought the Lord in prayer for his wife Rebekah who was barren for twenty-three years and God turned the situation around. *"And Isaac entreated the Lord for his wife, because she was barren: and the Lord was entreated of him, and Rebekah his wife conceived."* The siege of barrenness was broken, and the virtue of fruitfulness was released through prayer! She received for her shame double blessing in the school of fruitfulness as Esau and Jacob became the products of intensive prayer!

Prayer is an ordained weapon for total delivery of the inheritance of the saints in God. *"And there was a widow in that city; and she came unto him, saying, Avenge me of mine adversary... And shall not God avenge his own elect, which cry day and night unto him, though he bear long with them? I tell you that he will avenge them speedily."* [Luke 18:3,7,8a]. Prayer is the channel through which every believer presents his/her case to the Lord for a change of story. It is a medium through which we communicate our desires to the Lord for His divine, fatherly involvement. There was an account of a woman who left the country on divine instruction because of the great famine in the land and later returned after seven years. On her return, she discovered that all her land and properties had been taken by strangers and she went after the king to **cry** for restoration. *"And it came to pass, as he was telling the king how he had restored a dead body to life, that, behold, the woman, whose son he had restored to life, cried to the king for her house and for her land. And Gehazi said, My lord, O king, this is the woman, and this is her son, whom Elisha restored to life. And when the king asked the woman, she told him. So the king appointed unto her a certain officer, saying, Restore all that was hers, and all the fruits of the field since the day that she left the land, even until now."* [2 Kings 8:5-6]. Prayer is a cry to the King to secure restoration of lost virtues including properties, assets, health, peace, *et cetera*.

In the school of fulfilment, prayer is seeking God's will in order to know what to act upon. Finding His way in order to know what path to take and calling on Him to vindicate and justify us in His righteousness. Prayer is calling for help to win the battle over our life. Also as a child of God, Prayer is not weeping (to secure God's pity) as we thought it to be, it is neither begging nor appealing even as confirmed in Psalms 37:25 *"I have been young, and now am old; yet have I not seen the righteous forsaken, nor his seed begging bread"* Prayer is not reading the bible and or reciting the word in a religious manner. Prayer is the medium through which our requests are being presented before our Father (God) for divine intervention. Prayer is the channel through which we pour out our heart to the Lord concerning a specific issue. It is commanding heaven for swift intervention to the present situation as instructed by God to all His children *"Thus saith the Lord, the Holy One of Israel, and his Maker, Ask me of things to come concerning my sons, and concerning the work of my hands command ye me"* [Isaiah 45:11]

Prayer is the weapon for pulling strange and mighty things which are unknown to mankind. It exposes the treasures in darkness for possession by the saints of God. *"Thus saith the Lord the maker thereof, the Lord that formed it, to establish it; the Lord is his name; Call unto me, and I will answer thee, and shew thee great and mighty things, which thou knowest not"* [Jeremiah 33:2-3]. To experience a change of levels, it is prayer and fasting, so every time you desire a change, change your approach towards prayer. Reading the account of the Apostles in Acts 4: 16 – 32, after the notable miracle at the beautiful gate, the community leaders rose up and threatened them not to preach in the name of Jesus Christ. But they went and gathered themselves to seek God's intervention and be empowered with boldness to carry out God's mandate as divinely ordained.

> *"And when they had prayed, the place was shaken where they were assembled together; and they were all filled with the Holy Ghost, and they spake the word of God with boldness. And the multitude of them that believed were of one heart and of one soul: neither said any of them that ought of the things which he possessed was his own; but they had all things common. And with great power gave the apostles witness of the resurrection of the Lord Jesus: and great grace was upon them all. Neither was there any among them that lacked: for as many*

as were possessors of lands or houses sold them, and brought the prices of the things that were sold, And laid them down at the apostles' feet: and distribution was made unto every man according as he had need" [Acts 4: 31 - 35]

They pulled the virtues of boldness, authority and heavenly backing from the throne of grace through the weapon of prayer and they experienced instant change of story! The people who threatened them were now selling their properties and laying them at the feet of the Apostles for the propagation of the same Gospel of Christ that they detested. Prayer is the transforming force that humbles every principality and power and establishes the dominion of the saints. It is an ordained weapon for contending against the enemies, triumphing over them and restoring our inheritances in redemption.

Prayer draws virtues, but value must precede prayer as it is the composer of every heartfelt supplication! Worth strengthens approach while expected virtues enhance faith to consistently press until there is delivery. It takes a great measure of value to command results in the school of prayer.

PRAYER AND ITS BASIC REQUIREMENTS

Prayer requires patience because every vision is for an appointed time and patience is what secures answers to prayer. *"In your patience possess ye your souls"* [Luke 21:19]. Secondly, *"And all things, whatsoever ye shall ask in prayer, believing, ye shall receive."* [Matthew 21: 22] Prayer is impotent without faith, *"Let him not think he shall receive anything from God"*, and faith has to be consciously cultivated in the heart. Prayer is not an assumption but by cultivating faith through the word we have been hearing and channel our petitions in line with the knowledge and understanding of the authenticity of the word. It is not the asking that guarantees receiving but the belief that when prayer is made, answer to it is inevitable. The basic requirements therefore are knowledge, belief, faith, temperance, patience, hope, trust and confidence. These basic requirements among others are the boosters of our part in the divine nature of the prayer capability of our Master, Jesus Christ. *"And beside this, giving all diligence, add to your faith virtue; and to virtue knowledge; And to knowledge temperance; and to temperance patience; and to patience godliness; And to godliness brotherly kindness; and to brotherly kindness charity. For if these things be in you, and abound, they make you that ye shall neither be barren nor unfruitful in the knowledge of our Lord Jesus Christ"* [2 Peter 1: 5 - 8]

HOW DO I PRAY?

Prayer does not start with supplication, declaration and or intercession. Prayer starts with preparation. Preparation is the pre-eminence to divine intervention; it precedes prayer and it is the master key to the heart of God. Prayer should not be a hasty activity, rather it should be seen as a spiritual activity with adequate preparation. Prayer could be approached as a marriage. If you rush into it without adequate preparation, you are heading towards rushing out without a positive result. Preparation ensures absolute guarantee for answer to prayer (John 11: 1–17, 41). Preparation secures the faith required to channel your prayer and gives you the privilege to have control over the said situation, irrespective of the distressing state. Preparation draws answers from the throne for *"The preparations of the heart in man, and the answer of the tongue, is from the Lord"* [Proverbs 16:1].

Bishop David Oyedepo said in one of his teachings on prayer and I quote: 'There has to be that preparation to secure divine intervention, I want to think that the reason for so much frustration in the school of prayer, is the lack of adequate preparation. We rush into supplication, we rush into intercession and we end up in frustration, because we lack the adequate preparation to secure the divine intervention'. Inadequate preparation ensures inevitable frustration but when preparation is adequate, virtues are drawn even before prayer. *"And it shall come to pass that before they call, I will answer; and while they are yet speaking I will hear"* [Isaiah 65: 24] That is the effect of adequate preparation!

WHAT IS PREPARATION THEN AND HOW
DO WE PREPARE FOR PRAYER?

Most prayers are religiously and fanatically done to demonstrate our ego and display our dexterity through grammatical expression. However, the kingdom of God is not in the content of the complex and grammatical weight of your word but in the power of your adequate knowledge, and preparation is what secures the knowledge required for effective delivery in the school of prayer! Until the preparation is in place grace is not made available and when grace is not available mercy is withdrawn. It is mercy and grace that secure hel*p. "Let us therefore come boldly unto the throne of grace, that we may obtain mercy, and find grace to help in time of need."* [Hebrews 4:16]. The boldness needed for securing grace and mercy is acquired through adequate preparation.

Preparation begins with building the altar of God in your heart (1 king 18: 29 – 33). Secondly, we prepare by securing adequate knowledge of God's will regarding the petition. This is done through thorough exploration of His word to find out what He has said concerning the issue. Daniel revealed the secret of how he discovered the plan of God concerning Israel in Babylon and how he appropriated his prayer and fasting with the plan to secure an answer. *"In the first year of his reign I Daniel understood by books the number of the years, whereof the word of the Lord came to Jeremiah the prophet, that he would accomplish seventy years in the desolations of Jerusalem. And I set my face unto the Lord God, to seek by prayer and supplications, with fasting, and sackcloth, and ashes: And I prayed unto the Lord my God, and made my confession, and said, O Lord, the great and dreadful God, keeping the covenant and mercy to them that love him, and to them that keep his commandments;"* [Daniel 9: 2 – 4] He went in search of the will and plan of God concerning the state of Israel and he got the key (read Jeremiah 29). He knew God's determined timeline for their release from Babylon and understood God's recommended approach to get His plan executed for Israel. His adequate preparation secured divine guidelines on the steps to take and ultimately procured a swift answer. Friends, there is nothing new under the sun and there is no issue that the word of God does not address with a direct and reliable answer. So, we get into the word of God, and we *"Search the scriptures; for in them ye think ye have eternal life: and they are they which testify of me."* [John 5:39].

The essence of preparation is to secure the confidence required to enhance our faith and strengthen the value we have for the Vessel. Preparation also fortifies our hope and trust in God who answers prayers. Once the truth is revealed to us through the word, we move to the next phase of our preparation by setting our heart to get to God. Remember that prayer is not a one-way communication, but a two-way corresponding process. You are instructed to call, and God is committed to answer in response to your call. *"I will stand upon my watch, and set me upon the tower, and will watch to see what he will say unto me, and what I shall answer when I am reproved. And the Lord answered me, and said, Write the vision, and make it plain upon tables, that he may run that readeth it. For the vision is yet for an appointed time, but at the end it shall speak, and not lie: though it tarry, wait for it; because it will surely come, it will not tarry. Behold, his soul which is lifted up is not upright in him: but the just shall live by his faith"* [Habakkuk 2: 1 – 4]. Every virtue-drawing prayer must endeavor to build the required faith to get the desired result. Patiently sit down, study and discover what is required to have your desires met; then launch into prayer. Once your preparation is sufficient, the answer of the tongue will come from the Lord, for *"The preparations of the heart in man, and the answer of the tongue, is from the Lord"* [Proverbs 16:1]

THE POWER OF PERSISTENT PRAYER

"Pray without ceasing" for tenacity in prayer is the cure for failure. Persistent prayer is what secures consistent delivery! *"There was in a city a judge, which feared not God, neither regarded man: And there was a widow in that city; and she came unto him, saying, Avenge me of mine adversary. And he would not for a while: but afterward he said within himself, Though I fear not God, nor regard man; Yet because this widow troubleth me, I will avenge her, lest by her continual coming she weary me"* [Luke 18:2-5]. Furthermore, Isaiah 62:6 and 7 says *"I have set watchmen upon thy walls, O Jerusalem, which shall never hold their peace day nor night: ye that make mention of the Lord, keep not silence, And give him no rest, till he establish, and till he make Jerusalem a praise in the earth"*. It is your level of persistence on the mountain of prayer that guarantees your eternal rest.

Victory in life is subject to the ability to maintain consistent and persistent faith culture which states two notable principles in the school of prayer thus: **the fire must keep burning** *"And the sons of Aaron the priest shall put fire upon the altar, and lay the wood in order upon the fire:"* [Leviticus 1:7] Secondly, **the fire must never go out** as strictly instructed in Leviticus 6:13 *"The fire shall ever be* *burning upon the altar; it shall never go out.*" Because "*Where no wood is, there the fire goeth out: so where there is no talebearer, the strife ceaseth*" [Proverbs 26:20]

The products of persistent prayer are innumerable in its delivery. Persistent prayer irrespective of the magnitude of the situation will produce testimony to prove God's faithfulness and commitment to answering prayers done from a pure heart! Persistent prayer is the proof of our genuine unwavering faith in God which in turn commits Him to carry out His acts in our lives. In other words, persistent prayer is what enforces undeniable testimonies since God's response to our consistent and persistent prayers is the testimony we longed for.

Every prayer done with expectation ultimately provokes the release of God's supernatural power to prove that He is the God that answers prayer. This act is called testimony for "*Praise waiteth for thee, O God, in Zion: and unto thee shall the vow be performed. O thou that hearest prayer, unto thee shall all flesh come*" [Psalms 65:1-2]. And "*I called upon the Lord in distress: the Lord answered me, and set me in a large place*" [Psalms 118:5]. The evidence of the release of virtues is testimony, therefore, testimony must emerge to prove that the request has been granted.

We saw the practical demonstration of persistent prayer during Elijah's time.

> "*And Elijah said unto Ahab, Get thee up, eat and drink; for there is a sound of abundance of rain. So Ahab went up to eat and to drink. And Elijah went up to the top of Carmel; and he cast himself down upon the earth, and put his face between his knees, And said to his servant, Go up now, look toward the sea. And he went up, and looked, and said, There is nothing. And he said, Go again seven times. And it came to pass at the seventh time, that he said, Behold, there ariseth a little cloud out of the sea, like a man's hand. And he said, Go up, say unto Ahab, Prepare thy chariot, and get thee down, that the rain stop thee not. And it came to pass in the mean while, that the heaven was black with clouds and wind, and there was a great rain. And Ahab rode, and went to Jezreel*" [1 King 18: 41 - 45]

Testimony is that tangible proof of undeniable response of heaven to persistent prayer.

Beside instant testimony, persistent prayer produces tremendous power for triumph. In Genesis 27: 41 "*And Esau hated Jacob because of the blessing wherewith his father blessed him: and Esau said in his heart, The days of mourning for my father are at hand; then will I slay my brother Jacob.*" He vowed to kill Jacob once their father dies and Jacob ran away to *Paddan-aram* to dwell with Laban his uncle. On his return, he sought God persistently on the mount of prayer purposely for a change of status that would help him secure triumph over his brother. He desired a change of name and held on the angel of the Lord until there was a delivery. "*And Jacob was left alone; and there wrestled a man with him until the breaking of the day. And when he saw that he prevailed not against him, he touched the hollow of his thigh; and the hollow of Jacob's thigh was out of joint, as he wrestled with him. And he said, Let me go, for the day breaketh. And he said, I will not let thee go, except thou bless me. And he said unto him, What is thy name? And he said, Jacob. And he said, Thy name shall be called no more Jacob, but Israel: for as a prince hast thou power with God and with men, and hast prevailed*" [Genesis 32: 24 - 28]. He left home as Jacob who was awaiting destruction by his brother but arrived as Israel that cannot be destroyed. Do you desire a change of name that supernaturally singles you out as a touch me not entity? Then persistent prayer is the answer! Effectual fervent prayers carry tremendous power for a unique delivery.

The irresistible power for conquest, victory, triumph and fulfilment in life is generated through persistent prayer life. It is the earnest (heartfelt, continued) prayer of a righteous man that makes tremendous power available which is dynamic in its working. This is the '*Go again seven times*' kind of determination that delivers undeniable results in the school of prayer and supplication. What provokes the persistent spirit is the determined settlement of the outcome of the prayer before engaging in it. There is an expected settled result and the 'no looking back' zeal until it is delivered as expected!

"*And Elijah said unto Ahab, Get thee up, eat and drink; for there is a sound of abundance of rain. So Ahab went up to eat and to drink. And Elijah went up to the top of Carmel; and he cast himself down upon the earth, and put his face between his knees, And said to his servant, Go up now, look toward the sea. And he went up, and looked, and said, There is nothing. And he said, Go again seven times. And it came to pass at the seventh time, that he said, Behold, there ariseth a little cloud out of the sea, like a man's hand. And he said, Go up, say unto Ahab, Prepare thy chariot, and get thee down, that the rain stop thee not. And it came to pass in the mean while, that the heaven was black with clouds and wind, and there was a great rain. And Ahab rode, and went to Jezreel. And the hand of the Lord was on Elijah; and he girded up his loins, and ran before Ahab to the entrance of Jezreel."* [1 Kings 18: 41 - 46]. Elijah defined his expectation, set himself for the actualization and got the result as expected. So, persistent prayer is setting the goals, pursuing them and ensuring they are accomplished before returning from the mount of prayer.

The Amplified version of James 5:16 – 18 described the tenacity of Elijah in a very unique and provocative way, admonishing that you should *"Confess to one another therefore your faults (your slips, your false steps, your offenses, your sins) and pray [also] for one another, that you may be healed and restored [to a spiritual tone of mind and heart]. The earnest (heartfelt, continued) prayer of a righteous man makes tremendous power available [dynamic in its working]. Elijah was a human being with a nature such as we have [with feelings, affections, and a constitution like ours]; and he prayed earnestly for it not to rain, and no rain fell on the earth for three years and six months. And [then] he prayed again and the heavens supplied rain and the land produced its crops [as usual]."*

A great virtue is drawn from the throne of power when we persist in the school of prayer.

THE IMPACT OF PRAYER IN RELEASING VIRTUES

Virtue transforms destiny, but it must first be released before the impact can be seen. Prayer must be engaged by the recipient before he/she can experience transformation. Every release from heaven is traceable to a definite, earnest, heartfelt prayer of the righteous. Jabez was born as a child of sorrow, he grew up in sorrow and lived in destitution but when he realized the worth of the God of Abraham, Isaac and Jacob, he went after Him with all his heart in prayer and there was an overturning of events. A man of sorrow was transformed to an honourable man among his brethren. *"And Jabez was more honourable than his brethren: and his mother called his name Jabez, saying, Because I bare him with sorrow. And Jabez called on the God of Israel, saying, Oh that thou wouldest bless me indeed, and enlarge my coast, and that thine hand might be with me, and that thou wouldest keep me from evil, that it may not grieve me! And God granted him that which he requested"* [1 Chronicles 4:9-10]

Virtues are not released on the platform of religion, but they are enforced through effectual, fervent, continued pressure on the vessel through the weapon of prayer. Bartimaeus the blind whose condition had subjected him to a mere highway beggar *"when he heard that it was Jesus of Nazareth, he began to cry out, and say, Jesus, thou Son of David, have mercy on me. And many charged him that he should hold his peace: but he cried the more a great deal, Thou Son of David, have mercy on me. And Jesus stood still, and commanded him to be called."* [read Mark 10: 46-52] His persistent cry brought Christ to a standstill for swift intervention. Thus, failure in the school of prayer is to give up seeking when your petitions are yet to be granted *"And in that day ye shall ask me nothing. Verily, verily, I say unto you, Whatsoever ye shall ask the Father in my name, he will give it you. Hitherto have ye asked nothing in my name: ask, and ye shall receive, that your joy may be full."* [John 16: 23 – 24].

He that asketh not receiveth not! He that seeketh not fineth not! He that knocketh not shall remain without! Until we ask in faith through prayer, we cannot receive no matter how strong we may claim to be spiritually. *"Ask, and it shall be given you; seek, and ye shall find; knock, and it shall be opened unto you: For every one that asketh receiveth; and he that seeketh findeth; and to him that knocketh it shall be opened. Or what man is there of you, whom if his son ask bread, will he give him a stone? Or if he ask a fish, will he give him a serpent? If ye then, being evil, know how to give good gifts unto your children, how much more shall your Father which is in heaven give good things to them that ask him?"* [Matthew 7: 7 – 11]

LET THIS NATURE BE SEEN IN YOU TOO

"For Zion's sake will I not hold my peace, and for Jerusalem's sake I will not rest, until the righteousness thereof go forth as brightness, and the salvation thereof as a lamp that burneth. I have set watchmen upon thy walls, O Jerusalem, which shall never hold their peace day nor night: ye that make mention of the Lord, keep not silence, And give him no rest, till he establish, and till he make Jerusalem a praise in the earth." [Isaiah 62: 1,6,7]. God is a persistent God who made all things perfect through His persistent nature. And God said…and God said…and God said… until God began to see all that He persistently said (Read Genesis 1).

Christ came and exhibited this persistent nature during His earthly ministry and now by redemption we can enter into the same order of operation without weariness and or loss of appetite in securing the hands of God in our lives even as Christ practically enjoyed the Father's hand at all times through His persistent nature. We are entitled to this nature if we so desire to be as He is for *"Whereby are given unto us exceeding great and precious promises: that by these ye might be partakers of the divine nature, having escaped the corruption that is in the world through lust."* [2 Peters 1:4]

Christ is a prayer warrior! He was a prayer addict throughout His ministry on earth. He persisted in prayer and enjoyed the father's acts throughout His time on earth. And I must tell you with all truth, that it was prayer that sustained Him on earth and secured His eternal throne at the right hand of the Father. He was launched into His ministry through prayer (Luke 4: 1 – 14); He was baptized praying (Luke 3:21 – 23); He began the morning by separating himself into a solitary place praying as recorded in Mark 1: 35 *"And in the morning, rising up a great while before day, he went out, and departed into a solitary place, and there prayed"*. He chose his disciples praying. He walked in the city doing the Father's will praying always and without ceasing. He raised and trained His disciples praying and appointed them into various positions and responsibilities praying. He engaged in eating with prayer, He supplied food in the wilderness to innumerable number of people praying with thanksgiving. He walked into the cross praying and even on the cross He was still praying. He resurrected praying and no wonder He enjoyed ceaseless open heaven.

It will amaze you that even now, Jesus Christ, the Saviour is still sitting at His glorious throne praying and making intercession for all the saints as recorded in Romans 8: 34 *"Who is he that condemneth? It is Christ that died, yea rather, that is risen again, who is even at the right hand of God, who also maketh intercession for us."* You are never ushered into your place at the right hand until you embrace the prayer nature of your Master. It takes persistent prayer to maintain progressive advancement in your endeavours.

Finally, the essence of prayer is not just to pull virtues from the Vessel, but more importantly to enhance your spiritual life and sustain your daily connection to the Source of life. It is the force that stimulates the breaking forth of light! If you steadfastly engage in prayer combined with a chosen fast, *"Then shall thy light break forth as the morning, and thine health shall spring forth speedily: and thy righteousness shall go before thee; the glory of the Lord shall be thy rearward. Then shalt thou call, and the Lord shall answer; thou shalt cry, and he shall say, Here I am. If thou take away from the midst of thee the yoke, the putting forth of the finger, and speaking vanity; And if thou draw out thy soul to the hungry, and satisfy the afflicted soul; then shall thy light rise in obscurity, and thy darkness be as the noonday: And the Lord shall guide thee continually, and satisfy thy soul in drought, and make fat thy bones: and thou shalt be like a watered garden, and like a spring of water, whose waters fail not. And they that shall be of thee shall build the old waste places: thou shalt raise up the foundations of many generations; and thou shalt be called, The repairer of the breach, The restorer of paths to dwell in"* [Isaiah 58: 8 - 12].

Prayer is the key to unlock the breakthrough door of destiny. Every prayerless child of God ends up a victim in life. If prayer is taken out of your daily life, then weakness and failure would take hold of your spiritual life. Nothing works except it be pressed and prayer is the only ordained pressurizing force that can enforce the swift delivery of your inheritance in Christ Jesus.

Therefore, A prayerless Christian is a potential backslider. Your spiritual growth is dependent on your consistency in prayer. It takes the force of consistent and persistent prayer lifestyle to enjoy progressive delivery of your inheritance in God and to maintain daily growth in your spiritual journey. Engage in prayer to pull virtues of heaven for your release. Prayer is essential.

About the Author

Pastor Ola Jones Duyile is the Senior Pastor and Founder of Victory Chapel Ministries International (a.k.a. Victory House). He was called into the Ministry as a Messenger with a mission to expound the word of **knowledge** to Zion for her lifting from the pit of ignorance. He has served in various ministries as a Minister, Teacher and Associate Pastor. He is an author, a team builder and motivational speaker and as part of his engagements, he is well known for his passion for human development and empowerment. Ola Jones is fully committed to expounding the word of knowledge, and the anchor of his teaching is **FAITH**. He believes that faith in God is the master driver of destiny according to his usual statement of faith *'As long as Jesus Christ is the Way, there is always a way out of every situation'*

Pastor Ola Jones is fully in tune with the move of God for the end time armies as recorded in Joel 2: His mandate is to "Open the heart of men (by the help of the Holy Spirit) and plant the reality of their kingdom royalty as the 'True Heir' of God and Joint Heir with Christ; provoking men (through the word of God) to see the truth about their vantage position in redemption".

Pastor Ola Jones is also a Chief IT Consultants with prominent IT firms in Europe. He is the CEO and Founder of SDRD Systems & Services ApS, a company devoted to the quality standard of software products.

Pastor Ola Jones is married to Lilian Irowa Duyile and they are blessed with children.

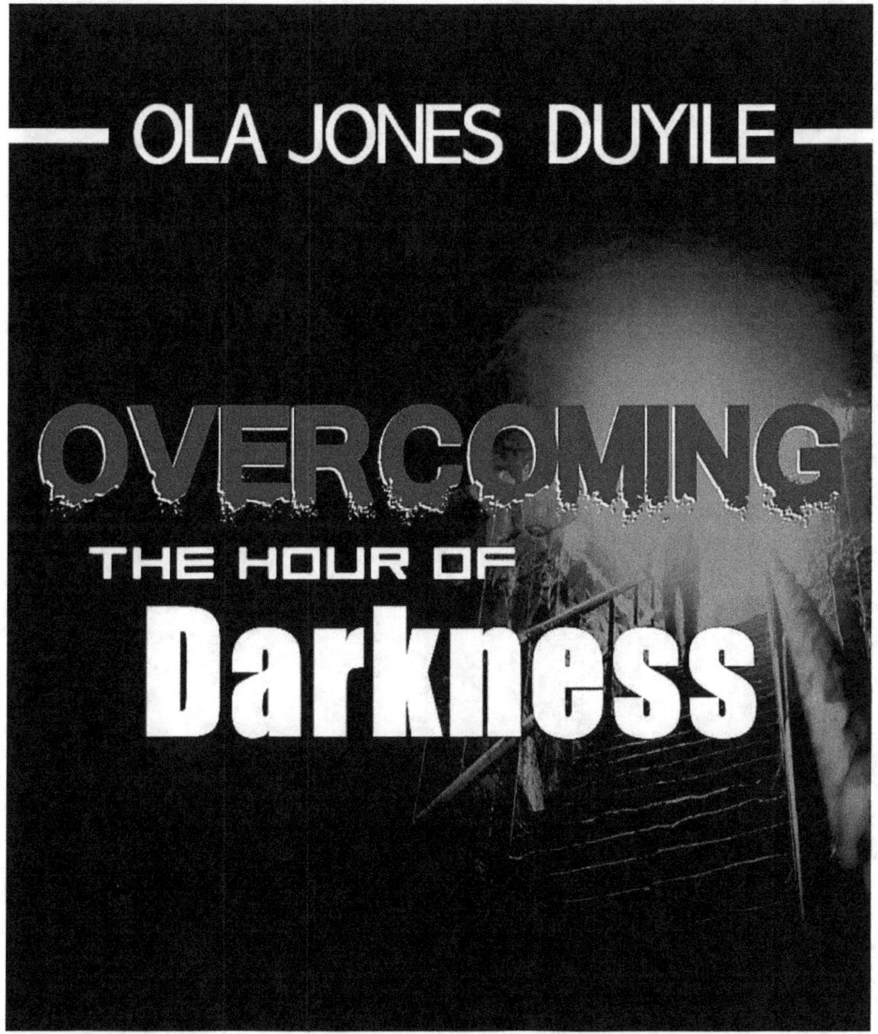
OLA JONES DUYILE
OVERCOMING
THE HOUR OF
Darkness
UNDERSTANDING HOW TO SCALE THROUGH
YOUR DARK MOMENT

Trading Values For Greater Virtues

Determining the magnitude of *virtues* by the level of *values*

OLA JONES DUYILE